Past Praise for
Dianne Ebertt Beeaff

For *Homecoming: A Book of Poetry*

"A loving book of poetry . . . illustrated by Beeaff's graceful, graphite artwork."— THE ARIZONA DAILY STAR

"A book of haunting poems that captures the spirit of Great Britain, its history, landscape, and wild weather." — SUE FELL, EIRINN MAGAZINE, UNITED KINGDOM

For *A Grand Madness: Ten Years on the Road with U2*

"A wise drummer (Clem Burke of Blondie) once said, 'The ultimate fan transcends fandom and does it himself.' Although Beeaff, a freelance writer living in Tucson, Arizona, has not founded a band in her heroes' names, she has provided an earnest, perceptive account of the Irish band's last tours in diary form. Recommended." — LIBRARY JOURNAL

"*A Grand Madness* certainly conveys the excitement of running away with the rock 'n' roll circus."— HOT PRESS, Dublin

"A candid, uncompromising account which captures the essence of the Irish rock band U2 from a fan's perspective . . . laced with warmth, intelligence, and humor."— MIDWEST REVIEW

For *Power's Garden: A Novel*

"*Power's Garden* takes us back to 1917 with vivid imagery, heartfelt emotion, and rich historical detail. Captivating! An excellent read!" — JENNIFER STEELE-CHRISTENSEN, *Utah Public Radio*, *Deseret News* correspondent

"Quietly impressive, meticulously researched . . . A surprise ending polishes off the finale!" — ARIZONA DAILY STAR

For *Spirit Stones: Unraveling the Megalithic Mysteries of Western Europe's Prehistoric Monuments*

"Part antiquarian, part shamanic . . . this evocative book felt more like a journey! I can't recommend it enough." — ALEX WHITAKER, Ancient-Wisdom, United Kingdom

"This lively and engaging work explains why the ancient monuments continue to renew our sense of the wonder and mystery of life." — FOREWORD REVIEWS

For *A Grand Madness: U2 Twenty Years After*

"Like Bono's lyrics, multicolored and yet full of shade and shadow, Beeaff's memoir envelops readers in the euphoria of fandom with the personal impact that U2's music has had on her life. Brimming with insights into one of the most adored rock bands of our time, *A Grand Madness* offers readers a rousing depiction of one fan's experiences on the road. It is sure to capture the hearts of die-hard U2 enthusiasts as well as those with a penchant for the intrigue and adventure of a travel narrative." — *The Music Universe*

"A swirl of fabulous energy . . . The author knows her stuff with stellar access and attention to detail, from setlists to song symbolism. This book checks all the boxes for a music fan whether on or off tour and makes that insider fantasy come true."— *Writer's Digest Book Awards*

For *On Tràigh Lar Beach: Stories*

"An ambitious ocean-spanning collection of objects and tales . . . Beeaff's prose is of such high quality, page to page, that readers won't want to put it down."— KIRKUS REVIEWS

"Richly written, thought provoking, and utterly compelling. Every story is full of tiny twists and turns, and every story has a thoughtful ending. In many ways, this is the sort of book that would go down well with a reading group; there's so much to discuss, so many links to explore." — A WISHING SHELF

"An engaging and beautifully crafted short story collection readers of Karen Russell and Curtis Sittenfield will devour."— SILVER REVIEW

Infinite Paradise

witnessing the wild

a memoir

Dianne Ebertt Beeaff

SWP

SHE WRITES PRESS

Also by Dianne Ebertt Beeaff

Homecoming: A Book of Poetry

A Grand Madness: Ten Years on the Road with U2

Power's Garden: A Novel

Spirit Stones: Unraveling the Megalithic Mysteries of Western Europe's Prehistoric Monuments

A Grand Madness: U2 Twenty Years After

On Tràigh Lar Beach: Stories

Published 2025
Printed in the United States of America
Print ISBN: 978-1-64742-932-4
E-ISBN: 978-1-64742-933-1
Library of Congress Control Number: 2025906227

For information, address:
She Writes Press
1569 Solano Ave #546
Berkeley, CA 94707

Interior Design by Tabitha Lahr

She Writes Press is a division of SparkPoint Studio, LLC.

Names and identifying characteristics have been changed to protect the privacy of certain individuals.

Permissions

All quoted material is either cited with proper permission, resides in the public domain, or falls under the Fair Use Doctrine of the US or British copyright statute. Thanks to these inspirational figures for permission to quote more extensively from their work:

Page xiii: To Rabbi Abraham Joshua Heschel. Permission granted through his daughter, Susannah Herschel.

Page xxi: To Diana Beresford- Kroeger quote in *To Speak for the Trees, My Life's Journey from Ancient Celtic Wisdom to a Healing Vision of the Forest*, Random House, Canada, 2019. Used with permission.

Page xxiii: To Wendell Berry, for permission to use his outstanding poem, *The Peace of Wild Things*.

Page 57: Robinson Jeffers' poem *The Inhumanist* in *The Collected Poetry of Robinson Jeffers*, Copyright © by The Board of Trustees of the Leland Stanford Jr. University. All rights reserved. Used by permission of the publisher, Stanford University Press, www.sup.org.

Page 55: Fenton Johnson, author of *At the Center of All Beauty: Solitude and the Creative Life*, W. W. Norton, 2020. Quote taken from *Beyond Belief: A Skeptic Searches for an American Faith*, Harper's Magazine, 1998. Used with permission.

Page 63: Terry Tempest Williams, *When Women Were Birds*, Farrar, Straus and Giroux, 2012. Printed with permission.

Page 228: To Jim Hohenbary, author of the novel, *Before the Ruins* (Blueberry Press, 2019) for permission to use his amazing poem, *The Witch*.

All photographs are by Dianne Ebertt Beeaff unless otherwise noted.

Pencil drawings of the daffodils (page 1), raccoons (page 91), mushrooms (page 185), and deer (page 241) are © Dianne Ebertt Beeaff.

For Dan

and

For my parents

Edna (OTT) Ebertt and Russell Ebertt

"As you sit on the hillside,
or lie prone under the trees of the forest,
or sprawl wet-legged by a mountain stream,
the great door that does not look like a door, opens."
— STEPHEN GRAHAM

"Our goal should be to live life in radical amazement,
to look at the world in a way that takes nothing for granted.
Everything is phenomenal; everything is incredible;
to be spiritual is to be constantly amazed."
— RABBI ABRAHAM JOSHUA HESCHEL

"There are some who can live without
wild things and some who cannot."
— ALDO LEOPOLD

Infinite Paradise

Contents

Prologue

I WAS NINE YEARS OLD when I first glimpsed Paradise.

Crushed and buff-colored winter grasses flowed off the hilltop where I stood, and the scatter of April's lilacs, hawthorns, and crab apple trees below had just begun to leaf out in a blush of lime green. I could track the tea-colored Conestoga River, left to right (east to west) as it sliced through a spongy water-meadow of wet spring earth to make a sharp turn south at the cedary western edge.

Neighboring farmer Robert Ritch had grazed his cattle for decades on much of this land, keeping at bay the eastern white cedar forest that already covered almost a third of the property's sixteen acres. On lazy summer days, these animals made their sluggish way home, moving up the slash of gully that drained the pastureland on the far side of the dirt road behind me, lumbering under a concrete bridge to my left. On the first of May in that year—1957—my parents purchased those sixteen acres then in Peel Township, Southern Ontario, Canada, for a thousand dollars.

Two vinyl-sided five-room cottages now grace the property's northside hill. Built by my dad in the late 1950s, they have been maintained for over sixty years, the last twenty or so by me and my husband Dan.

We took full ownership of the land in 2010.

Like most children, I was too young in the beginning to fathom the fragility that lay before me, to walk among elementals, as Jan Shepherd wrote in her engaging book, *The Living Mountain: A Celebration of the Cairngorm Mountains of Scotland*. That the natural world could bring infinity within sight was beyond my understanding. Nor was I aware, as John Muir was, that "between every two pines is a door leading to a new life." In my case, that door would lie between eastern white cedars.

But I knew the magic of night air. I prized the owl-light that came with sundown. I believed trees could have spirits. And though I could never have voiced it, I knew nature's undersong could illuminate the ordinary world.

ALL OF LIFE IS FORGED IN NATURE. At a time when "media is the big idea" (U2, "Kite," *All That You Can't Leave Behind*) and our world is fully plugged in, we find ourselves on the cusp of losing any kinship with the natural world. Yet groundbreaking studies have shown that in the sea of circuitry that comprises contemporary living, wild spaces, large and small, are essential to our mental and physical well-being. A walk in the woods can alter the whole tone of life, promoting relaxation, addressing chronic illness, combating stress, and improving creativity, sleep, and social ties in each of us. Encountering nature with each of our senses is the very definition of being fully physically alive.

"You should sit in nature for twenty minutes a day," a Zen Buddhist koan advises, "unless you're busy. Then you should sit for an hour."

Nature sparks in us a renewed sense of wonder, a longing for oneness with the earth and its creatures.

Today, when our battered world reels with erratic energies indifferent to humanity, optimism seems mercurial. We clear-cut our forests and shroud them in acid rain. We drive our fellow creatures to extinction with over-hunting and habitat destruction. We poison our oceans and our skies so that little remains that is either idyll or ideal. Catastrophic forces in the form of monster hurricanes, deadly wildfires and tornadoes, drought, flooding, and pollution have intensified in our lives, with the predominantly human scourge of climate change.

And yet life is eternally buoyant. Constantly on the move. Persistent and flexible. Riches remain. We have only to look with fresh eyes on all that is still right with our world.

Each one of us is a child of the landscape that surrounds us. We can make a choice to stay open to the splendid life-forms that live close by near our homes, in our yards and gardens, in our neighborhoods, and in our parks, preserves, and refuges. No piece of nature is insignificant, and, as Florence Williams writes in her book, *The Nature Fix: Why Nature Makes Us Happier, Healthier, and More Creative*, "Pretty much any slouching screen fiend can spend time in a pocket of trees somewhere."

The early environmentalist Henry David Thoreau believed that landowners were imbued with responsibilities to the land. Robert Macfarlane, in his remarkable book *Landmarks*, wrote, "Once a landscape goes undescribed and therefore unguarded, it becomes vulnerable to unwise use and improper action." The beauty and meaning of such places may be lost forever. As botanist Diana Beresford-Kroeger said in her book, *To Speak for the Trees: My Life's Journey from Ancient Celtic Wisdom to a Healing Vision of the Forest*, "Today it is necessary to see the world around us with a new vision and to understand it with new words."

The core of living lies in what we love, and the key to knowing a place inside and out is to return to it over and over. I don't know if it is possible to love the whole planet, but we can love a place we can see and touch and smell.

It is my hope that the stories I tell here will transcend the singular space from which they come. That the pure perception born of my own fascination with the natural world will move past the subjective to touch the collective spirit. That by describing openly and honestly the sixteen acres in rural Southern Ontario that my mother called Paradise, I will not only honor this unique place through seasons and storms, through time and tranquility, through life and death, but as Stephen Graham stated, "the great door that does not look like a door" will open, and you will fall in love again with the complexity and endless beauty and power of the natural world.

"When despair grows in me
And I wake in the middle of the Night at the least sound
in fear of what my life and my children's lives may be,
I go and lie down where the wood drake
rests in his beauty on the water, and the great heron feeds.
I come into the Peace of wild things
who do not tax their lives with forethought
of grief. I come into the presence of still water.
and I feel above me the day-blind stars
waiting for their light. For a time
I rest in the grace of the world, and am free."
— THE PEACE OF WILD THINGS, WENDELL BERRY

"I believe in the forest and in the meadow
and in the night in which the corn grows."
— HENRY DAVID THOREAU

"I believe in God beyond God."
— JOSEPH CAMPBELL

The Footpath Tour

An Introduction

A FOOTPATH MEANDERS through Paradise, from Wood's End in the west to Castor's Landing in the east. Here at the west side, we look out to the river, framed in cedar boughs, as through a window. Snatches of opaque umber water flash above a sweep of wildflowers and high summer grass. On this late July morning, the air swells with birdsong. We hear northern cardinals, red-winged blackbirds, robins, house wrens, song sparrows, and many more.

The owners of the first farm on the main road to Drayton have slung their summer fence across the river, and we can see russet-colored cows cropping the lea that forms the tip of the thumb of land where the river turns south. Belted kingfishers will soon perch on the top wire to launch their small blue-gray bodies into the river like arrows, looking for a meal. In a month or so, Canada geese will begin to gather in the deep curve of the river, just out of sight, beyond a jut of hillside.

The oldest trees of The West Woods almost encircle us, stalwart and indomitable, with four-, five-, even six-trunk collectives. Behind us, to either side of the pathway, their offspring, no longer limited by grass and brush, march off across the western slope to angle northward toward the two cottages—Edna's and Russell's.

We'll turn our back on the river now and move deeper into The West Woods, where the slope of the western hill is shallower, cool, and still. A patch of toothy-leaved herb Robert, its tiny pinkish blooms already nearly done, spreads out in emerald-green beneath a rift in the canopy of young cedars. In a few short weeks, we'll see the yellow-orange spurred slippers of spotted jewelweed in their place.

But for a smattering of mushrooms on tree trunks and forest floor—bronze to amber, pale ivory to teakwood—The West Woods lacks an understory or even any ground cover. Our footsteps fall in silence on a cushion of compacted leaves and fallen twigs. Near the top of the western slope, a sag of wooden fencing marks the boundary of the neighboring property, and to the right, the green-wall growth of the water-meadow glimmers between bared trunks. And then, passing under an arched arbor entrance, we leave The West Woods behind, emerging in the open space of Russell's Cottage.

Named for my father, Russell's was built in 1958 and serves as our guest accommodation. Aside from the parking area on the hilltop from which I first viewed Paradise, Russell's boasts the only other bit of mown-lawn domesticity. The canopies of the sixty-foot-tall sugar and Norway maples already rustle with the crispness of summer's nearing end, as do the trembling aspens in a stand at the bottom of the north slope behind us.

Russell's overlooks the water-meadow, reduced in size over the years by tree lines advancing from east and west and by the broad umbrella of a gigantic white willow on the riverbank. Annual spring run-off and occasional seasonal flooding have curbed any competition from white cedar, though American elm comes and goes, leaving behind gray skeletons, matchless staging areas for our blackbird murmurations.

Today, the meadow shimmers in green with apple, beryl, olive, sap, and jade stems and leaves. We know the dips, hollows, and hillocks shelter red-winged blackbird nests, garden spider webs, and rodent byways. On warm July nights, fireflies replace the cabbage butterflies, monarchs, painted ladies, and white admirals of late-summer afternoons, and the buzz of July's cicadas will soon give way to crickets and the odd mournful gruffness of bull frogs.

The glowing apricot trumpets of orange day lilies lean southward from the lip of the hill, nodding over four-foot-high grasses. Across the meadow, the soft radiance of spotted Joe-Pye weed in dusty mauve and amethyst has opened up and will stay until mid-fall. We see hardy, yellow-rayed elecampane growing on lofty stalks. There's Queen Anne's lace, black-eyed Susan, and water parsnip. By summer's end, sprays of deep-purple New England aster will dominate, along with a half-dozen species of goldenrod, the white froth of calico and swamp aster, and Canada fleabane.

The open space where we're sitting, and on through to the far side of Edna's Cottage, has been formally designated by local botanist, Jim Dougan, as Cultural Woodland—a mixture of ornamental perennials with planted or regenerated coniferous and deciduous trees scattered among outbuildings and other purposed structures. Two five-room cottages. A viewing deck. Sheds. Wooden swings. Picnic tables. A covered Greek-key shower with a span of adjacent wooden steps. A fifteen-foot pressure-pump well dug midway between the cottages. A railed polymer staircase dropping down from the top of the hill.

Fifty feet east of Russell's, Edna's Cottage, named for my mother, lies in the deep shade of soaring sugar maples, white spruce, black walnut, and eastern white cedar. Those nostalgic childhood winters we spent threading toboggans through leafless lilac bushes and hawthorns over snow-covered slopes vanished long ago. But on late summer evenings and long summer nights, raccoons, red fox, rabbits, skunks, and groundhogs are still afoot. Even now, midafternoon, eastern chipmunks and red squirrels scurry branch to branch, shadow each other through the periwinkle and lily of the valley, or scold us from the safety of a tree limb like fishwives.

Beyond Edna's Cottage shed though, the forest is well-established. We'll leave the cottage behind and make our way to the seasoned eastern woods. The footpath, paved from here to The Gully with irregular stone slabs, inclines to a three-tiered walkway (built by my son Dustin) that spans an occasional seep that trickles down from the slopes above. Water often pools in the hollows here, the water-meadow having crept closer, and the glimmer of meadow grass flickers behind widely spaced trunks of maple, spruce, and willow.

Just past the walkway, an abandoned one-room cabin—sagging porch, peeled paint, and mossy roof—molders beside a five-foot-high tract of early goldenrod on the verge of blooming. Last summer, a mother raccoon with four feisty babes set up an intermittent den there.

Stopping for a moment, we'll take in the woodsy wet-earth smells as the west wind rummages in the treetops. Behind us, stretching to the river, the water-meadow rolls out its glowing summer greens and cedars on the northern hillside shimmer in dappled sunlight.

At the base of The Gully, just short of its plank bridge, an apple tree uprooted in a windstorm in early spring has opened a window to the flood plain for us. Already, fallen apples litter the ground. By mid-September, the tang of ripening fruit will infuse the air. Towering over The Gully Bridge, a single American basswood with twin intertwined trunks dwarfs creeping bellflower stalks at its base, their blue elongated flower clusters tilting over the footpath. Now we can see a fringe of willow shoots on the opposite riverbank draped with tendrils of wild cucumber like strings of pearls.

Today, The Gully's channel draining the apple and cedar groves at the top of the hill is nearly dry. The uncluttered-V of its past is glutted with vegetation. We watch as water trickles under a boardwalk (thrown together by my brother David, nicknamed Ebe) to vanish in the burgeoning undergrowth of the flood plain.

Midway through our footpath tour, the true forest begins. Tunneling up a hillock of cedars, the track opens a door from the lush green of the water-meadow to the haunt of beaver, muskrat, mink, deer, heron, and goose. Below, the river slips westward, bordering the southside cedars, where another blanket of herb Robert ruffles in the breeze.

A beaver dam once crossed the stream at The Dam Rapids. One year my parents watched it rise through an entire summer.

We've made our way now from The Gully to Harold's Tea Deck, planted on the shoulder of the first hill in the eastern woods, in the footprint of a long-gone cabin. A cement slab marks the entrance stoop to that first-built cottage on the property, a two-room building raised in the summer of 1957 for my maternal grandfather Alvin Ott and his eldest son, my Uncle Harold. A silence, broken only by buzzing cicadas, sporadic but distant traffic, and the occasional caw of a high-flying crow, settles on us amid mottled green goutweed plantings, blue violets, wood sorrel (still sprinkled with tiny yellow cups), and ostrich ferns brought over years ago from the patch of wild across the river.

The footpath wends across an undulating hillside on a muffle of fallen leaves, skirting old beaver cuttings, and then, banking left, moves deeper into the woods. Before we follow, we'll drop down to sit a while at Black Bass Bend, where the river has widened behind a bristle of gray trunks.

Any watercourse embodies perpetual change. The slice of bank where we're resting has recently subsided and collapsed, revealing a thousand roots stretched like pulled taffy. One or two cedars overhang the water, mirrored in its surface. They'll be gone with next spring's flood, if not before.

The far shore is shallow and stone-lined. But we're four feet or more above the water-level here, and the stand of cedars beside us has been raked and mauled to another four feet by the ice of last spring's thaw. Wide and silent, Black Bass Bend curls out of sight in a sharp bend to the left. To the right, we can just make out the gentle burbling at The Dam Rapids.

A jungle of shoreline vegetation defines the small but pristine wilderness across the river. Never grazed or farmed, this ancient floodplain, backed by a forest of mature cedar, elm, and willow, is bordered by dense, chest-high ostrich ferns and by chains of tufted vetch, riverbank grape, Virginia creeper, false bindweed, ground ivy, and wild cucumber. A primeval forest dedicated to all things wild, this is the dwelling place of Jan Shepherd's elementals, a labyrinthine sanctuary of old flood channels, where the smell of the earth is the smell of life itself . . . where shadows conjure a northern woodland white-tailed deer . . . where great blue heron stalk the water's edge.

The cedars across the river, along with others on this side, comprise the mother trees of the forest, some of them over a century old. But there are also elms and maples, and on the riverbank, white willow.

As we make our way to Castor's Landing, which lies just short of a beaver lodge (a jumble of driftwood, fallen logs, gnawed saplings, and animal trails), the forest widens, broader hillsides littered with deadfall: stumps, sprigs, fallen limbs, and leaves. And where there's a break in the overstory, we can see stippled sunlight firing up further pockets of herb Robert and the broad, heart-shaped, emerald fronds of coltsfoot. In the marshy bottomland near the river, pickerelweed flourishes among old beaver cuttings, and farther inland, a colony of terrestrial crayfish has raised a scatter of mud chimneys over their burrows. White-tailed deer tracks on the pathway will lead us to Castor's Landing.

With an embankment chewed by meltwater year by year, the river has created a table at Castor's Landing from what was once a backless bench between cedars. We're well above the waterline here, with old mother-trees at our back. Some of them, anchored by an imposing scramble of roots, have up to sixteen variously conjoined trunks. Beyond us to the east, the path rises to the road, but a deer trail carries on through the woods, down past the beaver lodge, and into the high grasses of the eastern rapids, where flood plain, pathway, river, boundary fence, and grazing cattle meet.

A hundred yards on this side of the rapids, beyond a bed of wild mint and between two white willows, lies the beaver lodge, and on the far shoreline, half a dozen cedars list over the river, the ground beneath them undercut to snaky roots. Willows dip their arms in the water and banks of ostrich ferns fade into enchanted wildwood openings on the forest floor.

Castor's Landing breathes tranquility in sweet white clover, damp earth, and cedar. Over the whir of summer cicadas, tree branches click and creak in the wind. As autumn approaches, these eastern woods will resound with the clamor of roosting blackbirds.

The temptation to sit for hours in the peace of a riverbank beguiles with a promise of turtles, muskrats, racoons, deer, beaver, pike, bass, Canada geese, and great blue heron.

"Occasionally one sees something fleeting in the land," Barry Lopez writes in his *Arctic Dreams: Imagination and Desire in a Northern Landscape*. "A moment when line, color and movement intensify and something sacred is revealed."

One long-ago afternoon in late May, Dustin stretched out in the high grass of the now vanished slope below Castor's Landing, the buzz of cicadas in his ears, eyes closed to the sun, and wind in his hair.

"The only thing that could make this moment more perfect," he said, "would be to open my eyes and see a beaver swim by."

And then he did both.

"Never hurry through the world, but walk slowly and bow often," the great Mary Oliver advised in her poem, "When I Am Among the Trees." Somewhere, something incredible is waiting to be known.

Part One

SPRING

"Sit quietly, do nothing, spring comes,
and the grass grows by itself."
— ZEN SAYING

"All in the wild March morning, I heard the angels call."
— ALFRED LORD TENNYSON

❖ *1 March* ❖

THE WIND swirls a fistful of snow in my face as I scramble down the snow-banked steps to Edna's Cottage. With the thermometer hovering at 31 degrees Fahrenheit, I've no intention of loitering or even stepping inside. Ice-patched tufts of brittle, brown grass in the clearing at the top of the hill are being raked by frost fingers and will soon vanish in a billow of drift. Elsewhere, a mantle of heavy, wind-driven snow lies two or three feet deep in places, capping evergreens and bare winter limbs. And when I've slogged my way to Russell's Cottage, I see an unblemished depth upward of three feet on the meadow. The day stands crisp and motionless.

Except for one or two shredded blots where a gush of water has breached the ice, the Conestoga is locked in winter's whiteness, as are most of our year-round residents. Combined winter flocks of goldfinch, black-capped chickadees, white-breasted nuthatches, Canada blue jays, downy woodpeckers, and northern cardinals might be flitting about, woods to woods, if we were game enough to watch for them.

The first of March marks meteorological spring in the Northern Hemisphere, though no hint of it has thus far escaped the bounty of snow. Life rekindled awaits the future. No gray-white mist. No hollow blatter of rain. No pleading nestlings, watery sun, or hints of bloom. Nothing disturbs the black and white melancholia of winter.

Yet we know that March as a month is all action. Our red squirrels, striped skunks, cottontails, eastern chipmunks, raccoons, and mink breed in March, red fox and beaver as early as February. Always and forever, as the hit TV series *Game of Thrones* tells us "winter is coming," and the next generation needs to mature and toughen in order to survive.

So, too, do our year-round, winged residents. Over the past several days, I've enticed a half dozen inquisitive and hungry black-capped chickadees into eating sunflowers from the palm of my hand. A quarrelsome bunch with more than fifteen distinct vocalizations, each flutters over my hand scolding before its tiny feet prickle my skin. And then they eat with great gusto, zipping off into the trees between tidbits, dangling upside down from some snowy twig, munching insect eggs.

The fairy-tale flashes of a deep green summer are both a distant memory and a distant dream.

❅ *5 March* ❅

THE THERMOMETER on Edna's porch reads 42 degrees Fahrenheit. We might half expect some nuzzling rain. March bridges the abyss between winter's last stand and the foreshadowing of spring. It means nothing to us if not capricious weather, and tomorrow may throw up a blizzard.

Edna's steps were nearly clear of snow this morning when we arrived, but the snowy meadow still hunkers against the cold, the snowbound river sluicing between ice sheets.

March marked the first of the year to the ancient Romans. The opening of their campaign season is named for Martius/Mars, the Roman god of war. For many, March is almost always a battle.

The First Nation Ojibwe/Chippewa, who live an hour's drive north of us on the shores of Lake Huron, call this the Broken Snowshoe

Month. Late winter can compress snow into such a hard-packed ice-crusted mass that snowshoe lacings are easily rasped away.

Mirroring the ice-blue tinge of our Paradise snowdrifts, the primary gemstone of March is the aquamarine, a variety of beryl, an aluminum silicate mineral related to the emerald. A pale-to-rich deep blue with an occasional tint of green, aquamarine, known as "the gem of the sea," results from small quantities of iron that have been trapped in beryl crystals as they formed in ancient slow-cooling igneous/magma rock known as pegmatite. Ferrous iron gives aquamarine the trademark blue color many of us are familiar with. Ferric iron lends a green tint. Beryl has no hue, and raw aquamarine, more of a greenish blue, is heat-treated to remove most of the greenish hue.

Some aquamarines appear almost colorless by daylight, taking on a deeper tone indoors or by candlelight. Darker stones can also change dramatically in color when viewed from a different angle.

"Aquamarine" comes from the Latin words *aqua* (water) and *marina* (of the sea).

Thought to be a prize of mermaids, stones were frequently worn by sailors and other seafarers as a talisman for protection against drowning, shipwreck, or seasickness. Sailing ships decorated with the gemstones were intended to attract tranquil seas.

Sumerian, Egyptian, Greek, and Roman references to "sea-green beryl" have proven that aquamarine was well known and used as far back as the 6th century BCE. The Flemish mineralogist and physician Anselmus de Boodt first suggested the name aquamarine in his 1609 work, *Gemmarum et Lapidum Historia* (*The History of Gems and Stones*). The earliest modern-day discovery of aquamarine came from the mountains of Siberia in 1723.

Today, commercial stones come largely from mines in Brazil and Mozambique, and to a lesser degree from Nigeria, Pakistan, Myanmar, Madagascar, Colorado, and other areas.

Santa Maria Aquamarine describes stones of a deep vibrant blue from the Santa Maria de Itabira mines in the Marambaia Valley of

Brazil. With the original mine exhausted, Santa Maria Aquamarine is extremely rare. Mozambique stones of similar clarity and tone are known as Santa Maria Africana or Santa Maria Afrique. Rich, sea-blue Pedro Azul Aquamarine comes from the Minas Gerais region of southeastern Brazil, a leading source of the gem.

Aquamarine symbolizes courage and hope, something few of us can afford to be without in these, the dark days of March.

Though the morning broke mild and spring-like, satiny mounds of old snow still lie across the water-meadow in velvet-blue—aquamarine—shadow. Conjuring daffodils out of snowdrifts may seem preposterous, but the daffodil has long been designated our flower of March. One of the earliest blooms of the year, its brilliance signals warmer days ahead with the promise of rebirth and new beginnings. Over sixty years ago, Uncle Harold planted a dozen butter-yellow double-daffodil bulbs outside his eastside cottage. A handful still fire up the tea deck every spring.

The daffodil, an ancient perennial also called trumpet narcissus or jonquil, belongs to the *Amaryllis* family. Native to the Iberian Peninsula, Southern France, and North Africa, and introduced to the Far East around the 10th century, the daffodil now grows in temperate climates all over the world. Six smooth white or yellow petals surround a trumpet-shaped corona, long, narrow leaves rising from the base of a single stem.

The word *narcissus* has been linked to the Greek word *narcotic*, originating with the Greek physician Galen, referring to substances that numb or deaden. Galen, in turn, probably based *narcotic* on the Greek word *narcosis*, used by Hippocrates in describing the process of numbing. Among several other plants, narcissi produce an alkaloid that can be poisonous if ingested, a property exploited in the production of the alkaloid galantamine used in the treatment of Alzheimer's disease.

"Daffodil" likely derives from *affodell*, a variant of *asphodel*, a name the narcissus/daffodil was frequently given in antiquity. Asphodel comes from the Greek *asphodelos* meaning "lily." Why the initial "d" was added remains a mystery, though from at least the 16th century, the daffodil, sometimes known as the lent lily, was also called daffydowndilly.

The national flower of Wales, the daffadowndilly often blankets the Welsh countryside by March 1, St. David's Day. We are not so lucky here in Paradise. Still, those golden beauties at Harold's Tea Deck will no doubt have bloomed by the end of the month.

❈ *6 March* ❈

A BLANKET OF OLD SNOW deep under the cedars and packed in hollows and shady spots like raw unwashed cotton spreads across the water-meadow, where earlier this morning the thick-wet of fog crept up from a partially open river. On the maple slope at Russell's, the day's unseasonable mildness has laid bare patches of frozen earth for the first time since winter's descent. The Finns call March the Earth Month for this reason.

In the coming weeks, after the spring snowmelt has come and gone, we'll prowl the land again, taking note of the adjustments winter's passage has affected—trees collapsed or vanished under the weight of ice or snow or water and the shift and flux of the riverbank.

Wherever we live, ancient landscapes have emerged and crumbled with time and catastrophe for eons. Paradise, a pinprick just off the southern edge of the Canadian Shield, is, like all of the planet, the culmination of vast swaths of geological time.

Southern Ontario blossomed from ground moraine, a vast wrinkled sheet of till—assorted clays, silts, sands, pebbles, cobbles, and boulders—that formed the bottom of an ancient glacial lake extending broadly from the base of the Canadian Shield.

Also known as the Laurentian Plateau, the Canadian Shield, over a hundred miles to the north, makes up 50 percent of Canada's land mass and extends in a horseshoe shape from Labrador and the Arctic through most of Quebec, much of Ontario, Manitoba, the Northwest Territories and Nunavut, into northern Saskatchewan, northeastern Alberta, and the northern states of New York, Wisconsin, and Minnesota.

The only exposed portion of the North American Craton—the earth's underlying Precambrian continental crust that stretches from Greenland to Northern Mexico, making up the greater part of the Canadian Shield—was forged three billion years ago by the workings of plate tectonics, glaciation, and erosion. The expanse contains some of the oldest rocks in the world, mostly granites. Blocks of core crust, fused by collision, created the Grenville Mountains, perhaps the largest range ever to exist on earth. Spreading from Quebec to Texas, the Grenvilles eroded away at least 800 million years ago, leaving behind the Canadian Shield's present low profile.

The youngest portion of the Canadian Shield, the Grenville Province (170–570 million years old), spans an area from Sudbury, to the southeast, to the St. Lawrence River.

During the Paleozoic and Mesozoic eras (from 570 to 63 million years ago), basins off the Canadian Shield—the Hudson Bay and Moose River Basins in the north and the Superior, Southern, and Grenville in the south—filled up with sediment, with limestone from the sea creatures of primordial reefs, salt deposits from evaporated inland seas, and conglomerates, sandstones, and shales from ancient mountains and the Shield itself. From Windsor to Goderich to Sarnia, a massive saltwater lagoon flourished, though few pockets of its thick sedimentary bed remain.

About 66 million years ago, at the end of the Mesozoic Era, ice began to thicken, triggering the advance and retreat of glaciers in the Quaternary Period, which began 1.75 million years ago. This development, incidentally, led to our ancient ancestors, Cro-Magnon humans, venturing into Alaska on a land bridge from Siberia.

The Laurentide Ice Sheet, which began its final advance 115,000 years ago, covered all of Ontario and much of the northern United

States. The Laurentide began to melt about 18,000 years ago, ending about 8,000 BCE. Sea levels then rose, and the land began to rebound.

Some of it still rebounds.

Over eons, these retreating ice sheets laid down the glacial deposits that produced the fertile soils still farmed today in Southern Ontario, the most common precipitate being till. Heaps of such rubble, formed between the fingers or arms of a glacier, are known as glacial moraines. The nearest moraine to Paradise, which lies in the Grenville Basin, is the Oak Ridge Moraine, located on high land that rises between Lake Ontario and Georgian Bay.

Sitting on the crest of the north hill, our eyes skim the snow-covered tips of maples and white cedars. The apple trees beside us, gnarled and stooped, spread out their limbs like open arms. We all await another springtide, breathless in the cold for what seems like eons more.

❈ *9 March* ❈

THE FULL CROW MOON or Full Snow Crust Moon—the first full moon of spring—is riding high in the southeast as I step out into a bitterly cold but crystal-blue night. This year's March full moon appears especially large and bright, a supermoon making one of its closest orbital approaches to the earth for the year. We'll witness a second supermoon next month.

Moonlight has painted a luminous haze-fire on the skim of snow that has freshened the meadow's foot-deep crusted remnants. The ribbon of river runs swollen with ice chunks and glittering like a snow globe. We can hear it singing below, a frost-bound promise of warming days, clattering crows, and a thawing landscape.

❖ *19 March* ❖

THIS MORNING, AN ice jam has flooded the flats, smaller floes coursing downstream between riverbanks still locked in ice. On March 21, 1971 (as my father's cottage notebook reports), snow, drifted to twelve feet, clogged the top of the steps. More than we'd ever seen before. More than we've seen since. A shallow ridge of snow on the hill-top and a staircase hardened with rime seem trifling by comparison. Even with a forecast of eighteen inches or more in blizzard form, we can still withdraw in safety in an hour or so, before the first squall rolls in. Survival is not an issue.

Not so for the First Nations tribes, the French explorers, fur traders, missionaries, European immigrants, Loyalist refugees, and freed slaves who came before us. Regional histories rarely advance neatly or simply. Just to furnish some sense of the place Paradise holds in time, I'll keep this one brief.

Paleo-Indians lived in our area as early as 9000 BCE, Archaic cultures flourishing from 5000 BCE to the early centuries CE. A thousand years ago, a woodland people known as the Attiwandaronk Nation held the central and southern portions of Ontario's southwestern peninsula in which Paradise lies. They slipped through the thick forests on high ground or river trails that crisscrossed the land from Lake Ontario to Lake Huron, from Lake Erie to Georgian Bay. Some of them may even have walked or paddled the river just as we will in the weeks to come.

The name Attiwandaronk comes from the Huron/Wyandot Nation, a tribal people with whom the Attiwandaronk traded. The Huron/Wyandot, allies of the northern Algonquin, were then living on the shores of Georgian Bay. (The Algonquin, including the Ojibwe/Chippewa bands still holding reservation land to the north of Paradise on Lake Huron, Georgian Bay, and the Bruce Peninsula, originally lived in eastern Ontario and southern Quebec. The large group of

Algonquin-speaking people, which stretches from Virginia to the Rocky Mountains and Hudson Bay, was named after the tribe.)

The Iroquois all but annihilated the Huron/Wyandot or Wendat people in the mid-17th century. "Attiwandaronk" translates as "people who speak a slightly different language," referring to the difficulty the Huron/Wyandot had in understanding their southern neighbors. At the time of the European invasion into what was to them the New World, the Attiwandaronk—at least twelve thousand strong— occupied about forty small villages in Southern Ontario. They grew squash, beans, and maize, and gathered nuts and fruits. They also mined lead, copper, and flint fifteen miles to our southeast, just north of present-day Fergus.

The Attiwandaronk also bartered for tobacco with the Tionontati or Petun (the Tobacco Nation) of Lake Huron, and they traded flint to Huronia's old enemy, the Iroquois, who were then living to the south in present-day New York State. French explorers and fur traders probably referred to the Attiwandaronk as the Neutrals for this reason.

In 1651, during the French and Indian Wars (1642–1698), the Attiwandaronk/Neutrals abandoned their villages in the interior fol-lowing a battle with the Iroquois in what is now Hamilton, Ontario. Some Neutral survivors of this skirmish fled north, hiding out in the caves of Elora Gorge, twelve miles southeast of us, this side of Fergus.

French explorer Samuel de Champlain, who first arrived on the St. Lawrence in 1603, formed an alliance with both the Algonquin and the Huron. Champlain traveled along the shores of Lake Huron on a voyage of discovery, spending the winter of 1615 among the native people at Manisetung (present-day Goderich) about sixty miles directly west of the cottage, on Lake Huron. Returning to Georgian Bay, he crossed the height of land to the north, possibly passing very near to Paradise.

Also living among the Attiwandaronk at that time were French missionaries. Father Joseph de la Roche Daillon, a Recollect (the Order of Friars Minor Recollect, a reform branch of the Franciscans), back-packed the peninsula from one end to the other, staying a year in an

Attiwandaronk village near Drayton. Father Jean de Brébeuf, a Jesuit who worked predominantly among the Huron, was eventually killed by the Iroquois in the captured Huron village of Taenhatenteron (St. Ignace). As reported in Paul Raguenau's *Manuscript of 1652*, Brébeuf wrote about the falls on the Grand River at present-day Elora in the heart of old Attiwandaronk Land, in the realm of the Neutral Nation.

Many of these explorers focused on the forever stands of walnut, chestnut, and sycamore to the south or on the great gloom of the endless coniferous Boreal Forest to the north. By contrast, French soldier and adventurer Antoine Laurmet de la Mothe, Sieur de Cadillac, described the region in 1702 as so temperate, so good, and so beautiful, that it could justly be called the earthly paradise of North America. By 1759, when French rule in what they called the New World fell to the British on Quebec City's Plains of Abraham, Ojibwe tribes—principally the Mississauga from northern Lake Huron—had moved southward. By the time of the American Revolution, they occupied the entire tract of Attiwandaronk land but lost a large portion in 1784 when they ceded to the Crown an area bounded on the west by a line running northwest from near Burlington on Lake Ontario to the Conestoga River near Arthur, just six miles northeast of us.

In October of that same year (1784), Joseph Brant (Thayendanegea), sachem and warrior of the Five Nations Iroquois, signed a treaty with Sir Frederick Haldimand, the British Governor of Canada, by which a tract of land six miles to either side of the O:se Kenhionhata:tie River (now called the Grand River), from Lake Erie to the river's source, was bestowed upon the Iroquois Mohawk Nation. Formerly of New York State, the Iroquois had been settled in Southern Ontario by their British allies. Acreage to the north, east, and west was set aside as Crown and Clergy Preserves. United Empire Loyalists fleeing the American Revolution had previously been granted 3.2 million acres in Upper Canada, most of these refugees settling along the St. Lawrence River. This necessitated establishing a western expansion of the Preserves.

In 1827, territory that included old Peel Township in which

Paradise lies was given by the Chippewa Nation to the Crown in the form of a soldier and British agent to the region's Indigenous tribes, James Givins, who had participated in both the American Revolution and the War of 1812.

Among the first non-aboriginal settlers of our area were fugitive American slaves who had escaped on the Underground Railroad and had taken their names from their American masters. Beginning in the 1830s, they homesteaded along the Conestoga, building churches and schools in wooded areas that became known as the Queen's Bush. Most of these settlers were subsequently cheated out of their lands over many decades, though their descendants lived in the area for over a century. European immigrants, many of them tenant farmers from the British Isles or German Mennonites from Pennsylvania, began to arrive beginning in the 1840s.

From May to October 1843, Robert Kerr, assisted by John Cary and John Burns, was assigned to survey Peel Township, naming it for Britain's then prime minister, Robert Peel. In his diary, which is kept in the Wellington County Museum and Archives in Fergus, Ontario, Kerr describes the Drayton area as "swamp, with cedars, maple, elm, basswood and hemlock, clay soil, some stones." He goes on to claim that there were "some banks or hills of small elevations along the creeks and streams which flow thro [sic] it. Along the Conestogo River and on some of the larger streams, the land is elevated on one side, the bank steep and abrupt but on the opposite side it is low level and for a considerable distance. . . . The soil of the Township is generally composed of clay having the surface covered with a deep layer of vegetation."

This describes the Paradise we know and love to perfection.

Fully half of old Peel Township had to be drained due to the flat topography and the clay/loam soil. The Gully in Paradise still siphons off the excess water from the neighboring fields on the north hill.

When Peel Township opened for settlement in 1845, lots were scooped up within ten years. Our own sixteen wild acres, on the south half of Lot 1, had been part of a hundred-acre plot given by the Crown to Thomas Wilson, whose family still lived in the area when I was a child.

❋ *20 March* ❋

HERE I AM ALONE AGAIN on the hilltop, in the vast serenity of night. Twenty-plus inches of freshly fallen snow have released a radiance of stillness and midnight blue. Wrapped in arctic air, the world above and the world below shiver through the silence and streaming like scattered jewels across the zenith of a rare, black-velvet sky, starlight's daggers of ice dazzle the Milky Way.

In ancient Egypt, the goddess Nut bestowed blessings on the earth each night by offering up celestial milk to nourish trees and other vegetation.

May the magic of her starlight suffuse the air, penetrate the frost-hard ground beneath our snowdrifts, and touch the multitude of dormant seedlings in Paradise.

This very day marks the Vernal Equinox, the astronomical first day of spring in the Northern Hemisphere. An equinox occurs the moment the center of the visible sun idles directly above the equator. Day and night stand in parity.

Here in Paradise, with ever-lengthening days and the gradual warming of temperatures, we know that the struggle between light and darkness and between life and death has ended for another year, at least symbolically.

This glorious balance of day and night—twelve hours each—has been commemorated around the world for millennia: in the thousand-year-old Persian (Iraqi) New Year, Nowruz (Farsi for "New Day"); in Stonehenge's Neolithic equinox alignment; and in Chechen Itza's Mayan Kukulkàn Pyramid on the Yucatan Peninsula, where shadows from the late-afternoon equinox sun snake down the northern staircase. Easter, a key component of Christian resurrection mythology, falls on the first Sunday after a full moon that occurs on or after the spring equinox. The name derives from the Germanic/Anglo-Saxon Ostara or Eostre, a spring goddess associated with hares, eggs, and rebirth.

The Druid plant of the equinox was the trefoil or three-leafed shamrock, which represented the Celtic Triple Goddess. Like many other cultures, the Celts held the number three to be sacred. One represented individuality. Two, duality. Three referenced a deeper reality beyond human comprehension, the great mystery of the cosmos.

Definitive spring is, of course, subjective, varying from place to place and from year to year. In Paradise, we number a sustained flow of sugar-maple sap, the calls of returning Canada geese, red-winged blackbirds, and robins, and perhaps, on a warm snow-melt day, the rumble and hum of a bumblebee.

But for now, all of these lie dormant, buried beneath a bed of snow. But better days lie ahead, the spring equinox tells us. When the fading grays of winter finally give way, seeds will germinate, bud, and blossom, and animals will stir in their dens. New life will, once again, pierce the darkness.

❖ *25 March* ❖

UNTIL JANUARY 1752, when England adopted the Gregorian calendar to align the Empire with Continental Europe, this day ushered in the New Year in England and the colonies of what was then considered the New World.

The first calendar of the ancient Romans had a ten-month year, which also began in March. Julius Caesar revised that date to the first of January. Despite this, the Middle Ages saw a host of countries reverting to the March date until, in 1582, Pope Gregory reinstated January first as the opening day of the New Year. His Gregorian Calendar was widely adopted in Europe.

On this frigid March morning, Paradise lies largely free of snow but for shadowy spaces underneath the cedars and the dips and hallows of the water-meadow. Slabs of loosened ice on the river have backed up the flow again, under a freezing rain and a land-lash of high wind.

❋ *28 March* ❋

TODAY, FRINGES OF FOREST stand smoke-gray and empty in a dark but gentle rain. Mud-brown and dirt-black, a gloominess enfolds us on the hills of Paradise. Winter trees hunker down singly or in long bare lines. Under a skim of snow, ice rafts have clogged the river, though not so much as to overrun the banks. The temperature hovers near 50 degrees Fahrenheit.

Though underfoot the ground feels claggy with lumps of mud, our hearts have gladdened. We've just heard the first staccato drumming of a ruffed grouse. We've glimpsed the first robin, the first Canada goose, the first red-winged blackbird, the first starling. Puffs of pussy willow have popped out, and the red squirrels have begun to lap at sapsucker drillings in the sugar maples.

At long last, it's springtime in Paradise!

"Suddenly sunshine and perfect blue—
an April day in the morning."
— HARRIET PRESCOTT SPOFFORD

❖ *1 April* ❖

A GALE OF WINTER wind in the night left four inches of fresh snow on the ground this morning. All through the day, falling snow stitched the sky into a hushed and heavy earth-bound haze, which cleared by evening, when it turned much colder.

A sluice of water is showing on top of the river ice. With characteristically unpredictable weather, Mother Nature has stifled any talk of spring, fitting for April Fool's Day.

The origins of this day are still a mystery to us. John Aubrey labeled April first as "Fooles holy day" in 1686, though the concept of practical jokes and hoaxes can be traced back to at least 1582, when parts of Europe switched from the Julian to the Gregorian Calendar. This branded those who failed to see that a new year had begun as fools. Further back still, an ancient Roman festival at the end of March— Hilaria—had citizens dress in disguise, something of a foolish notion in itself.

"April," from the Latin *aprilis*, may have come to us from the Latin *aperire*, to open, this month—sacred to the Roman goddess Venus— being the time when flowers and trees begin to bloom. Alternatively, *aprilis* may have been taken from *aphrilis*, from Venus's Greek counterpart, Aphrodite (*Aphros*).

The flower of April, the common daisy (*Bellis perennis*), belongs to the *Aster* family. Also known as lawn daisy or English daisy, Bellis perennis, native to Morocco, southwestern Asia, and Europe, has been naturalized in most temperate areas, including the Americas. In general, flowers bloom from early to late summer. Our common daisies here in Paradise can be found from late April into early September.

Most of us are familiar with the daisy form. Leaves form small rounded or spoon-shaped rosettes. The flower heads themselves, produced on a stem without leaves, consist of a yellow center of disk florets and a halo of white petals (sometimes tipped red), called ray florets, each one an individual flower. All bits work together to attract insects. The daisy also exhibits a phenomenon called heliotropism, where flowers follow the position of the sun.

The name *Bellis perennis* likely came to us from the Latin *bellus* (pretty) and *perennis* (everlasting), though the plant has astringent/ antiseptic properties and ancient Roman physicians accompanying legions gathered flower heads for their juice. Soaked bandages would wrap sword and spear wounds. So "bellis" may be related instead to the Latin word *bellum*, meaning war. Daisies are still used in homeopathy.

The word "daisy" is probably a corruption of "day's eye," the flower heads closing at night and reopening at dawn. Chaucer called them "the eye of the day." As a nickname for Margaret, Daisy traces back to the French word for the oxeye daisy, *marguerite*.

Symbolizing childhood innocence and purity, the daisy well suits the sense of new beginnings we attach to the month of April. What could be purer or more innocent than the wild babes of April? Our raccoon, red squirrel, or cottontail kits? Our eastern chipmunk pups?

The stone of April, the diamond, is also a symbol of purity and innocence, so perfect for these newborn days of spring. (The origin of birthstones is thought to date to the breastplate of the Biblical Aaron, which contained twelve gems, each representing one of the twelve tribes of Israel.) The Greek name for diamond is *adámas*—unbreakable or unconquerable.

Diamond is a rare form of carbon, the atoms of which have a crystal structure called diamond cubic. Solid carbon comes in different configurations known as allotropes, depending on the type of chemical involved. The two most common allotropes of carbon are diamond and graphite.

As we know, a pure diamond transmits visible light and appears clear and colorless. Tinted diamonds result from structural defects or chemical impurities, principally the substitution of some other atom for a carbon atom in the crystal lattice. We call this a carbon flaw. Nitrogen produces yellow or brown stones, the most common diamond. Boron results in blue stones. And graphite clusters form black or carbonado diamonds. Radiation exposure produces green diamonds. The rarest stones of all are red, followed by pink, colors for which the cause is not yet known. In December 2009, a five-carat vivid pink diamond was sold for US$10.8 million in Hong Kong, at that time the most money ever paid for a diamond.

Most natural diamonds formed in the earth's mantle at depths of from 93 to 155 miles and are between 1 billion and 3.5 billion years old. Under extreme pressure and temperature, fluids containing carbon dissolved various minerals, replacing them with diamonds, which were eventually brought to the surface by volcanic activity and were deposited in igneous rocks known as kimberlites, lamproites, and lamprophyres.

Until recently, diamonds had the highest hardness of any natural material on both the Vickers and the Mohs scales, an attribute that makes them particularly suited to gemstone jewelry. A diamond could only be scratched by another diamond, so they easily resisted the rigors of everyday wear.

In 2022, I read that scientists had confirmed the existence of the mineral lonsdaleite, which has a hexagonal structure as opposed to diamond's cubic atomic form. This makes lonsdaleite 58 percent more durable than diamond. Discovered in a meteorite from a dwarf planet billions of years old, lonsdaleite formed from the massive release of pressure when an asteroid collided with the planet. If we had access to such a mineral, lonsdaleite would no doubt further strengthen industrial tools like saw blades and drill bits.

The hardest diamonds, used to polish other diamonds, originate in New South Wales, Australia. Diamonds also have the highest thermal conductivity of any natural material, which makes them invaluable in industry.

Seven countries have been the major producers of gem-quality diamonds for more than a decade, as with other gem extraction circumstances, sometimes under horrific consequences for native people. These are Russia, Botswana, Canada, Angola, South Africa, Democratic Republic of the Congo, and Namibia. Each generates more than a million carats per year.

Reflecting all the colors of the rainbow, diamonds represent purity, abundance, and clarity, all of which we're hopeful we'll see heaped and glittering in tomorrow's April sunlight.

❊ *7 April* ❊

NEARLY A WEEK AGO NOW, the spring ice-out began. With frost still seizing fields, flats, and forest embankments, snowmelt had nowhere to go but into flood. The river swelled, mud-brown with silt under a gloom of gray sky.

We watched the flow surge past, shouldering mini ice floes, tree limbs, and root boles. A slosh of dirty snow still littered the ground, punctured by dead grasses and a twiggy profusion of russet willow withies. Patches of mud streaked the open slopes beyond The West Woods.

As the day progressed and the skies cleared to sapphire and sunshine, the waters, reflecting a deep cerulean blue, further expanded until they swirled sixty feet from edge to edge. Miniature icebergs and chunky ice rafts floated by or rammed themselves up on both near and distant shorelines. Snow remnants on open ground shrank before our eyes, persistent in the shadows, dark and dappled.

By early the next day, the river had sprawled across the whole of the water-meadow. We watched as it lapped at the base of the northern hills. The cedar posts supporting The Willow Deck stood knee-deep in floodwaters that inundated the entire western peninsula, where open land and woodland normally encompassed by the river turn south. A gigantic sheet of ice water stretched across the landscape. A silver-gray lake peppered with cedar groves, fringe hardwoods, and exposed high ground, rose here and there above the surface. Snow lingered under the edge of the cedars and in a low ridge at the top of the hill. Shreds and scraps lay about on the open saturated ground.

This morning, under soft gray skies, spring's thaw still sluices over the water-meadow, slicing deep into the forests and fields to the south, the boiling current at its center coursing east to west. We can see that the water has now receded to within a dozen feet of The Willow Deck, yet sodden arms still reach back from the perimeter in spits and seeps, ponds and puddles. Little snow remains—just a patch or two on an open hillside or under the cedar trees.

All day long, newly returned red-winged blackbirds flitted about the bird feeders in the company of our overwintering wild canaries, chicka-dees, and cardinals. And we've already spotted a half dozen robins, several red squirrels, a handful of chipmunks, and even a groundhog or two.

All of Paradise lies in wait. Expectant. Scoured and silted. Primed and prepped. In the pink of health and vitality.

Fittingly, the Full Pink Moon, the second supermoon of the year—named for the color of wild ground phlox or moss pink (*Phlox subulata*), one of the earliest and most widespread of spring flowers—has just now topped the eastern woods, sailing through a crisp and silvered atmosphere. Paradise does not support wild phlox, though we know that dame's rocket (*Hesperis matronalis*)—an invasive species often mistaken for wild phlox—will flood the water-meadow with a flush of blanched violet and rose-pink by early May.

Also known as the Full Sprouting Grass Moon, the Full Fish Moon, the Full Hare Moon, or the Full Egg Moon, the Full Pink Moon reflects all the frenzied activity of April. In early springtime, everything happens at once. As the month progresses, fish will become more plentiful, many birds will lay their eggs, cottontails will breed, and new grasses will bud.

A poet whose name I've long forgotten once declared that in spring he believed in God again. In my mind, he must have been thinking of April, the month that so fiercely embodies the miracle of life. That force of love and logic in the Universe. A power, an energy and flow beyond comprehension. Beyond imagination. Beyond expression. Beyond words.

To me, any spiritual prohibition against speaking the name of God seems meant not as a taboo but as a simple spiritual truth. How can one single word encompass a concept as broad and embracing as God without diminishing or reducing its totality?

The human mind cannot know what it cannot name, it's been said. And so countless manifestations of the Divine—the sun, the sea, water, fire, fertility, vegetable and animal life—all those specific transcending principles and energies that invigorate our world, have been ranked and quantified through time and space, given a pecking order according to human impulse and understanding. Many have become gods and goddesses themselves.

"Love needs to find form. . . . Essence has to manifest itself." (Bono)

Whatever animates the universe seems to inhabit all things, all creatures, all places, all people, perhaps incarnating more strongly or more consciously, in one place or one person over another. Yet to my mind, as Dame Julian of Norwich wrote in the Middle Ages in her book, *The Revelations of Divine Love*, "It is a greater honor to God for you to see him in everything than in one special thing."

As Paradise rebounds, we're gearing up for the spring tour, for I believe, as Joseph Campbell wrote in *Hero of a Thousand Faces*, "God . . . is in the forest and in the fields and on the mountains when the rain comes."

What hollowed tree trunks will have fallen under the weight of winter? What ice-pummeled embankment will have washed away? What nips and tucks will the river have taken in its course?

❧ *12 April* ❧

ON THIS EASTER AFTERNOON, we're tinting a dozen hard-boiled eggs steeped in tea leaves. Our very own Easter bunnies, Eastern cottontails—symbols of birth and renewal—rolic and leapfrog on the greening turf outside the west window, a courtship dance filled with the high kicks of back feet, with loops and twirls and spritely leaps.

Bede the Venerable claims in his 6th century *Ecclesiastical History of the English People*, that the word "Easter" traces back to the Anglo-Saxon equivalent of this month—*Oster-monath*, or *Eostur-monath*—named for the Anglo-Saxon fertility goddess Eostre or Eostrae, whose festival took place at this time of the year.

On this mild Sunday, the river is running well over its banks, though the water level has dropped substantially. Hazy sunlight punches now and again through the dull overcast, scraps of snow stipple the landscape, and cast-off ponds glisten across the water-meadow. Flattened by the weight of a vanished snowpack, the browned grasses of winter sprawl everywhere.

With warming days and still sub-freezing nights, our tree sap is rising, maple sugaring in full swing. The red squirrels negotiating an aerial freeway of interlaced trunks and branches have begun to chew at the oozing from sugar and red maples, some lapping at holes drilled by yellow-bellied sapsuckers. Red squirrels can even suss out the difference between maple species, singling out those with the highest sugar concentrations. The Ojibwe to the north, on Lake Huron, call April *iskigamizige-giizis*, the "maple-sap-boiling moon."

According to oral tradition, the First Nations of northeastern North America processed maple syrup as a source of energy and nutrition long before European settlement. At the start of the spring breakup, they incised V-shapes in the trunks of maple trees, inserting a reed or concave piece of bark to collect the sap in birch bark buckets into which hot cooking stones were added to boil off most of the water. They also set pails outside overnight to freeze. Under a layer of ice, the sugary sap would settle to the bottom by morning.

Today, small-scale sugar-making proceeds at much the same pace. During the day, containers hung on nails in holes drilled into tree trunks gather sap, which is then heated in sugar shacks to evaporate the water. Subzero Fahrenheit temperatures will inhibit the sap flow overnight, but the pots remain in place, ready for the daytime surge.

Because of the high sugar content of their sap—roughly 2 to 5 percent—three maple species dominate syrup production—the sugar maple (*Acer saccharum*), the black maple (*Acer nigrum*), and the red maple (*Acer rubrum*). Sugar maple flourishes in Paradise, though hardly in sugar-bush numbers. Their fissured, gray boles reach up in double digits in the open spaces around both cottages. In late winter and early spring, starch stored in the trees before winter converts into sugar, which rises in the sap as the days warm.

Maples are usually tapped at thirty to forty years of age and can continue delivering sap until they are well over a hundred years old. Depending on the diameter of the trunk, each tree can supply between one and three taps a piece. An average maple generates five to fifteen gallons (twenty to sixty liters) of sap in a good season, larger trees upward of three hundred, from which eight gallons of maple syrup can be produced. If sap is boiled too long, the resulting syrup will crystallize. Under-boiling will yield a watery liquid that spoils quickly. Syrup must also be filtered to remove a gritty precipitate of sugar and calcium malate called sugar sand.

The matchless end product of sugaring—pure maple syrup—has a sugar/water ratio of roughly two to one. Early run syrup has the pale golden flush of light amber. The end run resembles black coffee. As the weather warms and maple buds begin to burst, the sap undergoes chemical changes, which make any resulting syrup unpalatable. Red maples, opening the earliest, thus have a shorter sugar season.

As with April's spring weather, the sap run progresses in fits and starts, lasting anywhere from one week to over a month. Quebec may furnish up to 70 percent of the world's maple syrup, but sweet festivities in Ontario abound. Elmira, twenty miles to the southwest, wrapped up its delicious one-day Maple Syrup Festival back on April 4.

❊ *13 April* ❊

A PATINA OF RIME FROST glazed the riverbank willows this morning, following a half-inch snowfall ushered in by vicious overnight winds. Wisps of water vapor swirled across the river's surface at noon, before another heavy slurry of rain and snow closed in.

Just before dusk now, and we're cold and dark and drizzly, the ground turned to mush and mud, the river high with fresh bits of slush and ice.

On the sloping hilltops, though, and along the staircase, our lilacs show a hint of bud. Faint slivers of green have sliced through the brown of winter grasses in the water-meadow. Very soon, beyond the brooding blackness of the cedar woods, our hardwoods will begin to blossom.

The ancient glacial basin in which Paradise lies has thickened with thousands of years of forest growth, a mixed woodland/plain ecozone that covers all of Southern Ontario. We are part of the temperate Great Lakes-St. Lawrence Forest, which stretches from the northern shores of Lake Superior well above Sault Ste. Marie eastward to Gaspé Peninsula. Dominated by broad-leaved deciduous trees like yellow birch, sugar and red maple, basswood, and red oak, along with coniferous white spruce, red and white pine, eastern hemlock, and eastern white cedar, this mixed forest forms a transition zone between the great Boreal Forest to the north and the Carolinian or Eastern Deciduous Forest to the south.

The largest intact forest on earth, the formidable Boreal rings the Northern Hemisphere, about a third of it spanning the Canadian landscape from Newfoundland to the Yukon, predominantly on the Canadian Shield. Most Canadian Boreal trees are conifers, chiefly black and white spruce, but also jack and lodgepole pine and balsam fir, along with aspen, eastern white cedar, poplar, and birch, most of them wrapped in a vast and boggy wetland of more than a million and a half lakes. As we have seen in past years, the Boreal's awesome magnificence can be most easily experienced from the most northerly point of Lake Superior's north shore on the Trans-Canada Highway east of Lake Nipigon. An endless watery expanse of black forest, mossy outcrops, and pristine lakes, ponds, rivers, and fens, the Canadian Boreal Forest reaches northward to the muskeg and tundra of the Hudson Bay Lowlands. From overhead on a clear day, I've watched sunlight reflecting on this marshy expanse, glittering as though it were draped in black lace.

Moderated by the Great Lakes, the once great Carolinian Forest begins some thirty miles to the south of Paradise, just outside of Cambridge and Woodstock. The name alludes to the Canadian portion of a forest region known in the United States as the Eastern Deciduous Forest, which extends from the Carolinas into Southern Ontario. The southern-most portion of the mixed woodland/plain ecozone, as well as the northern limit of the Eastern Deciduous Forest, the Carolinian is characterized by broad-leaved trees such as black walnut, ash, elm, white oak, magnolia, birch, chestnut, tulip, and silver maple. Established on limestone concealed by a mantle of glacial till, scarcely 10 percent of this original forest survives in Southern Ontario, the greater part having been erased by centuries of agriculture, logging, and urbanization.

Between the Boreal and the Carolinian Forests lie the sixteen acres of Paradise, part of the more than fifty million acres that comprise the Great Lakes-St. Lawrence Forest region, the second largest in Ontario. From the St. Lawrence, this region spans the most populous areas of Central Ontario to Lake Huron and includes a small area west of Lake

Superior along the Minnesota border. Very occasional portions that have never been cleared or otherwise transformed—like our wildwood across the river from Black Bass Bend—are known as ancient, primary, or primeval forest.

❈ *14 April* ❈

ON THIS DISMAL AFTERNOON of numbing rain and descending gloom, I'm huddled on Edna's deck reflecting on our own transitional forest.

The predominant tree of our Paradise woods is the native eastern white cedar (*Thuja occidentalis*), a member of the *Cypress* family also known as northern white cedar, swamp cedar, or American arborvitae (the Tree of Life). *Thuja* derives from the ancient Greek word *thuia*, the name given to a kind of African juniper that was formerly included in the genus. *Occidentalis* means "of the western world."

A slow-growing tree, the eastern white cedar can reach 125 feet, though few in our woods rise above sixty. The bark of the white cedar is a furrowed reddish-brown that peels in narrow strips. The fan-like branches have soft scaly leaves formed in flat sprays that are relished by white-tailed deer. Slender cones, which begin yellow-green and ripen to a nut brown, each contain about eight seeds. With little understory, a cedar forest like ours with dense foliage can provide considerable protection for wildlife, especially in the depths of winter. In summer, these woods resound with mass roosting and the murmuration staging of thousands of starlings and other blackbirds.

In the late 1950s, when the damp eastern woods had barely reached the open glade where Harold's Tea Deck now stands, a clump of advancing trees stood in for a beer-heavy Beverage Room while Uncle Harold's cottage was being built. On the west side, at Wood's End, another marooned cluster became the make-believe Silver Cedar Ranch. White cedars have since spread westward from Abaco Heights, which is now in the center of the eastern forest, marching up to the margins of the water-meadow. They've replaced countless hawthorns, lilacs, thorn apples, dogwoods, choke cherries, and buckthorns.

White cedars are long-lived. Some, inaccessible to deer and wildfire, are upward of eight hundred years old. One fallen tree was found to have 1,653 growth rings. Another stunted tree, known as the Witch Tree—Manidoo-giizhikens (Little Cedar Spirit in Ojibwe)—still grows out of a bare-rock cliff face on Lake Superior in Minnesota. Sieur de la Verendrye, a French adventurer, first described it as being fully mature—in 1731.

The First Nation Ojibwe hold the eastern white cedar in awe, not only for its usefulness in construction and craftwork but for the age-old medicinal properties of its sap, bark, and twigs. Cedar foliage, for instance, rich in vitamin C, quite likely cured the scurvy of Jacques Cartier and his companions during the grim winter of 1535–36.

The eastern white cedars of our wildwood across the river and in the extreme reaches of Paradise, east and west, are likely only a couple of hundred years old. Yet to wander among them brings the comfort of familiarity and peace at almost any time of the year, a cushiony if sometimes quaggy haven backed by the often-faint rush of the rapids below.

Nookomis Giizhik—Grandmother Cedar, the stuff of legends—has given us stair railings, swing frames, and roofing poles for The Willow Deck.

For decades, the soaring majesty of the American elm (*Ulmus americana*) glorified the landscape of Paradise. Elm's classic vase-shaped profile has grown to heights of well over eighty feet, especially those on the narrow strip of grassland across the river or on the fringes of the water-meadow. Their stately crowns of lush, serrated leaves cascaded like fountains and their deeply furrowed grayish-brown trunks welcomed my dad's handmade house-wren homes. For decades more, in death, their bared but graceful frames supported blackbird murmurations. They still do.

American elms belong to the genus *Ulmus* (*Ulmus* is the Greek word for "elm") in the plant family *Ulmaceae*, which dates back twenty million years to the Miocene. The genus, an hermaphrodite, has small purple-brown flowers that are wind-pollinated. Their late-spring fruit is a light, flat samara, a circular papery wing flushed with chlorophyll surrounding a single seed.

Sadly, Dutch elm disease brought on by a microfungus dispersed by two species of elm bark beetle has decimated American elms. Beginning in Europe, DED spread to North America in the 1950s when infested English elms were imported to Ohio for veneer. The research and eventual development of DED-resistant cultivars began in the Netherlands around 1928, but the regal American elm has sadly not rebounded.

Saplings that germinate and grow on the boundaries of the water-meadow here may reach thirty feet. Just a step off the path to The Willow Deck, one has managed fifteen feet. Death has already touched its upper branches, so we know its days are numbered.

White willow (*Salix alba*), native to Europe, western and central Asia, and North Africa, ranges up and down the Conestoga's banks, north and south. *Alba* is the Latin word for "white" and *salix* for "willow."

All willows love wet places, and several sizeable trees shade the beaver lodge beyond Castor's Landing. The massive matriarch below Russell's Cottage—rising easily to eighty feet—is as wide as she is tall. Her branches arch and bend. Some stretch for the sky. Some riffle the surface of the river. The lofty willows between the beaver den and the water-meadow, on both sides of the river, attract bald eagles, great horned owls, and red-tailed hawks.

A fast-growing, generally short-lived deciduous tree, white willow has a tough wood that easily decays, being susceptible to a variety of diseases. Trees may suffer great damage over winter or during violent storms.

Our water-meadow matriarch forfeited a hefty lower limb two years ago, lost to the weight of seasonal snowfall.

One of the first trees to leaf out in the spring and one of the last to drop leaves in autumn, the low-branching white willow presents a broad, pale-toned, rounded crown of grayish-green leaves, the undersides of which, covered with fine, silky, white hairs, gave the tree its name. The bark, grayish to yellow-brown, is deeply fissured, especially in older trees. Male and female catkins, on separate trees, are pollinated by insects. Male catkins are long and yellow. Female catkins, made up of capsules enclosing tiny seeds rooted in a white down, mature in midsummer, when they scatter with the wind.

Past and present, white willow has had innumerable uses: the bark for tanning leather, charcoal used in the production of gunpowder, withies for weaving, and (before the advent of plastic) artificial limbs.

The inner bark or leaves, steeped as tea or chewed, reduced fever and eased aches and pains for millennia. Salicin, the active ingredient isolated in crystalline form in 1828, produced the chemical derivative salicylic acid—aspirin.

No doubt harvested by countless bygone generations, white willow is a favorite snack of the beaver in Paradise. On a late summer afternoon stroll not long ago, as we neared The Dam Rapids on the edge of the eastern woods, a chestnut-colored boulder hunched up on the far-side sandbar resolved to a large adult beaver. Accompanied by three tiny kits, she'd been instructing them on the finer points of stripping bark from willow withies. Each gnawed on a sapling, eating the living plant membrane—cambrium—directly beneath the bark. A parade of gleaming white twigs—*wasacsena* to the Ojibwe—floated off downstream. An enchanting scene.

Another abundant tree of our Paradise woodland is the maple, which grows mostly around the cottages themselves. Some were transplanted years ago from the family home in Kitchener. Sugar and Norway maples dominate, both belonging to the *Sapindaceae* family, which includes soapberry and lychee.

Sugar maple (*Acer saccharum*), also known as rock maple, birds-eye maple, sweet maple, and curly maple, is native to eastern Canada and the northeastern United States. The word *acer* derives from Latin *acies*, which comes from a proto-Indo-European word meaning "sharp or pointed." *Saccharum* traces back to the Sanskrit word *sárkarā*, meaning "ground or candied sugar."

These trees love a cool climate, requiring a hard winter freeze for proper dormancy. Consequently, maple syrup production is impossible in the southern part of its range, where winters are just not cold enough. Sugar maples dazzle with their stunning fall foliage, from brilliant yellow-gold to burnished orange and fluorescent red. With five-lobed leaves in opposite pairs, rounded at their interior edges, sugar maples tend to color unevenly in the fall, some trees showing all the above hues at the same time. Swaths of leaves on a mature tree may change color weeks ahead of or behind the balance of the tree.

Exceptional sugar maples can reach 150 feet and survive three hundred years. The average tree however, like ours here in Paradise, only reaches between 80 and 115 feet, with a lifespan of one hundred to two hundred years.

Sugar maple's early-spring flowers are yellow-green; leaf buds are pointy and dark brown. The fruit—pairs of samaras (winged seeds)—drop in autumn and require at least forty-five days of temperatures below 39 degrees Fahrenheit in order to break their coating down. (Seeds soaked, with their wings removed, can be eaten if boiled, seasoned, and roasted.) Seeds germinate the following spring after the soil has warmed and any danger of frost has passed. The most shade- and soil-tolerant of any large deciduous tree, sugar maples have roots that draw water up from great depths, discharging that water into upper, drier layers of soil, which is, of course, beneficial to all the plants growing around them.

One of our most prominent sugar maples graces the rim of the slope to the water-meadow, left and front of Russell's Cottage. This spring, though its trunk is anchored tall and strong, a withering limb hints that the tree's allotted sixty years may be nearly spent.

Unfortunately, sugar maples are more susceptible to pollution than any other species of maple. They have been decimated by acid rain, soil acidification, and the decades-long use of de-icing salt. Ours still hold their own, but . . .

Enter the Norway maple (*Acer platanoides*), always ready to pick up the slack. Native to western Asia and eastern and central Europe, Norway maple arrived in North America between 1750 and 1760, brought into the Northeast as an ornamental shade tree. *Platanoides* (resembling a plane tree) comes from the word *platanus*, Latin for "plane tree" with the Latin suffix, *-oides*, meaning "like."

Growing sixty-five to a hundred feet tall, with a broad crown, Norway maple's bark is gray-brown and shallowly grooved, unlike most other maples, which tend toward a shaggier bark. Buds are a shiny red-brown, and the five lobes of each leaf bear one to three side teeth. Each leaf secretes a milky juice when broken.

Early spring flowers, yellow to yellow-green, open before the leaves do, as with all maples. They last two to three weeks. Paired seeded samaras, at an almost 180-degree angle, form the fruit, the seed a flattened disc. Autumn color is generally a modest buff yellow. Under ideal circumstances, in its home territory, Norway maples can live 250 years, though here in North America they barely reach sixty.

Norway maple's competitive edge makes them one of the few introduced species that can invade and colonize a native forest. Other maple seeds need that hard winter freeze and sun-warmed spring soil. Norway's require only three months of temperatures below 40 degrees Fahrenheit and thirteen hours of spring sunshine, and they will sprout about the same time as they leaf out. (Autumn leaf-drop requires ten hours of daylight.) Most North American trees rely on air temperature to bud, so Norway maples often open up well before native trees, which can be hampered by weather. In addition, the roots of the Norway maple grow close to the surface, drawing moisture away from other plants.

Norway maples are often marred by mites, which cause galls on the undersides of numerous leaves, and tar spots from fungal infections run rampant. Both infestations, though generally harmless, have afflicted many of our Paradise trees, including the giant at the front of Russell's Cottage near the entrance to The West Woods. This seasoned tree manifests a glory of crimson, tangerine, and lemon-yellow leaves every autumn. Just as magically, a dogwood has taken root in the fork of its two main, shaggy-barked trunks. The Norway maple cluster around Edna's Cottage also suffers from diverse fungi, which has led to isolated dead spots called cankers.

A third maple species, silver maple (*Acer saccharinum*), a medium-sized, fast-growing tree of graceful foliage and rapidly branching crown, favors the moist alluvial soils found along waterways and wetlands. *Saccharinum* combines the Greek word *sakkharon* meaning "sugar" with the Latin suffix -*inum* meaning "of or like."

Also called soft maple, river maple, silverleaf maple, swamp maple, water maple, and creek maple, silver maples are native to the eastern and central United States and southeastern Canada, including here in southwestern Ontario. Growing to an average of fifty to eighty feet and living upward of 130 years, silver maple demands more sunlight than other maples, so few of them have taken hold in Paradise where thick cedars abound.

The first of our maples to bloom, silver maple produces greenish-yellow flowers in dense knots, and as with other maples, male and female groupings may appear on the same tree. Branches and saplings have a smooth silvery-gray bark, which dulls with time and becomes shaggy. Aging trunks also develop cavities—perfect accommodation for racoons, owls, squirrels, woodpeckers, and others.

Silver and red maple—a close relative—are the only maples to bear a fruit crop of winged samaras in spring through early summer, instead of in the fall. Along with large, rounded leaf buds, this fruit feeds a horde of birds and small mammals at a time when stored winter supplies have been used up, acorns and other nuts already sprouted.

Growing on long, slender stalks, silver maple's broad leaves, with deep angular notching between five lobes, can create a magical shimmer, their downy silvery undersides flashing in the slightest breeze. Silver maples drop pale yellow leaves earlier in the fall than other maples. They may also cross-pollinate with red maples, producing a hybrid known as the Freeman maple.

Our most notable silver maple lives behind the cedar swing at Russell's. Though its brittle wood may be easily damaged, it has thus far fared much better than the adjacent Norway. This gorgeous maple's amber leaves will blanket the open space east of Russell's come September.

Manitoba maple (*Acer negundo*), also known as box elder, maple ash, or ash-leaved maple, prefers full sunlight and a flood plain. *Negundo* comes from the Latin form of an East Indian name for plants of the *Vitex* family and traces back to the Sanskrit word *nirgundī*, which means, literally, "that which protects the body from diseases." Our most evident Manitoba maple flourishes on the south rim of Wood's End and dips its toes in the moist clays of the riverbank. Some summers it's all but lost in the profusion of high grasses and cedar saplings.

A fast-growing, short-lived North American native, Manitoba maples grow across much of the United States and Canada, from the Atlantic Seaboard to the Rocky Mountains and south into Guatemala. With a typical lifespan of only sixty years, they may still reach over seventy feet, single trees sometimes producing several trunks that may eventually coalesce to form impenetrable thickets.

Pale-gray or light-brown scaly bark features clefs and broad ridges. Fresh, brittle, green irregular branches have a waxy powderiness to them. Small, yellow-green flowers appear in early spring and paired samaras with incurved wings drop in autumn. Miniscule bladder gall mites fashion small galls on the undersides of leaves that resemble those of the ash.

Indigenous tribes of North America from the Navajo and Cheyenne to Tewa, Dakota, and Omaha have valued Manitoba maple for centuries for carving bowls, drums, pipestems, and prayer sticks. The oldest known wooden flutes in the Americas (620–670 CE), unearthed in 1931 in northeastern Arizona by archaeologist Earl Morris, were fashioned from Manitoba maple.

On the brim of the water-meadow, our lone Manitoba maple seems almost weedy. With ragged crown, it's still hanging on in the shadow of The West Woods. But for how much longer?

❈ *15 April* ❈

AS WE'VE BEEN SMITTEN with one more gloomy gray day, I'll continue with my inventory of the trees of Paradise.

Also known as Canadian spruce, Alberta white spruce, cat spruce, or Black Hills spruce, white spruce (*Picea glauca*), the northernmost tree species on the North American continent, is native to both temperate and boreal forests. The word *picea* derives from the Latin *pic* meaning "pitch" as in pitch pine, and glauca from the Greek *glaûkos* meaning "silvery or bluish gray."

In late October 1967, Dad, my brother Ebe, and I planted two hundred white spruce trees in Paradise, bought at a penny a piece from the Ontario Forestry Service. We scattered them westward from The Gully to Russell's Cottage. Tramping the soggy grounds of late autumn, I remember a still but crisply cold day with occasional spits of rain and a glowering dark sky. Many of those striplings now top sixty feet.

A large slow-growing coniferous evergreen, white spruce normally grows from fifty to a hundred feet, though some have reached over one hundred and thirty. White spruce of two hundred or even three hundred years of age are not uncommon. Dwarf trees on the shore of Urquhart Lake in the Northwest Territories are well over three hundred years old.

White spruce bark, thin and scaly, flakes off in small circular plates, gray-brown or ash-brown in color, silvery when freshly exposed. Conic in young trees, narrow white spruce crowns become cylindrical with age. Needle-like, blue-green leaves—blue-white below—have a diamond shape in cross section. Slender cones droop from upper branches with thin flexible scales colored green, reddish, or pink, becoming pale-brown at maturity. These cones mature in late summer or early fall, with seed dispersal primarily through the air. A thin wing clasps each small oblong black seed inside. In Paradise, rabbits and white-tailed deer will browse white spruce foliage in the winter, and the seeds are prime fodder for our red squirrels.

One of the earliest signs of approaching autumn here in Paradise comes with the pounding of white spruce cones on Edna's roof. The red squirrel in whose territory it lies harvests this crop from the soaring white spruce overhanging the northeast corner of Edna's cottage. Work begins just after daybreak, continuing off and on for several days. Spruce cones slam sporadically on the shingles with the snap of gunshots. We'll find them a short time later piled near the bottom of the hilltop steps or at the base of the tree.

Norway spruce (*Picea abies*) or European spruce, native to northern, central, and eastern Europe, being more tolerant of humid summers than other spruce species, now occurs in the Rocky Mountain states, along the Pacific Coast, in the northeastern United States, and here in southeastern Canada. *Abies* probably developed from the Proto-Italic word "*abjets*", a word related to the ancient Greek word "*ábin*", referring to a silver fir or similar conifer.

A sizeable coniferous evergreen, mature Norway spruce, under prime conditions, can top out at eighty feet, growing three feet in a single year over decades. When a tree has reached sixty-five feet or so, this growth declines. Bottom branches that droop downward, at first die off as the tree ages and its crown thins. As late as 2019, the planet's tallest Norway spruce—at 204 feet—still lived near Ribnica na Pohorju in Slovenia.

Norway spruce bark consists of gray-brown, flaky scales in vertical lines. Needle-like leaves, quadrangular in cross section and dark moss-green on all four sides, have blunt tips. Seed cones with triangular-pointed scale tips—at three to seven inches the largest cones of any spruce—begin a greenish-reddish color, maturing to burnished russet. A tree begins to produce long black seeds in its fourth decade, each with a pale beige wing.

Individual Norway spruce can live up to three hundred years. In 2004, Umea University in Sweden discovered a Norway spruce clone subsequently named Old Tjikko living on the summit of *Fulufjället* Mountain in Sweden. A portion of the root system carbon dated as

9,562 years old. Old Tjikko had sprung up in 7550 BCE, spending its first few thousand years as a scrappy shrub.

A clonal tree such as Old Tjikko regenerates new trunks, branches, and roots over millennia. The oldest known individual tree—one that has not taken advantage of vegetative cloning—is a Great Basin bristlecone pine which, at over five thousand years old, germinated in 3051 BCE.

Spruce beer, produced by steeping the tips of fresh spruce shoots in water, once served as a preventative or cure for scurvy. These limey shoots of spring can even be plucked and eaten straight from the tree.

UNESCO designated another form of Norway spruce, Haselfichte or hazel-spruce, which grows in the European Alps, as an intangible cultural heritage. Stradivarius worked Norway spruce for his famous instruments. Additionally, Norway spruce provides much of the world with Christmas trees. In gratitude for their aid during World War II, Oslo yearly gifts London, Edinburgh, and Washington, DC, with a seasonal tree, set up in a major city square.

An ancient Scandinavian legend says that the Norway spruce was the Garden of Eden's original Tree of Life. Tempted by its juicy fruit, its broad green leaves, and glorious blossoms, Eve partook of the forbidden fruit. As punishment, it became a rough, dry cone, leaves withering to sharp, thin needles.

In Paradise, a scraggly grove of Norway spruce with a bristle of dead lower limbs took root many years ago and now extends in a broad band from just east of the cabin nearly to The Gully wash. Forage especially for our red squirrels, the ground here is littered with the heaped confetti of spruce seed wings every autumn.

Sitting on Edna's deck, I'm just a few yards away from two stately eastern American black walnuts (*Juglans nigra*), soaring to sixty feet or more beside the shed, right of the pathway to the cabin. They're shivering into blackness now, but their canopies will be a shimmer of green lace by late spring.

Juglans comes from classic Latin *iūglāns*, the Roman name given to the walnut tree, with the extended meaning being "nut of Jupiter."

Nigra, from *nigrum* the Latin word for "black," may trace its origin to the Proto-Indo-European word *neg* meaning "bare or night."

A deciduous tree in the family *Juglandaceae* and native to Southern Ontario and the eastern United States west to South Dakota and south to northern Georgia, Florida, and central Texas, black walnut does well in riparian environments like Paradise. The soils here can hold large amounts of water. These trees also release harmful chemicals from their root systems, which gives them an aggressive edge. Walnuts sustain a wide variety of animals, especially rodents and birds. Rare unclaimed seeds buried by squirrels help spread the species.

A black walnut can grow three feet in its first year, more in its second. An average tree can reach 70 or 80 feet over a 130-year lifespan. Valued for its deep brown, easily worked wood, eastern American black walnut is a pioneer species, like red and silver maple. It has adapted as a "weed tree," popping up along verges, forest margins, and in open fields.

In the woodland conditions of Paradise, walnuts can rise straight and tall, with a gray-black bark furrowed into thin diamond-shaped ridges. Male and female flowers open on the same tree, the female appearing before the male in clusters of two to five on the current year's growth. The drooping catkins of male flowers form on the previous year's growth. Pale, silky leaf buds covered in downy hairs unfurl to emerald-green pinnately compound leaves with a fuzzy underside, arranged alternately along the stem.

Leaf out occurs when daytime temperatures warm to 70 degrees Fahrenheit, sometimes as late as mid-May in Paradise. Subsequent leaf-drop begins mid-to-late September when the high slips below 65 degrees. Walnut fruits—those familiar spherical brownish-green semi-fleshy husks surrounding a crinkled tan-colored nut—usually fall in October. Fruit production is irregular, and a large crop can only develop after twenty years. Our majestic black walnuts have already yielded crops of some significance.

Some years ago, Dan and I set out to expand our black walnut range to the top of the hill, east of the parking area. We soaked and sorted and properly prepped a half-dozen prime fallen fruit. We installed a protective span of wire mesh atop our three-foot square plantation as protection against critter predation. Alas, black walnuts demand full sunlight and adequate weed control, neither of which we could supply. The following spring, not a sign of our efforts remained. Not even that scrap of wire mesh. Our plantation might never have been.

In May 1967, Dad planted a row of ten European black poplar (*Populus nigra*), a deciduous species belonging to the genus *Populus* (in the *Willow* family), on the hilltop to either side of the steps, as a windbreak against seasonal snow drifts. Today they have tripled to several dozen.

From Old Latin *populus/poplus*, back to Proto-Latin *poplos*, meaning "people, nation, public, or populace," *populus* refers to the fact that trees of this genus were often planted around public meeting places in Roman times.

Another fast-growing but short-lived tree, black poplars have a shallow but far-reaching root system. Their smooth whitish bark changes to deeply furrowed black with age. Individual trees can top a hundred feet and live up to sixty years. Yellowish to tan-colored twigs have leaf scars, and leaf buds are sharp, thick, and umber-colored. In April, male and female flowers sprout on separate trees forming catkins. The male droop in long and slender conical clusters, the female smaller and limey green.

Like cottonwoods and aspens, which also belong to the genus *Populus*, black poplars produce tiny black seeds, each wrapped in a woolly tuft of silvery hairs. These will thicken the late spring air like a snow squall. Tall and narrow, their triangular notched and glossy-green summer leaves will shimmer in the slightest breeze—a dance that turns to gold when autumn sets in.

Another member of the genus *Populus*, a burgeoning grove of quaking aspen (*Populus tremuloides*), also known as trembling aspen, American aspen, golden aspen, mountain aspen, and even white poplar, has taken hold at the base of the gentle slope behind Russell's Cottage.

Tremuloides comes from the Latin *trumulo*, meaning to "tremble," together with the suffix *-oides* from ancient Greek *eides*, meaning "resembling or like."

The most widely distributed deciduous tree in North America, quaking aspens thrive in the cooler areas of the continent, from Canada to central Mexico. A largely high-latitude or high-altitude tree, quaking aspens—the definitive species of Prairie Province parkland—extend through every Canadian province and territory, with the possible exception of Nunavut.

Aspens can reach eighty feet, growing five feet per year. Chunky, dark, horizontal scars and inky knots mark an otherwise smooth, greenish-white-to-gray bark. In early spring, pendulous male and female catkins (on separate trees) form well before any leaf buds. The fruit—four-inch-long dangling strings of capsules, each containing about ten tiny seeds embedded in a cottony fluff—saturate the early summer air with a feathery down. With a dull underside and small curved teeth, aspen's round, lustrous green leaves will flicker and flutter with the faintest breath of air. In all seasons. As enchanting and golden in autumn as the black poplar.

Rarely do aspens germinate from seed. They propagate primarily through their root systems, male and female trees forming broad but separate clonal colonies. All trees in a specific group are part of the same organism. A single-root system can underlie an entire hill and weigh upward of thirty-two tons.

Old Tjikko, that ancient Swedish Norway spruce we talked about a few pages back, has serious competition for oldest living clonal tree from Pando. A stand of 47,000 quaking aspen clones estimated by some to be between eighty thousand and one million years old, Pando ("I spread" in Latin) refers to a 108-acre clonal colony of aspens in the Fremont River area of Fishlake National Forest on the western edge of the Colorado Plateau in south-central Utah. Others argue that Pando could not have weathered the last glaciation, making it under ten thousand years old. I'll leave that to the experts, though by any measure, Pando is ancient.

In the drier areas of western North America, an individual quaking aspen might live for over two hundred years. Here in the east, however, they decay faster, sometimes surviving only sixty years. Our forty-foot quaking aspen grove clocks in at around a decade. As with all quaking aspens, the buds, bark, and foliage help sustain cottontails, white-tailed deer, ruffed grouse, and a variety of moths and butterflies.

A member of the *Oleaceae* or *Olive* family, green ash (*Fraxinus pennsylvanica*), also known as downy ash, swamp ash, red ash, and water ash, is native to eastern and central North America from Nova Scotia to Alberta, Colorado, Florida, Oklahoma, and east Texas. *Ash* comes from *æsc*, the Old English word for the tree. "*Fraxinus* goes back to Proto-Italic *fraksinos*, the name the ash tree was anciently known as.

The most prominent green ash in Paradise, a gorgeous tree rising from the bottomland east of The Willow Deck, soars straight and tall, with a full and regal canopy in high summer.

A medium-sized deciduous tree, green ash has an average lifespan of 120 years. Single trees can top out at 120 feet in its southern range, over sixty feet in the north. The smooth gray bark of young trees turns thick and fissured with age. Buds are a velvety reddish brown. Oblong and lustrous leaves, each with seven to nine leaflets with serrated margins, can turn a deep golden-yellow as early as the first week in September.

Inconspicuous flowers arrive in the spring in tandem with the new leaves. The fruit—a single seed with one long winged samara that turns from lime-green to vibrant yellow or dark brown—drops in autumn, as soon as it ripens. Large seed crops provide nourishment for a variety of birds and animals.

With the decimation of American elms from Dutch elm disease in the mid-20th century, green ash emerged as a prized ornamental tree. Elm and ash, both members of the ancient elm-ash-cottonwood bottomland ecosystem, gained popularity for their longevity, majestic natural beauty, and tolerance of severe urban environments. Green ash, lighter than white ash and with a bright sound and pleasing grain, has been used extensively by electric guitar producers like Gibson, Fender, and Ibanez.

Today, unfortunately, a relentless infestation of the emerald ash borer, whose larvae can girdle an ash tree, has proven to be much more devastating than epidemics like chestnut blight or Dutch elm disease. Both of the latter scourges spread more slowly, affected only one species, and did not kill a plant before it could reach maturity as the emerald ash borer does.

Native ash tree leaves, which lack tannins, have been a crucial food source for frogs, particularly tadpoles living in temporary or permanent ponds and puddles. Red maples, non-native ash, and various other invasive species have taken the place of failing native green ash. Though resistant to the emerald ash borer, these trees have higher tannin levels less suitable for frogs. Our Willow Deck green ash still enjoys enough recurrent flooding that, with any luck, at least some of our languishing Paradise frogs will persist.

With two gently intertwined trunks and a stately rounded crown, our prime American basswood (*Tilia americana*), dips its toes in the runoff wash from The Gully. American basswood favors frequent flooding like that from the drainage of the topside farm fields. In the *Malvaceae* family and native to eastern North America, American basswood stands as the sole representative of its genus in the Western Hemisphere.

The European species is known by the name "linden tree." *Tilia*, from Proto-Indo-European *pteleiā*, meaning "broad, as in broad-leafed," is the Latin name for the linden tree, a word corrupted from the Latin word *lentus*, meaning "flexible." Indigenous people used basswood's tough, fibrous inner bark—or bast—for making cords, thongs, and ropes. North American settlers subsequently called the tree "bast-wood," from which the word "basswood" comes.

A fast-growing medium-to-large-sized deciduous tree, individuals can reach 120 feet, the average being sixty. Basswood trees often double the annual growth rate of beeches and birches and can live up to two hundred years.

Basswood bark, gray to light brown, has narrow, well-defined fissures. The large roots are deep and wide-spreading. Twigs smooth and reddish-green change to a light-gray in their second year, dark-brown or brownish-gray at maturity. Pale-green downy leaves that open mid-spring, become dark green, smooth, and shining through the summer, yellowing in autumn. Fragrant yellowish-white flowers droop in clusters in early May and will form small dry cream-colored nutlets.

Basswood blooms provide nectar for many insects, including bees that produce a mildly spicy honey. Seeds provide nutrition for chipmunks, mice, and squirrels. The leaves feed a handful of caterpillars, and rabbits and voles will eat the bark, which was also used by Indigenous people for baskets, rope, and fishing nets.

These, then, are our giants in the earth, the regal beauties of Paradise. They surround and augment their lowlier subjects: shining willow, dotted hawthorn, alternate-leaved dogwood, common apple, red-osier dogwood, black cherry, sandbar willow, choke cherry, common buckthorn, heart-leaved willow, and others.

As I sit here now, in a blue funk of rain, with bleakness unabated and forlorn skies ever murkier and more cheerless, with a dull and twiggy haze of forest fringe near and far, I'm melancholy and chilled to the bone.

But one day very soon, the earth will move, and we'll awaken once again to a great glory of green.

❊ *16 April* ❊

THIS MORNING IN A GRAY gloom, the bulk of winter's snow and ice, crystal to liquid, has made for the river, leaving broad brown connected ponds on the water-meadow. From their perch on the horizon, water dogs, those small floating clouds that portend rain, moved in with English swiftness to snuff out a timid, cerulean-blue sky. A misted drizzle now taps on the rooftop. Blackbirds and geese, robins, redwings, and cardinals cry from the flats, from across the river, and from the tops of forest trees. The air has sharpened, sweet and fresh, and on this now watery day, with a thunder lump of rain cloud idling overhead, we'll soon set off on the first walkabout of spring.

In the early days, with countrified wildness, a woodburning stove, an outdoor privy, and kerosene lamps, our family life in Paradise mirrored a frontier spirit, though my father, remembering wood chopping and washboards would say, "I guess we were young and foolish."

But we did have a pioneering sense of place.

The world at large can overwhelm. We're overcome with so much grassland, so much mountain, so much forest, so much desert. Our ancestors, by necessity, have lived out their lives in one bounded and contained space, leaving fragments of themselves or their stories behind in a hill, a farm, a pasture. This waterway becomes Buthar's Mere. This pasture Naboth's Field. We anchor and we root and we live in settled permanence, within a specific locale, pieces of which we might have named.

Our sixteen acres of Paradise very quickly fostered such a sense of place. As Alistair Moffat writes in his *The Secret History of Here: A Year in the Valley*, "Every place has its history, its secrets. And all that is needed to unlock and learn them is love, patience and open eyes."

On May 1, 1957, Fergus farmer Bob Rich sold sixteen acres of land on his property for $1,000 to my parents Russell and Edna (nee Ott) Ebertt, my uncle and aunt Wilkin and Esther (nee Ott) Lavery, my uncle Harold Ott, and my grandfather Alvin Ott (Pa). A few short weeks earlier, we'd checked out another offering—a flat, fieldish slice of farmland, short-grassed and muddy, with hardwood forest fringes and a drainage creek sluicing down one side.

By comparison, Paradise, grazed by Mr. Rich's dairy cattle, opened up wide and spacious, hillsides and meadowland brimming with spring wildflowers, budding thorn apple tree, and lilac bushes.

The first weekend on the land passed by in peaceful seclusion. The following saw a steady stream of vehicles crawling along the old concession road, which then traced the rim of the north hill. Mr. Rich had let word slip that he'd sold the land to a nudist colony.

We're at Wood's End now, in the chill tranquility of midmorning. After-drops of rain freckle the swollen river, which has crept across the water-meadow to the wood's edge. We've had to move our plastic Muskoka chairs to higher ground. As children, we christened this Wood's End clump of trees Silver Cedar Ranch, the neighboring adjacent bluff, Mexico Bay Cliff.

The shifts and adjustments of spring can sometimes seem absent, deceptive, or veiled. Not so at Wood's End this season. The long dead elm tree high to the right as we face the river has fallen across the path. A gray-white hulk gleams in the April gloom. Last spring, as we stood on that very spot chatting touch-me-nots and herb Robert, the bole of a multitrunked cedar on the brim of the water-meadow not ten feet away gave a sudden snap and within seconds had collapsed toward the river with a resounding thud. As rare a sight to witness as a calving glacier or a boulder slipping off a rock face.

A private home on the hilltop beside us, built in 1979, marks the site of a Zion Hill Wesleyan Methodist Church, which in the building's eighty-fifth year, held an official closing service on June 3, 1962. In the five years that followed the purchase of Paradise in 1957, we'd often caught snippets of exuberant Sunday morning hymn singing—sometimes we even joined in—and the horse-and-buggy stables of old Zion fed our childhood imaginations. Each separate stall became a ranch house of its own, stacked beams and stored planks morphing into sleeping or sitting quarters.

After the church's 1963 sale to a neighborhood woman who attempted something of a revival, we would stop on the drive to the cottage from Kitchener to fetch altar bouquets from her garden. My sister and I occasionally sang in the choir. All I remember of those rumored performances is a single harmonized duet where I managed the alto line of "Lead Kindly Light."

The old brick building with its wooden buggy stables and once-up-on-a-time blacksmith shop quickly fell into disrepair. Rooting around in the ruins of its final days, Ebe and I unearthed a smattering of hand-made nails and one or two rusted tin plates.

In The West Woods now, yesterday's heavy rains have left the ground mushy end to end. At least a dozen cedar saplings uprooted by snowpack, wind, or melt water have slumped across the spongy track to Russell's, their pale root plates bared and boney. We managed to toss the bulk of them farther down the slope and have squished up to Russell's.

Little changes year to year around the cottages themselves. And yet everything has changed. Built in the summer of 1958, both took shape in a rolling, grassy landscape now brimming with trees. During construction, a mortar mound of sand at Edna's became a diamond mine. Cut-glass "diamonds" pried from pieces of old jewelry still survive in a tin box commemorating the 1953 coronation of Queen Elizabeth II.

Over the years, Uncle Harold and Pa strolled over to Mom and Dad's after supper for a round or two of Ramoli or Stock Ticker. We kids were in bed long before they finished. I would lie in my bottom bunk listening to their muted voices in the night . . . that same safe and secure, clear and comforting nighttime sound of my parents' conversation outside our tent whenever we went camping.

Fuzzy, our pet rabbit (who also went by the names Fizzy or Fizzerine), often came up to Paradise too. A soft, pristine white with pink eyes, pink foot pads, a pink nose, and pink insides to her translucent ears, she originally came from Uncle Harold's stock across the road in Kitchener. Fizzy lived inside the garage at the Kitchener house, in a roomy pen at the rear of the garage. From the ceiling of her chicken-wire cage, Dad had suspended a long wooden hutch with an entrance ramp. We boldly claimed that Fizzy could count and add. We gave her problems to solve, and she always "answered" with repeated comings and goings up and down the incline or with successive turns around its lower end.

Using a burgundy ribbon leash, we grazed her in the clover patches of the church-next-door's front lawn and would whine and moan shamelessly about having to collect more. Fizzy loved warm milk and vanilla ice cream, and we wrapped a head of iceberg lettuce in tissue paper for her every Christmas.

Once, while she was upstairs in my sister Carol's bedroom, Blacky, our Labrador retriever, allowed only in the basement, somehow slipped through the kitchen door and came bounding up the second-floor stairs. Fizzerine bolted under the bed and thumped her back foot madly.

When she came to the cottage, Fuzzy would kick out her back legs and plop down on the shelf of our Pontiac sedan's rear window, her pink nose twitching. She had a small straw-filled house in an outdoor chicken-wire enclosure built around a long-gone thorn apple tree at the front west corner of Edna's.

One summer night, the latch of her cage had not been properly secured and a red fox took her. Our hearts shattered. Pa buried her remains down on the water-meadow.

Inky but for a white tip on his tail and a white patch on his chest, Blacky often visited the cottage too. At home, he lived in a large, fenced enclosure with a straw-filled doghouse attached to the outer back wall of the garage. A whirling-tail-loves-everybody dog, Blacky, also known as Beebert, liked to sit with Dad on his doggy porch, regularly wheeling round to give Dad's face a thorough licking top to bottom. We would run him in the country sometimes, and barreling through the woods on one occasion, he leapt across a creek. What he thought to be solid ground turned out to be scum on top of the water. Of course, he splashed right in, abject horror on his face. Blacky was never much for swimming.

Not much for hunting either. He would follow in Dad's footsteps through the snow so that each time Dad lifted a foot, Beebert's chin clapped and his teeth clicked. But he would never desert his post.

Here in Paradise, the cattle grazing across the river produced a frenzy of barking. Whenever a beast shifted in his direction, Beebert would duck for cover, usually behind Mom. Ebe would often walk Blacky past the church while a service was in progress. Beebert never failed to walk right in.

My aunt and uncle owned what is now Russell's Cottage, leasing it out until Dan and I acquired the entire property in 2010. Most of my indoor childhood memories spring from Edna's Cottage. I remember lamplight flickering on the painted plywood walls. Dad playing five-string banjo by the fireplace or down in the cabin. Toast crisping over an open hot plate on the wood stove. Mom knitting by the fading light from the west window. Bedtime snacks of pretzels, potato chips, or cheese puffs in small, colored-plastic bowls—mine was blue.

Here we are then outside Russell's, above the water-meadow. Our majestic white willow, scrappy with age, rises from the river-bank below. She's knee-deep in spillover today, lower limbs fractured or sweeping the current. Dark pools flood the sinks and pockets of the meadow, some of them prickled with blanched and half-drowned driftwood. The skies have marbled with a spit of rain. The stale and flattened grasses of winter lie brown and beaten, belying a summer-time future of black-eyed Susans, goldenrod, daisies, and purple Joe-Pye weed.

In the early days, we called this humble floodplain The Flats . . . part of a narrow stretch of bottomland that continued beyond the river's west bend, where the remains of a Boy Scout Camp once stood.

Marsh marigolds will soon bloom there.

Each spring, Dad would burn a heap of raked leaves and post-ice-out debris down on The Flats. He would also light a measure of the meadowland to encourage new growth and simplify adult baseball games. In March 1961, his blaze ran wild. Flames raked through the tamped winter grasses fingering the wood pile just outside of Edna's. With good fortune, we doused the fire with wet rags and well water.

With time, the meadow grew high and wide. We hunted red-ringed blackbird nests, garden spiders, and budding wildflowers, each in its season. Wild canaries swooped overhead. Cowbirds, catbirds, wrens, and robins piped from the thorn apple trees. And in those days, too, when we would stride along the iris-bound riverbank we flushed out frogs and muskrats with each step. When the long, warm, blue, and bright days of summer turned frosty, and winter sufficiently froze the river beyond the meadow, we slipped on our ice skates and played tag. In from the fierce cold, we'd thaw our frozen feet on the open door of the woodstove.

We're here now on a bench at the east side of Edna's Cottage. The scrap of ground in front of the shed is a mire of mud and dead leaves. A half-dozen black Angus cattle invaded from the farm upriver in the late 1990s, churning up the ground beyond repair. Nothing much grows there anymore beyond a handful of lily-of-the-valley, forget-me-not, and periwinkle. So, we sit here by the hour feeding chipmunks and red squirrels by hand or liberally flinging out peanuts.

Past the shed to the left, a staked sign skewed by the subsiding hillside and seasonal snow, marks the site of Dad's old telescope platform: the Russell Newton Ebertt International Observatory. Little sky blinks through the canopy of apple trees and cedar now. But in a more unobstructed past, we indulged in close-ups of the full moon, the Milky Way, a planet or two, or a lunar eclipse.

Nearly opposite the observatory, the remains of the cabin have inched farther toward the water-meadow, a few more breaches in its roof. One dark maw now at the right rear corner of the roof could accommodate a red squirrel, a small fox, or a raccoon. At the base of the porch, a depression holds a pool of dark floodwater that conjoins another drowned sinkhole bordered by willows lying to the west. From cabin to gully another scatter of snapped or uprooted cedar saplings has fallen across the pathway.

At The Gully, frothy meltwater rages from the foot of the ravine's leafless trees and cedars to fan out across the flatland below the bridge. Swelling patches of umber overflow have already gathered there. A whisper of green above the meltwater line has faintly tinged the margin of the meadow's winter die-back as it joins the eastern woods. Here, the overgrown track to The Dam Rapids, impassable at the best of times, has vanished under a channel of floodwater. Broken limbs hang over-head, and up-churned root balls protrude above the water's surface.

Another spit of rain darkens the day as we climb the first hillock in the cedar woods to take shelter at Harold's Tea Deck. The outdoor fireplace, the cement slab at the base of the deck, stacks of concrete blocks and rotting timber slats, and a decaying flight of cement stairs hidden in the wooded slope behind are all that remain of the first building in Paradise.

This roofed tea deck occupies the western half of the old cabin's footprint. After Uncle Harold and Pa both passed away and the contents of their cabin were removed, the emerald-green cottage faded away. During the summer of 1986, my dad and Ebe dismantled the remnants, sawing up usable wood for Edna's outdoor fireplace.

Cedar trees surround us here, but for transplanted goutweed and ferns brought in from the wilds across the river. Both will soon sweep through the eastern portion of this forest glade. And with any luck, Uncle Harold's double daffodils will bloom again.

At the western edge, beside the fireplace, a single wild apple tree holds on with scrappy fingers. Sprinkled with barely visible spring buds, one limb in a tangle of dead branches reaches for any sliver of skylight. Nothing recognizable remains of the Beverage Room, that cluster of old cedars that housed cold drinks during the cottage's construction. Ice blocks buried in the damp spaciousness of its understory kept things cold through that entire summer.

Across the hillside path to Black Bass Bend, another smattering of cedar saplings, uprooted in the aftermath of winter, will have to be removed. As we work these off the trail, dragging them farther down the slope, we can see that the seat of the wooden bench fastened to twin cedar trunks at The Dam Rapids has been split in two horizontally by ice floes. River water courses under the fractured slats. Even if the bench proves usable after the flood subsides, the bank below has eroded away, leaving scant footing—rather sad, as that bench had been built in 1978 so Mom and Dad could watch the raising of the beaver dam.

For decades, we've taken in the extraordinary wildlife of Paradise fromThe Dam Rapids. White-tailed bucks across the river browse on wild cucumber. Does lead their speckled fawns upriver for better grazing. Raccoon families fish in the shallows. Blackbirds gather crayfish for their nestlings. Great blue heron stealth-hunt from midstream sandbars. Muskrats scull home at dusk. Beaver harvest willow withies.

And that full summer, Mom and Dad watched the construction, maintenance, and repair of the beaver dam. Forepaws large and small cemented boulders from the river bottom into place with mud and twigs, shrinking the rapids, where in earlier days we'd set up our Dinky Toy villages.

Above The Dam Rapids, Dad taught us to swim. Clear, warm, and shallow, the tea-colored water on the far shoreline turned silty near the grayish-clay of the north bank where it deepened. Minnows nibbled at our thighs. Cold springs shocked as they seeped in from the river bottom. On still and breathless summer evenings, we puddled until sundown in our rubberized water-shoes. When wisps of mist crept in from upriver and swirled like rising steam, we made our shivering way back to the cottage, plagued by deer flies.

Carol and I waded there once. Mom—who couldn't swim—kept watch on the bank. A couple of bantering teenaged boys slowly paddled downriver after leaping in at Black Bass Bend. Glimpsing Mom on the shore, they smoothly paddled back and disappeared.

With the tea deck's hillock path cleared, we're headed over to Black Bass Bend, the widest east-end curve on the river. Years ago, Dad reeled in a substantial black bass from out of this pool. Black Bass Bend takes the brunt of the spring thaw, ice floes slamming into the rim of the cedar forest, leaving trunks scarred and shredded.

One summer, my grandfather snagged a snapping turtle in Black Bass Bend. I can clearly see him holding his catch, its mouth clamped on a stout stick. We no longer swim in the river, so snapping turtles can now roam freely.

The actual Black Bass Bend sitting area lies underwater at present. One white cedar that sagged over the riverbank all last summer has vanished, embedded perhaps in the river bottom. Time will tell. Our

Black Bass Bend chairs remain in winter "storage" halfway up the hill behind me. In a very short time, this west end of the forest will echo with the cacophony of a thousand roosting black birds. As we make our way to Castor's Landing, a watery sun vies against the cloud cover, and the air has marginally warmed.

Season to season, nothing much changes inside the eastside cedar woods, though once again, an array of toppled saplings, some holding on by a root or two, spans the track. Abaco Heights, the rising land where the eastern cedars once began, now lies midway through the forest. Floodwater extends from Black Bass Bend's sitting area to the scoured lowland west of Castor's Landing. Our terrestrial crayfish hamlet remains submerged.

At Castor's Landing (named for the North American beaver *Castor canadensis*), the ground beneath the table/bench has eroded further. (The name "castor" derives from the Greek word for this same animal, *kastor*. "Beaver" comes through old English *beofor*, tracing back to an Indo-European root word meaning "brown.")

Across the river, several listing cedars on the bank have been severely undercut, the tops of their root plates bristling with exposed filaments.

With summer's dense shoreline jungle of ferns, climbing vines, and tall grasses, we don't often venture across the river. Springtime makes for better footing.

On rare occasions in the past, Dad would lash together fallen, harvested, or driftwood logs, pile his raft with cut wood, and sail it downriver, guided with a hefty walking stick. Transferring his shipment to the north bank, he'd haul the load up to Edna's. These Tom Sawyer days really had him in his element.

Just after we bought the land, an ancient elm tree deep in the wilds across the river went down. The six-foot stump left behind—which we called Spooky Hollow—really augmented any fingerlings of evening mist. Carol and I also once rescued a fledgling robin from a long-gone inlet on the far side, which we then christened Swimming Bird Cove.

A hundred yards upstream from Castor's Landing, the beaver lodge, reinforced with sprigs and sprays, is circled with residents' footprints. This year, the sheltering willow at the den's riverside edge leans even farther toward the streambed, another fractured limb just visible above the current.

Beyond Castor's Landing, the trail deteriorates step by step to dissolve on neighboring farmland in a quagmire of splayed winter grasses and mud. Where the river courses south from the Big Bridge to slip through the eastern rapids into Black Bass Bend, Canada geese have already settled in below Rainbow Cliff. Their voices pierce the afternoon stillness.

All walks in Paradise, end to end or place to place, awaken, enlighten, and renew. As we do every year, we've vowed that as the weather softens, many more strolls will follow.

❈ *22 April* ❈

FOLLOWING A SHARP frost in the night and dense fog earlier this morning, Earth Day has dawned, warmish and bright. Under fresh spring breezes, the river, glutted and gorged, rolls through a blush of lime-green grass shoots, budding lilacs, and pussy willows in velvet. A robin has already nested in the white spruce at the northeast corner of Edna's Cottage. Bevies of blackbirds, starlings, and redwings flit about overhead. In the bird feeders, chickadees and goldfinches clamor, while a harassment of barking crows settles in the water-meadow willows.

Inspired by the protests of the 1960s, Wisconsin Democrat Gaylord Nelson proposed Earth Day as a national day of environmental awareness. Nelson had been elected to the US Senate in 1962, the same year Rachel Carson's *Silent Spring* exposed the devastating consequences of the prolific use of the pesticide DDT. Earth Day, first observed in the United States on April 22, 1970, led to critical pieces of environmental legislation: the Clean Air Act, the Water Quality Improvement Act, the Endangered Species Act. And in December of that same year, President Nixon established the Environmental Protection Agency. By the 1990s, Earth Day festivities had swept around the globe.

Today over a billion people participate.

In tune with the day, the air in Paradise has ripened with burgeoning life. April is the month of action. Grasses sprout. Fish rise. Animals breed. Birds nest.

Life relentless. Life tenacious. Life persistent, dogged, and determined.

"How completely and utterly miraculous in the scheme of things it is for life . . . to be here at all. Life just wants to be," states Bill Bryson in his book, *A Short History of Nearly Everything*. In the clamor and chaos of life, what bird or plant or animal, besides the human, spends any time at all in wonder about its purpose? Life just roars along until it doesn't.

Some years ago, on a brief road trip, I listened in as National Public Radio interviewed an atheist whose name I no longer recall.

"What was the meaning of life?" he was asked.

"There's two ways to look at it," he answered. "The first is to create—our art, our science, our family. An immortality of sorts. Secondly, the meaning of life is—"

As we entered the rifts and hollows of Texas Canyon on Interstate 10 in southern Arizona, the radio transmission mutated to crackling interference. All a bit Douglas Adams.

So, as it's what humans do, here's a few random thoughts for Earth Day on *Life, the Universe, and Everything* (Douglas Adams).

For many people, organized religion fills a need they have to retain something animate and conscious after death. From megalithic stone circles and burial chambers to Egyptian embalming and the magical flooding of the Nile. From the halls of Valhalla in Norse mythology to the Christian Rapture. For many of us, it's all about what comes *next*. Countless ancient lives have come and gone and nothing definitive (in regard to an afterlife) to show for it. We plot and we plan. We hope and divine. We ask the same questions. Invent the same answers. And all the while, "life just wants to be." The present is all we have.

As poet, professor, and essayist Fenton Johnson once wrote in *Harper's Magazine*, "For a moment you are given to understand . . . that here and now you are made in the image of the divine, that paradise is a mirror in which you see yourself, that what we have to become is what we already are" ("Beyond Belief: A Skeptic Searches for an American Faith").

In her wondrous work, *Pilgrim at Tinker's Creek*, Annie Dillard writes that Jewish Hasidism "has a tradition that one of man's purposes is to assist God in the work of redemption by 'hallowing' the things of creation." Not to praise God but to glory in the glory of God. To manifest the glory of God within, as a poplar shimmers in moonlight.

The ego implied in eternal praise to God has always bothered me. So . . . not praise *to* a power but in praise *of* a power that encompasses all things great and small. No exclusions, no elitism, no ultimate authority.

"There are only two ways to live your life," Albert Einstein is thought to have written, as recorded in the personal notes of US geographer Gilbert Fowler White in 1943. "One is as though nothing is a miracle. The other is as though everything is a miracle."

Any "Supreme Being" must be somewhat embarrassed by the state of the world through history. Not much has changed in all the millennia that have piled up behind us, though there may be some eternal, underlying, cosmic harmony toward which human activity should direct itself, however off course we might have become.

Spiritual striving often muddies the water with dogma and restrictions . . . with rules and regulations, hierarchies, and prohibitions. All possible notes when sounded together without limit only produce noise. Cosmic harmony depends on limitation, as a musical composition creates beauty out of disharmony. Our present reality reflects our failure to focus on commonalities and thus our failure to produce harmony in our world.

Similarly, the quantum physics quest for a Grand Unified Theory strives to discover that ultimately each force in the universe is the same thing. They just occur in different ways. The same could be said about humanity's concept of God, defined in Merriam-Webster as "the supreme reality." That most of us can explain—scientifically—a sunset or thunder, childbirth, a tree, or the stars, doesn't make them any less miraculous. Can you make a tree? Past and present civilizations have appreciated and revered the divinity of the universe by fixating on water or the sun, on fire, Jesus, or Buddha.

Perhaps the core of religion should be spiritual unity. That *all things* are divine. That God, whatever that is perceived to be, is and has been in all worlds. That worship of animal life, corn pollen, Allah, or the moon represents the same impulse to revere a divine force, manifested in a specific form. God in all worlds. In history and prehistory.

We are each a singular manifestation of the divine into the universe. And yet, practitioners and priesthoods hammer out commandments and decrees, arrange pecking orders and internal controls, interpret and define and exclude. So that religion warps into *the chosen few*, leaving believers of one system or another to decry any loss of power, control, or moral superiority.

Nothing *spiritual* about any of that.

Perhaps the supreme reality of spirituality and the Grand Unified Theory of quantum physics are the same—one essential energy that makes up the universe—galaxies to microbes, expressing itself in a multitude of ways, ethereal, unknown, and unknowable. Everything animate and inanimate is formed of something indefinable, except to say that energy is energy. It just is. Life just wants to be.

First Nations/Native Americans have long looked on the world from such a perspective. Their viewpoint, as expressed with eloquence by the early 20th-century writer and conservationist, Grey Owl (born Archibald Stansfeld Belaney, in England, 1888) seems to have great merit in our troubled world when he wrote in his book, *The Men of the Last Frontier*:

"The Indian's God does not reside in the inaccessible heights of majestic indifference of most deities. The Indian feels his presence all his waking hours, not precisely as a god, but as an all-powerful benevolent Spirit, whose outward manifestation is the face of nature. . . . They do not fear him, for this God jogs at their elbow, and is a friend, nor do they worship him, save through the sun, a tree, a rock, or a range of hills, which to them are the outward and visible signs of the Power that lives and breathes in all creation."

In his eloquent poem, "The Inhumanist," Robinson Jeffers expresses this with supreme beauty:

"Does God exist?—No doubt of that," the old man says. "The cells of my old camel of a body

Because they feel each other and are fitted together,—through nerves and blood feel each other,—all the little animals

Are the one man: there is not an atom in all the universes

But feels every other atom; gravitation, electromagnetism, light, heat, and the other

Flamings, the nerves in the night's black flesh, flow them together; the stars, the winds and the people: one energy,

One existence, one music, one organism, one life, one God: star-fire and rock-strength, the sea's cold flow

And man's dark soul."

Can we gather that energy, manipulate it, direct it? Are all parts of it inter-connected to the extent that one part might contact another? How much more wonderous to see the universe in terms of an evolving, slow-working system of diversity and growth, in contrast to some cosmic magician's sleight of hand.

To understand the energy of life on the physical plane requires that we seek balance and harmony between humanity and the sciences, that we seek an appreciation that people function on different non-physiological levels: Cultural. Social. Ethnic. Physical. Psychological. Motivational. Even if life could be reduced to an accumulation of neurons and energy cells, the spark of life means looking at *people* not chemical interactions—at people who raise children and churches and flower gardens, who make love and plans and war, who paint pictures and houses and backyard fences. Without balance, we lose sight of our own humanity and risk becoming reclusive, locked in self-imposed exile, studying minutiae under a microscope instead of experiencing the flash and play of life itself.

Divine energy permeates all life and resides in each of us singularly. In many ways, Christianity and other religions look to separate God from humanity by making the divine transcendent, heaven nonphysical. Perhaps our earthly challenge is to recognize that divinity, here and now. In our time. In our place. Technology has given us a much higher standard of living but often no sense of what living is all about—a lived truth in terms of the wider world of nature, with all things essentially related. Every moment creates.

The best comment about all of this may be from St. Augustine of Hippo, who writes in his *The Confessions of St. Augustine*, "I am aware of something in myself, like a light dancing before my soul." That's all we really have, isn't it?

As German mystic Meister Eckhart says in his *Selected Writings*, we should be aware of something in ourselves "whose shine is our reason."

If we could only grasp that, we might know all truth.

Maybe we're here just to keep the story of life going.

❈ *26 April* ❈

WE'RE RELAXING AT BLACK BASS BEND at the close of an exquisite day. Of late, each morning has broken more springlike than the last, and the cedar forest at our back now breathes a woodsy freshness dispersed by cool and gentle breezes. From the tops of the elms and willows in the airy far-side wilderness, blackbirds buzz. The river still flows broad and brimming, though this morning, at The Dam Rapids, we managed to wade across for pussy willows.

Sleek new grasses shoot through the dead mat of drab winter vegetation and a dazzle of fragile leaf buds, lime-green to amber and pale pomegranate, burnishes all the deciduous trees, near and far. A delicate wispy reflection of their rich and latent autumn glory.

The greening of springtime has begun!

We opened the day with a cursory sorting of Edna's shed. A family of field mice had nested in a folding chair, and three pups, naked and blind, dropped down to the scatter of nutshells on the floor. We replaced them in their cozy home, though it's doubtful they'll survive.

Life unfurled everywhere after that. By midmorning, a half dozen white-tailed does had bolted from Wood's End to slip across the river. A pair of striped skunks nosed about at Russell's. Cottontails in twos and threes browsed by the well. And as we raked the moldering after-winter leaves at Edna's Cottage, a trio of chipmunk kits peered out from under the deck steps, ducking in unison if any wayward glance fell their way.

From dawn to dusk, the air held a pastel wash of lucid blues and pink blushes.

Now the metallic gold of sunset dominates. We've just come from hot dogs at Harold's Tea Deck, where his double daffodils once again flashed their butter yellow at the far side of the fireplace.

As the evening air chills now, wraiths of fog purl along the surface of the water, a pair of wood ducks cavorting in their midst. Two Canada geese honk past, tracking the river east to west, and a red-tailed hawk settles in an elm tree, a sleek black point above the thickness of the cedars.

Befitting this moment of new life and new leafing, today marks international Arbor Day, when the world extolls the glory of trees and their planting. The first documented tree festival took place in the village of Mondonedo in Spain in 1594. Another Spanish village, Villanueva de la Sierra, observed the first modern-day celebration in 1805. Arbor Day gained ground in the United States when Nebraska newspaper editor J. Sterling Morton promoted the concept on April 10, 1872. A million trees were then planted in his state. By 1883, enthusiasm reached Canada, Europe, and Australia, with President Teddy Roosevelt issuing a National Arbor Day Proclamation on April 15, 1907, the last Friday in April.

Canada celebrates National Forest Week over the last full week in September, the last Wednesday of that month being National Arbor Day, also called Maple Leaf Day.

Trees make up an integral part of global carbon storage. Stalwart and commanding, breathing in and out, connected to each other by underground networks of mycorrhiza—the symbiotic relationship between fungus and a plant's root system—trees oxygenate the earth. As with many plants, they infuse the world with chemical and biological agents called phytoncides—antimicrobial organic compounds—which have proven physiological effects and are key to many antibiotics.

One phytoncide, the soil bacteria geosmin, a turpine in the family of aromatic hydrocarbons and a major component of natural resins, is produced by a specific type of blue-green algae and causes the glorious scent of damp earth after a rainfall.

Savoring the natural world, especially forests—which the Japanese call *shirin-yoku* or forest bathing—can combat stress, obesity, migraines, high blood pressure, anxiety disorders, diabetes, ADHD, high cholesterol, and respiratory disease. Natural environments can boost immune functioning, stimulate creativity, promote relaxation, and improve our social ties.

A park. A garden. A wilderness. A tree-lined roadway. The cedar forest at our back. Each has its value. Each has its music. The trills and twitters of songbirds. The rustle of wind in leaves and limbs. Each tree has its own beauty.

❋ *27 April* ❋

ON THIS BALMY, BRIGHT, and blue April day, maple and willow flowerings have refreshed the landscape and the overstory of the cedar forest with a delicate lace. Filmy tendrils of morning mist climb up from the river and cross the water-meadow to finger Russell's front door.

We sit like cats after that, watching clouds sail by, watching musk-rats swim home, a watery sun warming our skin.

"Sit down. Keep quiet. Wait ten minutes," David Attenborough, British broadcaster, biologist, and author once advised on a *Call of the Wild* podcast. "You'll be very surprised if something interesting didn't happen within ten minutes."

Despite April's spring dance of showers and sunshine, sizzle and chill, birds rule the world today. Grackles and starlings—*little stars*—swirl in the air above the Canada geese and mallards who passed the morning at the bend of Mexico Bay Cliff. And a pair of painted wood ducks—enroute farther north—rest a moment on the arm of Russell's outdoor fireplace. Seven crested female mergansers float in a queue downriver, while a flock of crows, putting several of their twenty-three individual calls to work, harry a red-tailed hawk who'd just snagged a mouse.

One of the "solitary people of the sedge"—a great blue heron—stalks the riverbank opposite our white willow matriarch, while male red-winged blackbirds, with a rash of trills, stake out their territories on the water-meadow. Their ladies will join them in a week or so. A desperate robin rages against a red squirrel who sits in her spruce tree nest calmly munching her eggs, and three male finches, molting into their golden spring plumage, join the crowd of warblers, sparrows, and mourning doves in the west-side bird feeder.

With the exception of those three resident wild canaries, these are some of the early birds of the spring migration. Others—no doubt present, though not yet seen or heard—include flycatchers and phoebes, cowbirds and juncos, turkey and black vultures and thrushes, and that punk-rocker of the avian world, the belted kingfisher.

Depending on how far individuals or a species must travel from their winter quarters in the southern United States, in Mexico, or in Central and South America to reach their breeding grounds, the spring migration begins anytime from late February to early April. Arrival times peak in May and June. Some participants won't appear until well into July.

The birds of Paradise predominantly utilize three of the four major flyways in the New World: the Atlantic, which follows the Eastern Seaboard; the Mississippi, which mirrors the river; and the Central, which parallels the eastern side of the Rocky Mountains.

Hundreds of bird species navigate these routes (along with the Pacific Flyway) to reach their summer breeding grounds in Canada and the northern United States. They orient themselves by the stars, the sun, topography or coastline, wind direction, magnetic fields, even odors. Most of them will leave again in September. So, in the weeks and months ahead, our summer visitors will be augmented by—among many others—osprey, buntings, flickers, hummingbirds, swallows, grosbeaks, tanagers, redstarts, catbirds, owls, and eastern blue birds.

In tandem with the spring migration, the dawn chorus, that frantic and fantastic shouting match comprised of the world's most beautiful voices, has also broken out. Performers are bent on attracting a mate or proclaiming territory. Occurring March to July, the production excels from late April through early June. Lasting several hours beginning at four in the morning, the recital peaks at a half hour before to a half hour after sunrise. At this cooler and drier time of the day, voices travel farther and have a better range.

Larger members of the chorus (in Paradise, our robins, thrushes, doves, and cardinals) open the proceedings, loud and lively. Wrens and warblers fill the second tier. And our smallest birds—the sparrows and finches—join in last when there's enough light to see. Everyone fills their allotted niche at their allotted time.

This morning, robins take center stage. Shivering on Edna's deck before sunrise, I'm drenched in a dozen of their gloriously bell-like trills, resounding from all directions. Rich cardinal airs and arpeggios soon amplify this glory of sound with clear, rising whistles. And in short order, the whole world is saturated with joyous birdsong.

Sadly, pesticides may be killing the planet's voice. So in listening to a dawn chorus, we remember that life is precious . . . that we should all strive to sing our own song while we can.

"Once upon a time, when women were birds," Terry Tempest Williams writes in her book, *When Women Were Birds: Fifty-Four Variations on Voice*, "there was the simple understanding that to sing at dawn and to sing at dusk was to heal the world through joy. The birds still remember what we have forgotten, that the world is meant to be celebrated."

The View from Wood's End

Russell's Cottage

Watermeadow

Edna's Cottage

Willow Deck

The Gully Bridge

Harold's Tea Deck

View from The Dam Rapids

View from Black Bass Bend

View from Castor's Landing

Spring Thaw, April 1987; photo by David Ebertt

American Robin, April; photo by Dan Beeaff

Eastern Red Squirrel, April; photo by Marie Laure Fontaine

Canada Geese, May; photo by Dan Beeaff

Northern American Beaver (Beaudelaire), May

Rose-breasted Grosbeak, May; photo by Marie Laure Fontaine

"The May month flaps its glad green leaves like wings."
— Thomas Hardy

❈ *1 May* ❈

THIS LAST MONTH OF SPRING likely takes its name from the Greek earth goddess and midwife, Maia, the eldest of the seven nymphs of the Pleiades, a daughter of Atlas and mother of the messenger god, Hermes. Her ancient May festivities, laden with May flowers, honored the triumph of summer over winter, new life and rebirth over death. The Roman poet Ovid writes of a possible second etymology in which the name derives from the *maiores*, Latin for "elders," June being named for "young people," the *iuniores*.

All over the world, May Day—held on either May 1 or the first Monday in the month—upholds the Maia tradition.

In 1889, various political factions chose May 1 as International Workers' Day, commemorating Chicago's Haymarket Affair, which involved a bombing, the police killing of a worker, and a peaceful rally in support of an eight-hour workday. This is, of course, a horse of a very different color from conventional May Day observances.

The earliest known May Day ritual occurred during the Roman Republic in the 1st century BCE with the Floralia, a festival held from April 27 to May 3 in honor of Flora, the Roman goddess of flowers. Today, we celebrate May Day, especially in Europe and North America, with prancing around beribboned maypoles, with the crowning of May queens, and with costumed Morris Dancers who "dance in the May."

The Gaelic May Day festival of Beltane/Beltaine/Bealtaine, one of four Celtic seasonal celebrations, fell on May 1, halfway between the spring equinox and the summer solstice. Beltane signaled the coming of summer when livestock would be driven to summer pastures. The word "Beltane" probably derives from old English *belo*, from which comes "bale," meaning white or shining as in bale-fire, and *tene*, denoting "fire."

Druids or herdsmen would run their domesticated animals between two Beltane pyres in hopes of promoting fertility or protecting against disease. These fires also bestowed blessings on fields. Farmers would sometimes leap over the flames to ensure good fortune in the season ahead. They might even force dairy cattle to do the same, lest their milk be stolen by fairies, a belief likely tracing back to pagan gods or ancient nature spirits. Garlands of yellow and white May flowers—primrose, rowan, hawthorn, gorse, hazel, and marsh marigold—fastened to livestock, doorways, windows, and byres evoked these sacred fires. In Ireland, such customs persisted into the early 20th century.

This morning, through a powder-blue dawn, we have a robin-led May Day chorus that dazzles. One unfamiliar whistling soloist closes out the performance at six o'clock. After breakfast, thick fog resolves to a distant haze, full spring leaf-out in feathery greenness, before gloom descends and a fierce, cold wind ushers in an afternoon of rain. So cozy to be inside with a light drizzle tapping on the roof.

One lone cardinal up the north hill behind us piped pure and ethereal through it all. Such a sharp change from yesterday when the sun glimmered for us all day. The day before, we'd heard that a funnel cloud from heavy wet winds hovered over Fergus and left behind a blanket of hailstones, some of them an inch in diameter.

Around four thirty, the sun breaks through, and Dan renews tidying up efforts on the west-side path, organizes the east-side woodpile, and readjusts the old stair rails used there as a containment fence.

After supper, we feed peanuts to several chipmunks living under Edna's shed before strolling down to the river, running high and full from recent rains. A pair of mallard ducks cavort just above The Dam

Rapids and a sparse and muted chorus of frogs chirps downriver on the flats.

Best of all, a large adult beaver ambles out to browse the fresh lime-green grass shoots across the river. Our first beaver sighting of the season. Always a treat. We christen the big fellow Archibald Beaudelaire XXII, Beau or Bucky for short. Gliding ever nearer to our Black Bass Bend chairs, he crisscrosses the water back and forth, while a sleek muskrat paddles along the far shoreline, whipping his snaky tail side to side.

With the sun's retreat, we slip back into dusky gloom. As we head for home bundled up against the rising chill, a solitary brown thrasher above The Gully exalts in the failing light. Already, a scatter of lily-of-the-valley and amber dog-tooth violets have popped up along the fringes of the cedar woods. Shadowy hints of marsh marigold clusters will soon brighten the short, still-matted grasses across the river.

In a few short days, we, too, should be bringing in the May.

❋ *2 May* ❋

ON THIS COOL, GRAY DAY of black-bottomed clouds, spring's pastel lime greens, lemon yellows, and rust reds have dusted the land-scape. Farm fields all around have rolled out their fresh emeralds and chocolate browns. We've seen tulips in red, yellow, and pink springing up in gardens everywhere.

We spend the morning raking leaves, posting property signs, replacing staircase lighting and front door curtains, planting gladiolas, and finishing up a minor spring cleaning. I hang about in a hammock afterward, the whole world drenched in birdsong. Jays and robins and blackbirds. Crows and red-wings and gold finches. Cardinals, catbirds, chickadees, nuthatches, brown creepers, northern flickers, and Canada geese.

Just before noon, we spot the season's first ruby-throated hummingbird at Edna's east-side feeder. A glittering fairy of color and light.

In the New World, the Spaniards described hummers as *joyas voladoras*. Flying jewels.

A harbinger of global warming, hummingbirds require specific flowers in order to successfully overwinter in Mexico. As blooming schedules change, birds may fail to adapt, reaching their winter quarters too late to find enough food to survive.

Only one species, the ruby-throated hummingbird, is found in Eastern Canada. In the Chiricahua Mountains of southern Arizona, where we own a cabin, at least a dozen varieties will spend the summer. Beginning in April, a hummingbird count in the area, which carries on through the summer at two-week intervals, monitors their numbers.

Last year, on a "slow" April morning with only eighteen catches, a tiny adult male broad-tailed hummingbird with a shimmering iridescent green back closed out the day. Banded and measured—wing to wing and tail to beak—and rolled like a taco to be weighed, the little fellow drank and drank and drank when held up to a feeder.

"Who would like to release him?" his captor asked and placed two inches of utterly stunning weightlessness into my hand. I could feel the racing heartbeat, the feathery tap of a long thin black beak against my palm. Gently, I raised and lowered my arm, palm spread. And off he zipped, like a sprightly gem.

The bird world astounds us with variety, character, and tribe.

I once heard an ornithologist expound on that avian giant, the condor. He spoke of standing on a high canyon precipice in Peru when a roar something like a jet engine—a sound he'd never heard before nor has since—pushed up from out of the abyss. He waited with trepidation and a gigantic Andean condor with a ten-foot wingspan slowly rose up in front of him. Having dropped to the base of the cliff to escape the harassment of two Harris hawks, the condor had spread its wings, caught a thermal current, and just floated back up.

The second miracle of our morning arrives with a shock of brilliant-red ladybugs swarming the outside of Russell's porch door. Members of a widespread family of beetles called *Coccinellids*, ladybugs are beneficial in keeping aphids and other agricultural pests under control. When the numbers of their natural enemies decline, they may become a nuisance themselves, causing considerable damage to large-scale commercial crops like grains, potatoes, and beans.

In Great Britain and in other parts of the English-speaking world, ladybugs are known as ladybirds, a name derived from their association with the Virgin Mary, who was often depicted in early paintings wearing a red cape. The Lady Beetle or Our Lady's Bird morphed into ladybird. Their yellow, orange, or red oval bodies have rounded backs and flat undersides, black spots on wing covers, black heads, six short black legs, and black antennae. Primarily carnivorous, ladybugs in turn feed birds, frogs, wasps, spiders, and dragonflies. In temperate regions like Paradise, they will enter a winter diapause, a state of dormancy with a metabolic slowdown. As a result, they are often among the first insects to appear in spring, when they mate and lay several batches of eggs. Many cultures consider ladybugs a symbol of good luck.

By late afternoon, we've hauled our portable table and L.L.Bean chairs down to the river for a picnic supper, setting up just behind the old Dam Rapids bench. The river rushes by all fizz and froth with overlapping rhythms. A mallard duck couple executes a couple of flybys before skiing in for a landing at Black Bass Bend.

Surrounded by the twilight trills of red-winged blackbirds across the water-meadow, the chirping of robins, and the soft coo of mourning doves on the hillsides, we walk back in the gloaming, along the riverbank and up through The West Woods, the sun a deep rose-red slipping away in a frigid sky.

❊ *3 May* ❊

YESTERDAY, LATE AFTERNOON, we took our leftovers to The Gully wash where we'd discovered a likely raccoon den. Muddy pawprints shaped like five-fingered human hands splattered The Gully Bridge in chalky clay—lots of chattering squabbles in the night after that, along with honking geese and essence of striped skunk.

We wake up to blue skies and sunshine, though a drizzle had dampened the air earlier, even as the dawn chorus got under way. The morning passes with more signposting. We then tweak the stone steps on the far West Woods boardwalk and continue sorting Edna's shed. Sadly, another mouse family has succumbed.

From the start, mice have not fared well in the domestic portions of Paradise. A large number are house mice, descendants of stowaways from Europe centuries ago. Many more are native white-footed mice or woodland deer mice.

The very spring that Dan and I took over the property after years of unintentional neglect, we found a snug nest of shredded tea towels tucked away in a drawer of the living room buffet, complete with a cache of hard candy. Nothing remained of the inhabitant but a drift of rodent-shaped fur in the kitchen sink. Until the lack of a reliable water source hit home, she, too, must have thought she'd found Paradise.

We break for a lunch of cheese and crackers, nuts and fresh fruit, in front of Russell's, overlooking the water-meadow. Brewer's black-birds—five males and one female—at odds with a single brown thrasher and a gang of chickadees and sparrows, flutter and flap at the bird feeder. Nesting robins fend off interloping blue jays in the cedar forest and a handful of wild canaries gather for choir practice in one of the bare elm trees. From the scolding next door, the red squirrels are in open warfare over scattered peanuts. All of this activity spooks a ground hog, who'd peeked out once or twice from under Russell's shed.

Ground hogs have declined in Paradise with the advance of the cedar woods. They prefer open grassland.

One summer, long ago, Carol and I rescued two tiny, orphaned pups (Donny and Johnny) from down on The Flats. We so wanted to keep them as pets. They remained in the cottage just long enough for Mom to see that their pelts were seething with fleas.

In the early afternoon sunshine, we slip on our wellies and set off across the river again. We reach the north bank through the marshland twigginess of the water-meadow below Russell's and make our way along the shoreline to The Dam Rapids, picking up both the trills of American toads and the croaks of bull frogs.

New grasses on both sides of the river roll out like green velvet, pushing up through the dull, straw-colored carpets of winter. Negotiating the submerged and slippery rocks of The Dam Rapids proves a challenge. Rushing water laps at the tops of our boots, our walking sticks no match for the current.

A time or two we almost go down. But we stumble up and out still dry—for the most part—to prowl the open swath of spring forest that stretches back from the river sixty feet or more to the south property-line fence.

Grasses wedged in the forks of trees show that the spring floodwaters had reached at least ten feet high. Animal tracks and trails abound, crisscrossing the spongy understory—muskrat, deer, raccoon, skunk, and red fox. At the mushy east end, where bright patches of marsh marigold glow opposite the beaver lodge, we find colt's foot and dutchmen's britches with their tiny, white, pantaloon petals.

We return to the north bank by the swollen east-end rapids near Rainbow Cliff. Meadow violets in cornflower blue, grape hyacinth, blue-eyed grass, and trout lilies have sprung up on the margins of the cedar woods. At the beaver lodge, two jumbles of twigs and branches heaped above the waterline and ringed with fresh tracks, suggest ongoing renovations. The tenants have also scouted out an uprooted cedar tree and the limbs of a fallen white willow.

Back to Edna's then for a pork chop barbecue. And now here we sit on Edna's deck on a crisp but calm evening. Against an indigo sky, creamy clouds have slipped westward with the sun. Bumblebees and butterflies flit through rising darkness, the songs of robins and blackbirds resounding across the edge of night.

❈ *6 May* ❈

AFTER A TEA AND TOAST BREAKFAST, we browse through Dad's old cottage journals. All through the 1960s, '70s, and '80s, his early May entries speak of "patches of snow still in the cedars" or "snow gone except in the cedars." Since then, we've weathered the odd spring snow squall or two, but "snow still in the cedars" no longer resonates as a mantra of early May. Presumably one of the less subtle consequences of climate change in Paradise.

A 2021 Canadian study by the Intergovernmental Panel on Climate Change shows us that on average Southern Ontario and southern Quebec are warming twice as fast as the rest of the world, their northern regions by a factor of three. The progressive loss of snow-cover has resulted in these Canadian landscapes absorbing all the solar radiation they used to reflect back into space. Though such winter warming may decrease our ice-out, excessive rains may now bring more frequent spring and fall flooding.

Midmorning, we speak with one of our hilltop neighbors. On the heels of the apparent disappearance of our resident red fox, she heard coyote pups whimpering last night. It's tempting to attribute the expansion of coyotes into Southern Ontario to global warming. But they've been spreading east from their traditional range on the western prairies since the early 20th century, in response to deforestation and a lack of predators.

This cool day of overcast and drizzle banishes most thoughts of global warming. Even as gray-bottomed clouds crawl across the sky, hazy spring excels. In amber, limey-green, and reddish-orange washes through the woods. In golden-yellow willow blossom pendants. In the soft emerald blush of lilac buds. In cylindrical clusters of ivory choke-cherries abloom at Russell's.

Lots of action again at Black Bass Bend in the early evening. We watch as a half-dozen mergansers float in from around the bend. Spotted sandpipers bob on the shoreline. And at the edge of the woods, a lone wild turkey struts. Later still, under a resplendent waxing moon, rustles, snaps, and snarls at Edna's deck exposes a well-fed raccoon perched in the fork of a maple tree, hauling in the bird feeder paw over paw like a fishing line.

❈ *7 May* ❈

MAGNIFICENT SPRING! We woke this morning to warming blue skies over a splendidly burnished landscape. Spring grasses are now high enough for those water voles, the muskrats, to slip out of the river and vanish. The first red-breasted grosbeaks of the season feast at the west feeder. Side by side and just inches above the surface of the water, three spotted sandpipers whisk upriver with soft twitters, while a chattering belted kingfisher speeds past in the opposite direction.

Greener and greener the earth grows.

Alice Thoms Vitale writes in *Leaves in Myth, Magic, and Medicine,* "Every day, every hour of all the ages, as each continent and, equally important, each ocean, rolls into the sunlight, chlorophyll ceaselessly creates. Only when man has done as much, may he call himself the equal of a weed."

Oh, the power and the glory of the spring greening!

An abundance of wildflowers also blooms in May. Canada anemone, wild garlic, common bellflower, dog-toothed violets, sundrops, dogwood, wild blue iris, and lily of the valley, to name just a few.

"Earth laughs in flowers," poet Ralph Waldo Emerson once wrote in his poem "Hamatreya." He must have been thinking of the month of May.

In early days, I stitched together a small, red, cotton sack embroidered with FLOWERS AND SQUIRRELS, in which I carried a notebook, a pencil, and a compact wildflower book (a Christmas gift). I wandered the property recording flowers in bloom. What. When. Where. A habit I've never really lost.

One of the oldest seasonal flower celebrations, Anthesteria, held in honor of Dionysus, the god of wine, took place in ancient Greece in May when the last season's wine reached maturity. Flowers, symbolizing fertility and fruitfulness, prosperity and happiness, played a large part in the festivities, as they had in the Roman Floralia Festival.

In May 1561, Charles IX of France received a sprig of lily of the valley as a lucky charm. Each year thereafter, he offered the same to the ladies of his court. By the 19th century, lily of the valley, *Convallaria majalis*, had become a symbol of both springtime and happiness, and subsequently, the flower of May.

The English name comes from "lily of the valleys," as written of in the Biblical Song of Solomon, *Convallaria majalis* being the Latin equivalent.

A two-leafed woodland plant with sweet-scented, bell-shaped white petals hanging in pendant sprays of five to fifteen flowers, lily of the valley is a native of Asia and Europe. We also call them May bells, Our Lady's tears, and Mary's tears. Plants can form extensive colonies, using underground stems called rhizomes. The new shoots of summer, which lie dormant and connected underground through winter, become leafy foliage in the spring. All parts of the plant, including its small orange and red berries, are poisonous and can cause abdominal pain, nausea, vomiting, and irregular heartbeats. Glorious banks of blooming lily of the valley have spread in patches all over Paradise, especially west of Edna's.

Fittingly, May's Full Flower Moon will rise later tonight, known also as the Corn Planting Moon, Mother's Moon, and Milk Moon, from Old English *Rimilcemona* meaning "Month of Three Milkings." In times past, spring cows were milked three times a day. The Full Flower moon quite likely took its name from the profusion of May wildflowers.

In the icy stillness of late evening, we're outside sitting in front of Russell's. The full moon has cast shards of silver across the water-meadow. The river glides below, a pale ribbon shadowed with ghostly swirls of mist. On the slope, dampened blades of grass throw back the moonlight. The silence is lustrous. Magical. Freezing.

❀ *10 May* ❀

DAN SERVES UP A STELLAR MOTHER'S DAY brunch this morning: scrambled eggs, ham, toast, orange juice, and coffee. Outside Edna's west window while we eat, wrens spruce up their nests in Dad's old birdhouses. A pair of plump groundhogs browse on dandelions that had sprouted around the well. And, in time, a sharp breeze blows off the cloud cover, leaving an afternoon of sunshine.

While Dan sets about raking old leaves, I ramble back and forth across the property gathering kindling. At Wood's End, the river rolls wide and tranquil until two Canada goose couples swoop in from opposite directions and begin grazing on the foot-high grasses of the opposite bank. Within moments, a blazing territorial dispute erupts. Gentle mutterings swell to honking, squawking, hooting, and a great flapping of wings. Couple to couple, long necks low and snaky, with occasional bouts of preening, through all the yawps and yelps, bows and dips, they finally reach some sort of accord and waddle off again, in pairs, to disappear for the night in the long grass.

I know they're boisterous and messy, and I appreciate that they don't please everyone, especially those living on waterside property. And once they've successfully nested, they'll return again and again to the same spot in growing numbers. But I'm enthralled, absolutely enchanted by the sight and sound of any goose flock in V-formation.

Our Southern Ontario Canada geese—conservatively numbered at 400,000 breeding birds—are protected under Canadian law. Animals, eggs, and nests. When winter weather affects their feeding and roosting grounds, many will migrate as far south as Tennessee. With climate change, however, more and more choose to overwinter.

By their clearance of forests in the late 18th century, settlers greatly improved goose habitat and they flourished. However, unrestricted hunting so reduced the population that by the turn of the 20th century, they had all but vanished from most of their Southern Ontario breeding range. Consequently, in the 1960s and 1970s, birds were reintroduced, and with few predators, they more than adjusted to our parks, golf courses, and other open spaces, preferring the shorelines of ponds, rivers, and wetlands. Nesting geese have been found in trees, on rooftops, and in roadside ditches.

The Canada goose or *Branta canadensis* (*brante* Latinized from Old Norse *brandgás* meaning "burnt" in the sense of "black") mates for life and may live up to ten years, some reaching twenty-five. Females are often sitting on their nests by mid-April and hatching peaks in May. A few weeks after goslings arrive, adult geese molt their wing feathers. Flightless for up to six weeks then, they become reluctant to leave their nesting/molting areas. Goslings can usually fly by mid-July and by the end of the month, they've settled into roosting areas on larger bodies of water, flying off for daily foraging.

In the fall, the subarctic breeding Canada geese from farther north join our temperate birds for migration. Numbers soar through late October. Most migrating birds have left by mid-December.

As I later sit at Black Bass Bend with a sling full of firewood, a Canada goose, gander, and three six-inch gosling fluff-balls come paddling down from the upper rapids. As they slip out in silence to crop the riverside grasses, Dad on constant guard duty on the river's edge, I make my muffled way home.

❈ *15 May* ❈

HEAVY SPRING RAINS PASSED through last night, complete with thunder and lightning. They left behind a gray showery sky that hovered over the rest of the day.

We spend much of the morning on Edna's deck as sublime spring surges around us. Escaping hungry rodents, two tulips have even bloomed in Mom's old planters, one in cherry red, one in lemon yellow. Our few remaining lilac bushes have also broken out in tiny tight flower buds.

Through a mizzle of rain comes the first lowing of cows in some distant meadow. We might call this Dancing Cow Day, the traditional day in many parts of Europe when dairy cows are let out into the fields or taken to summer pastures. After spending the winter indoors, they will jump for joy, skip and dance with excitement, kick up their heels, buck and stretch, push and shove, in their pent-up quest for freedom.

In Denmark, Dancing Cow Day, also known as Økodag (Organic Day), falls in late April. Many Danes travel to nearby farms for the annual ritual in which thousands of dairy cattle are set free at noontime.

Despite the faintly falling skies, we manage an hour or two at Castor's Landing midafternoon, passing Harold's Tea Deck, where his dazzling daffodils glow through the gloom. Speckled with raindrops, the river burbles on in chocolate brown at The Dam Rapids and the open woodland to Black Bass Bend spreads out underfoot, soft with old cedar leaves and rich black earth. Up and down the river, spring trees stand in lacy lime and pale gold, with new leaves unfurled. Spring grasses wave in vibrant emerald against the dreary sky. Across the river, patches of rust-red reeds shiver in the rain.

❊ 21 May ❊

GREEN IS THE COLOR OF MAY—not the deep greens of summer or the faded greens of fall, but lime and beryl and chartreuse. Pea green, pale olive, and apple green. The green of unfurling fiddleheads across the river. The green of lilac leaves in counterpoint to their amethyst flowerheads. The fresh green delicacy in the burgeoning crowns of elms and maples, walnuts and willows, poplars, ashes, and aspens. Under the satin-gray clouds, we see that the earth in spring shimmers in green, enveloped in smooth and pliant softness, like a blanket.

The emerald, the traditional birthstone of May, echoes the pervasive hue of springtime. A variety of the mineral beryl, emeralds take on their green tones from traces of chromium and/or vanadium, though colors may range from yellow-green to blue-green. Top gems require a high degree of transparency along with a pure verdant green. Lighter-toned stones are usually referred to as green beryl.

The name emerald comes to us from Old French *esmeraude* and Middle English *emeraude*, which developed from Vulgar Latin *esmaralda/esmaraldus*, a variant of Latin *smaragdus* from the Greek *smaragdos* meaning "green gem."

Emerald ranks among the big five of gems, besides diamond, ruby, amethyst, and sapphire. Though emerald is found from Afghanistan and Australia to Zambia and Zimbabwe, Colombia has long been the world's largest producer.

India and Austria mined emeralds from the 14th century BCE, ancient Egypt from at least 1500 BCE. Their workings, later exploited by the Roman, Byzantine, and Ottoman empires, ceased with the discovery of Colombia's deposits.

New grasses high and wide across the water-meadow and up over the open hillsides embody emerald, as do our lush, now-blooming, lilacs. Needing full sunlight six to eight hours each day, few lilac bushes have survived on Paradise property. A hardy half-dozen struggle year to year near the top of the north-hill steps and another handful have sprung up at the top of the slope to the water-meadow. Zion's old churchyard, now manicured and trimmed with a few rescued grave slabs arranged out front in tidy rows, still hosts several dozen dense clusters each spring. The old moldering black wrought iron fences of the original graveyard lie buried in their depths.

Lilacs are my favorite flower. Their twenty-one species belong to the *Oleaceae* family, along with olives, ash, and jasmine. They can be found from Asia to Europe and North America. Known as the Queen of Shrubs, lilacs have been known to reach a hundred years of age or more. Pale white stands for purity and innocence. Violet or deep purple for spirituality. Lilac for first love. Blue for happiness and tranquility, and magenta for love and passion.

Their scientific name, *Syringa vulgaris*, derives from the Greek word *syrinks* which means "pipe." Ancient Greek myth tells us that Pan, the god of forest and field, fell in love with a comely nymph named Syringa. Being pursued by Pan through the forest one day, Syringa escapes by turning herself into a lilac bush. Failing to find her, Pan comes across the lilac, whose branches are hollow. And so, he snips a reed, creating the first pan pipe. The common name, lilac, referring to the light purple of the flowers, comes through the same French and Spanish word from Persian *lilak* and Arabic *laylak*, meaning "blue."

With the lilac's incomparable fragrance, the Celts considered them magical. Which, of course, they are. One of the earliest flowers of spring, lilacs last a mere two to three weeks, so they are not to be missed.

On this Memorial Day, when we remember all those who've fallen in war, we have been blessed with a singular warm and windy spring day, the air drenched with the intoxicating perfume of lilacs.

❈ *26 May* ❈

A SHORT GENTLE RAIN WAKES us this morning and the black-bottomed clouds that lingered from dawn to dusk, drop an occasional sprinkle through the day. The fireplace at Edna's Cottage blazes all day and in the cool evening dampness, we set off for Black Bass Bend with a thermos of hot mint tea.

The sun inches its way through the gathering darkness in the west, turning everything near and far to gold. High spring grasses. Newly opened purple irises. Rain-splashed elms, willows, and apple trees. The whole world glitters against the ebony skies, the river a sudden sweep of eye-piercing shards of light. Birds trill everywhere. Blackbirds, cardinals, and robins in the cedar woods. Sparrows and warblers across the water. The air, earthy and rich, lies crisp against our skin.

One of the first articles I sold as a professional writer, many decades ago, involved an enormous tree trunk that had washed up on The Flats in some now-distant spring flood. I remember lying on that log, keyed into the sights, sounds, smells, and feel of that one singular moment. The buzzing of the insects. The rush and rustle of the wind in the grass. The bird chorus. The pungent spring earth. The brush of a breeze along my arms. The shimmering blue sky overhead.

In his book, *The Nature Principle: Reconnecting with Life in a Virtual Age*, writer Richard Louv coined the term "nature deficit disorder," which he defined as "a diminished ability to find meaning in the life that surrounds us."

What happens when we lose touch with our own natural surroundings? Whether gardening outdoors, tending houseplants, or enjoying a natural landscape out an open window, we can all feel some connection with the natural world, which seems essential to a life well lived.

This wise quote, attributed to W.B. Yeats, sums up the power of nature: "The world is full of magic things, patiently waiting for our senses to grow sharper."

❊ *29 May* ❊

RIGHT ON SCHEDULE, we've had a froth of creamy apple blossoms explode across Paradise in a sea of white foam. Sprinkled through the woods, east and west, they're rampant on the hilltop. Only opening two or three weeks after the first leaf buds appear, they will only last three to ten days.

In order to bloom, apple trees require a proper chill during their winter dormant stage. With the likely coming of milder Canadian winters due to climate change, an inadequate freeze may mean the tragic loss of apple blossoms in the not-too-distant future.

But in this year, on this day, they've outdone themselves. Their pink-tinged clouds of perfumed ivory, eggshell, and pearl have brushed the landscape with blanches of frost.

What a glorious salute to summer!

Part Two

SUMMER

"Summer's lease hath all too short a date."
— WILLIAM SHAKESPEARE

"And since all this loveliness cannot be Heaven,
I know in my heart it is June."
— ABBA WOOLSON

❋ 1 June ❋

IN THE WOODS EAST AND WEST, on the bluffs north and south, across the water-meadow and along the riverbanks, a riot of plush green against the deep-blue sky shouts—*Summer!*

Even as fruit tree blossoms begin to fade on the hilltop and in forest glades, new leaves emerge, resplendent in emerald, moss, lime, and olive. So much living to be done in the few short months before the world grows cold again.

Summer! The longest and warmest of days. Easy living. A time of flamboyance, contentment, and abundance.

On this, the first day of meteorological summer, when Paradise temperatures still hover on the edge of late spring, we feel expectation and possibility in the air. A flock of Canada geese nearly a hundred strong gives bombastic voice to the season, streaming directly overhead in V-formation.

Summer in the Northern Hemisphere encompasses the months of June, July, and August. The name derives from Middle English *sumer*, from Old English *sumor*, related to Old High German and Old Norse *sumer*, from the Sanskrit *samā* meaning "year" or "season."

The Roman poet Ovid gives us two etymologies for the name of this month, the first being from Juno, the Roman goddess of love and marriage (equivalent to the Greek goddess Hera), spouse to Jupiter.

"Juno" is derived through the Latin *iuvenis,* meaning "youth," from a common Indo-European root word referring to a concept of vital energy or "fertile time." Summer incarnate. The predominance of June weddings probably originated with Juno, many ancients considering it good luck to be married in the month bearing Juno's name.

Alternatively, Ovid tells us, the name Juno may derive from the Latin word *iuniores,* meaning "younger ones," as opposed to *maiores,* "elders," for which the preceding month may have been named.

In ethereal, late-evening calmness, we're sitting on Edna's deck. Not a leaf stirs. Stars have broken out above and wild geese move upriver through the dusky night to settle in pairs for the night.

❋ *2 June* ❋

ANOTHER BRIGHT BLUE DAY broke this morning, filled with sunshine and perfumed late-spring air, a rush of wind in the trees, a float of wispy cloud on the horizon. Marcs' tails and angel hair.

And an occasional smother of mosquitoes. They, too, have thickened the late-spring air, drawn to movement, dark colors, odor, and carbon dioxide. *Be a good listener,* they warn us.

I startle a cottontail at the woodpile this morning, and several more chipmunks convene at the bird feeder when the red squirrels allow— legends of manna from heaven in these parts. The chipmunks have grown accustomed to our presence now and sit comfortably about with the Canada blue jays, munching peanuts. One territorial robin, who must have a nest nearby, harasses even the jays.

Yesterday, this neighborhood bully—or heroic family protector— bopped about on constant guard duty. Like a hawk, she swooped down on a chipmunk, raking sharp claws across the wee fellow's back.

Vestiges of apple blossoms remain shrouded in a glut of new leaves, and tall yellow flowers, possibly Jerusalem artichoke, now line the riverbank opposite. Ostrich ferns are already high and thick enough to shield the deer from view in the wilderness across the river. Green, green, green glimmers everywhere. You can almost see the grass growing.

A spectacular sunset, viewed from Black Bass Bend just short of nine o'clock, has swaths of powder-pink cloud reflected in soft coral on the water. Smoky blue evening trees rise between. As dusk settles, the surface of the water comes alive with fish jumping. Great splashes, in unison, a dozen at a time. Ripples spiraling in every direction in a remarkable water ballet.

One snapping turtle, a species older than the dinosaurs, swims close in to check us out as Beaudelaire materializes midstream. Paddling silently with one push of a back paw against the current, Beaudelaire moves down past The Dam Rapids. When I rush over for a shot of that stunning sunset, he cruises over to have a closer look, comes to within a dozen feet of me, and then dives and disappears. Always an enormous relief to know our beaver are still safely in residence.

❀ *5 June* ❀

ABOUT ONE O'CLOCK THIS MORNING, unable to sleep, I throw on a robe and sit an hour or so in front of Russell's under the Full Strawberry Moon. The water-meadow, hills and hollows, forests and fields, all stand in stillness, cloaked in a surreal and dusty glow. Not a sound but the distant murmur of the river below as the moon rides high and hazy behind a brightly overcast sky.

The Full Strawberry Moon, named for the short wild-strawberry season that peaks in June, is known in Europe as the Full Rose Moon, the Full Hot Moon—for summer's looming onslaught of heat—or the Full Mead Moon, from the Anglo-Saxon season of mowing meads or meadows. As it happens, Dan finished a second trimming of our own sparse Paradise lawn just yesterday.

Cultivated strawberries, members of the *Rose* family, developed from the common wild Virginia strawberry, native to North America. We've likely taken the word "strawberry" from the Old English *streawberige* or *streabariye*, plants sending out runners likened to pieces of straw. Alternatively, the name may have come from the practice of mulching the berries with straw. The first colonists in America shipped larger strawberry plants back to Europe as early as 1600. Presently, most cultivated strawberries come from California.

The wild perennial herb, Virginia strawberry (*fragaria Virginiana*), also known as mountain, common, or wild strawberry, grows less than a foot tall. The name "fragaria" comes from the Latin word *fragum*, from *fraga* meaning "fragrance." New plants develop along runners called stolons, which stretch sideways above ground taking root as they branch out. Leaves with toothed edges remain green throughout winter, new sprouts appearing with the green grasses of spring. Wild strawberries' delicate blooms, less than an inch wide, have five rounded ivory petals surrounding a pale-yellow center.

The red conical part of the strawberry we've most often thought of as the fruit is actually a receptacle for the true pips or seeds embedded on its surface. Strawberries, high in vitamins B, C, and E, provide food for many small mammals and birds. We've also used them as an ingredient in lotions and skin creams.

With their fragile milky petals, a few wild Virginia strawberries have returned to Paradise in patches of sunlight across the parking area at the top of the north hill staircase. With a bluish hue to their leaves, a related species, the woodland strawberry, has emerged on the edges of the cedar forests. Their tiny berries will ripen in a week or so.

When we were young, the hilltop road tracked down past Zion to meet and cross the main road coming north. We regularly picked berries along the dusty verges. Raspberries, chokecherries, blackberries, and itty-bitty, but oh-so-sweet, wild strawberries.

A mist of rain sent me back to bed last night, and with its gentle patter on the roof, I had soon drifted off.

In another midmorning spritz, we wander off through the sheltered West Woods, robins, cardinals, chickadees, red-winged blackbirds, crows, mallards, Canada geese, and two great blue heron all celebrating the season.

As we approach Wood's End, we startle a doe and a fawn, who both bounded for the river through a showy bank of lately bloomed mother-of-the-evening (*Hesperis matronalis*), more commonly known as dame's rocket.

Often mistaken for wild phlox (five petals), dame's rocket (four petals), our most prominent flowering plant of spring and early summer on the water-meadow, has over a dozen names, from damask violet and dame's gillyflower to summer lilac and Good & Plenty. A short-lived herbaceous perennial intolerant of summer heat, dame's rocket belongs to the *Brassicaceae* or *Mustard* family. Native to Eurasia and imported to North America in the 17th century, some plants escaped to become an intrusive weed species to many gardeners. The genus *Hesperis* most likely refers to the scent of the flowers becoming more conspicuous toward evening, *hespera* being the Greek word for "evening."

In the shadow of the water-meadow's white-willow matriarch, early spring furnishes the deep green mounds of their low-growing foliage, and now dame's rocket has burst into a scented fluorescence of soft pastels—lavender, amethyst, deep purple, pearl, salmon pink, and coral.

❊ *6 June* ❊

THOUGH TODAY'S FORECAST BOASTS "warm and sunny," a chilled overcast holds sway until midmorning, when heavy rain shuts off our power for over an hour. By six o'clock in the evening, the sun has breached the gloom, and shafts of sunlight fire up a bouquet of lilacs on the polished-oak dining table at Edna's. A warm and cozy hominess floods the room.

About eight o'clock, we make for the river again. The sun stands low and golden above the western hills. Just as we move up into the eastern cedar forest, two white-tailed does, tawny shadows in the trees below, dash across the river at The Dam Rapids.

From Black Bass Bend, another whitetail slips across the river at the far eastern rapids and melts into an island of grassland cedars. Blackbirds feast by the dozens on a million flying insects that roil and jounce above the river's surface.

Beau emerges midstream, gliding toward a far-side willow, and vanishes into a cove bank. Clusters of driftwood and sprays and sprigs on either side of The Dam Rapids suggest contemplation of a new beaver dam. As we watch and wait, Beau reappears and paddles midstream and back a time or two, as though waiting for his mate to arrive. And she does. He heads off downriver on his own then, stopping to rummage in a clump of yellow flowers in bloom on the far bank, and then climbs out to consider that pile of driftwood. For twenty minutes, with due diligence and true professionalism, he hauls up mud and pebbles from the river bottom, cementing them into place with sticks and twigs, branchlets, rocks, and gravel.

Close to nine o'clock, flocks of starlings swoop in to roost in the cedars. They fill the trees with a cacophony of buzzing, trills and squawks, warbles, whirs, and hoots. Yet we can't see a single bird. The trees themselves might have been singing.

When the sun sets in a blaze of pale fuchsia and deep rose, the darkening river water reflects silver striations above and below. The trees turn to black lace against the failing light, and the forest falls silent.

❋ 7 June ❋

ON THIS BRIGHT AND SUNNY DAY freshened by a cool breeze, we picnic again at The Dam Rapids. On our approach from high in the east woods, we spot a lone deer at the river-crossing below. We watch her drink until, startled by the inadvertent snap of a twig, she makes her silent retreat.

After lunch, we navigate the shallow rapids with ease and meander through the wild southside forest on well-worn animal trails. From the riverbank willows on through the open understory, most lead to the south-side property boundary and beyond. A brace of sweet-scented swamp rosebushes straddles the fence here, nearly five feet high and sprinkled with delicate pink-satin blossoms.

From the narrow lea opposite our own water-meadow, we back-track to reclaim our chairs. As we stretch out under the sun, the multivoiced river sluices by at our feet. Several branch-stripped cedar trunks, having floated down from upriver, lie in wait in the beaver dam construction zone.

The rose, in a hundred different species, flourishes especially during the month of June and serves as the primary birth flower of the month. Roses belong to the *Rosaceae* family. Developed from wild forebearers all around the world, from North America to Africa and Oceania, we've bred them for hundreds of years for habitat, color, size, fragrance, hardiness, longevity, and disease resistance. Roses span the spectrum of color, ranging from bright cerise, dark red, purple, pink, and coral, to yellow, bluish-lilac, orange, and white, to all the many colors in between.

Sacred to both Venus, the Roman goddess of love and beauty, and Bacchus, the Roman god of wine, roses of varying hues have symbolized love, sympathy, sorrow, friendship, innocence, purity, joy, gratitude, and more. Among ancient Romans, secrets fell "under the rose." Cleopatra had the floor of her palace strewn with rose petals in anticipation of her lover Mark Antony's arrival.

With small, oval, reddish-orange fruits called hips or haws and prickles incorrectly identified as thorns, the rose releases a pungent sweetness from tiny perfume glands on the petals. Vineyards will often plant a rosebush at the end of each row of vines, their health reflecting the health of the wine crop.

Old Roses, introduced prior to 1867 and referred to as old-fashioned or heirloom roses, come in hundreds of lush and fragrant varieties. Of our modern hybrid roses—those bred after 1867—tea roses, which have a single flower per long stem, are among the most popular, along with the English rose.

The blossoms of the third category, wild roses, which have bloomed from spring through late summer for thousands of years, have five pale-pink to rosy-pink petals. The wild rose of Paradise, the swamp rose (*Rosa palustris*, Latin for "rose of the marsh") grows from three to eight feet tall, with branching, often crooked stems, yellow stamens, and a center-flattened cluster of yellow, pink, or reddish-orange pistils. Native to much of eastern North America, swamp rose shrubs, which prefer full or partial sun and wet or moist acidic soils, flower for one to two months from early to late summer.

Catbirds, brown thrashers, yellow warblers, and cardinals, all denizens of Paradise, may nest in the taller bushes, and the fruits feed our ruffed grouse, cedar waxwings, white-footed mice, and striped skunks. White-tailed deer browse the twigs and leaves, and beaver will munch on the woody stems or use them as construction material. Our own beaver clan would be hard-pressed to harvest anything so far removed from the safety of the river as our swamp rosebushes at the southern boundary. But as an indicator of high-quality wetlands, we hold our swamp rose shrubs in high regard.

The bonus birth flower of June, the honeysuckle (*Lonicera*), an arching shrub or hardy climbing vine in the *Caprifoliaceae* family, has not yet reached Paradise, having only been discovered in Ontario's forests in 1976, invasive since 2007. The name "honeysuckle" derives from the sweet nectar of its intensely fragrant tubular flowers. *Lonicera* honors Adam Lonicer, a renowned Renaissance botanist. As the orange variety of honeysuckle has proven irresistible to hummingbirds, we would welcome them in Paradise.

Our restful nap by the river allows Beau to cruise past, dive, and then resurface twenty feet downriver, where he shakes his head with a faint splash—the only time he's ever made a sound. Into the high grasses he trundles, returning with a willow branch, which he swims upriver to the lodge.

With renewed energy, we head off through the woods, climbing up to the road and on down to The Big Bridge, where the river flows nut-brown and smooth as glass.

To the north side, on the left bank, sprawls the lofty grove of white cedars we called in early cottage days, the Queen's Palace.

A natural "moat" surrounded the "palace," at that time, comprised of watery inlets, furrows, and a modest spring. At one end, in a fabulous tangle of straggly willows labyrinthed with cow paths, lay the "palace garden," a place of endless royal intrigue. I loved the role of any evil queen, locking up innocent princesses and chopping off their hair. Late spring flooding involved the navigation of shin-deep puddling overflows and the grasping of tree trunks and low branches to keep our balance.

Across the river and reached at the time by a natural clap bridge of flat river stones, stands the Coronation Palace, another spread of white cedars with an open understory.

A cow path—the Coronation Walk—moved north out of the "palace" along the raised riverbank. Processions of regal splendor took place there. In flowing robes of woolen blankets and old bed sheets, we greeted our subjects—the mass of thorn apple trees that dotted the hills and fields right and left—with studied royal waves.

On one such august occasion, we noticed a fellow in the adoring crowd—probably a hunter—sporting a rifle. From then on, the precinct above the Coronation Palace and its walkway became Killer Country.

Weekends when Mom and Dad stayed overnight here in Paradise, we played Queens at home in Kitchener. Several turns around the kitchen table reached the peak of a palace turret. The cellar served as the dungeon. And the living room, with a scattering of my Great-Aunt Jessie's flowery hooked rugs, stood in for the royal gardens. Blanket fluff that balled up under all the furniture always gave us away.

On this early summer day, two small boys with fishing poles, one ten or twelve, the other seven or eight, peddle down the road to The Big Bridge on their bikes.

"What kind of fish are you after?" Dan asks.

"Well, there's a sucker over there. And over here's a pike."

"How do you know it's a pike?"

"Because it's so thin," the older boy answers and slips down the embankment to cast in.

His little brother—so little-brother-like—pipes in with, "Yeah, it's a pike. I can tell by his eye."

Of course, nothing but a long, thin, brown fish-back hanging motionless in the water can be seen.

❀ *8 June* ❀

A SHOWERY OVERCAST, cold and windy, opens the day. House wrens sing bubbly torrents nonstop through the sprinkles as they assess various nesting options. Dad's journals record "snow flurries" on this day in 1980. So, by comparison, we're ahead of the game.

Years ago, on another June 8, Mom came to Paradise for the first time since she'd had her stroke. A day that broke dull and drizzly brightened with sunlight just as she arrived. Dave Eveleigh, our treasured renovator/restorer, arranged her on pillows and blankets in the back of his small trailer and down she came behind his off-roader—Dave's Limo Service. While Dan and I trimmed a few wayward saplings from the line of view to the river, Mom and Dad rested for a time on Edna's swing. We would glance up to see them convulsed in laughter.

Clouds break late in the evening and, rare for cottage skies, stars pop up everywhere, a vague fringe of dusty cloud on the horizon.

I've been reading Chet Raymo's *An Intimate Look at the Night Sky*. He talks about how the Hubble Space Telescope created one photograph by focusing its camera on a speck of sky chosen randomly from the dark space between visible stars. An area the size of a pinhead held at arm's length. The resulting picture from a shutter left open for ten days shows two thousand galaxies, hundreds of others mere pinpricks of light. Twenty-five thousand such shots would just about cover the bowl of the Big Dipper. NASA's James Webb Space Telescope has probably more than quadrupled that awesome statistic.

Many of Raymo's students found these facts depressing, viewing themselves as barely a speck in all the universe.

But what an astounding privilege it is for each of us to be one singular, unique life-form manifesting in all of that space and time.

❋ 12 June ❋

ON A DAZZLING SUMMER DAY, balmy and bright, we're enjoying a late lunch at Harold's Tea Deck. The drowsy drone of a prop plane overhead—the very anthem of summer to me—hums on the still air. We've just come from the beaver lodge, where we harvested a batch of wild peppermint to dry overnight.

Yesterday, overlooking the water-meadow at Russell's Cottage, we took in the first lightshow of that marvel of summer nights—fireflies.

Members of the *Lampyridae* family of insects in the *Coleoptera* order of beetles, fireflies, sometimes called lightning bugs, chemically produce a yellow, green, or pale red "cold light" (meaning it lacks infrared or ultraviolet frequencies) from organs on their lower abdomen. We know this reaction as bioluminescence. The chemicals involved in this reaction are now being studied for use in the treatment of diseases like cancer.

The 136 species of these soft-bodied beetles (called glowworms in their larval state) can be found in both temperate and tropical climates. The oldest known fossil, *Protoluciola* found in Late Cretaceous Burmese amber in Myanmar, dates back ninety-nine million years.

Fireflies utilize their light to communicate with potential mates. Along with the use of chemical cues, light signals comprised of glows and flashes that vary according to color, duration, timing, and repetition, allow the insects to identify mates of their own species. Most fireflies contain steroids similar to those found in some poisonous toads. Like toads, too, they have proven distasteful to many predators who may also be alerted to this toxicity by distinctive light patterns in firefly flight.

Of the twenty-three known firefly species in Southern Ontario, Paradise supports predominantly two—*Photuris* and *Photinus*. Both have unique courtship flash patterns. *Photinus* females do not fly as a rule. They signal from the ground in response to males of their own species. Though they also dine on mosquito larvae, slugs, and worms, *Photuris* females, sometimes referred to as "femme fatale fireflies," will also mimic the patterns of other fireflies. They often target smaller Photinus males who, attracted to what appears to be a suitable mate, are then eaten.

Like so many other life-forms on our distressed planet, fireflies, which can indicate the health of the soil, have declined worldwide through loss of habitat, pesticide use, climate change, and especially light pollution.

As darkness sets in, these bewitching winged jewels of the night rise and dip on the sweet summer air. Their tiny, silvery-green, auroral sparks of light glow and glint off and on for hours, like little lanterns. They weave spells through tufts of meadow grass. They sprinkle the edges of the woodland with their magic and bounce and pulsate high overhead in the blackness of maples and elms and apple trees.

Fireflies remind us just how lucky we are to be alive. Their fleeting beauty says we should take nothing for granted.

"What is life? It is the flash of a firefly in the night. It is the breath of a buffalo in the wintertime. It is the little shadow which runs across the grass and loses itself in the sunset." (Attributed to Crowfoot, chief of a Canadian Blackfoot tribe about 1880.)

❋ *14 June* ❋

SINCE 2002, CANADIANS HAVE MARKED the second Sunday in June as Canadian Rivers Day, advancing the promotion, health, and maintenance of our river systems. Our own Conestogo ranks as one of the four principal tributaries of the Grand River, Southern Ontario's longest river at 300 kilometers or 185 miles. The remaining three rivers are the Speed, the Nith, and the Eramosa.

The largest river system in Southern Ontario, the Grand River watershed lies between Georgian Bay and Lake Erie. It drains 7,000 square kilometers or 2,600 square miles of mostly agricultural land, an area the size of Prince Edward Island. The system has supported human habitation for thousands of years, since the last ice age.

The Grand River rises forty miles to the northeast of Paradise near the village of Dundalk in Grey County. Coursing south southeast, the river discharges into Lake Erie at Port Maitland in Haldimand County. This southern flow makes the Grand something of an anomaly. Most regional rivers will find the nearest Great Lake. Yet the Grand's headwaters emerge near the Georgian Bay portion of Lake Huron and move south through some of the richest farmland in the world.

Known to the First Nation Mohawk as Willow River for the abundance of willows found along the banks of its watershed, the river became the Ouse in the early 1790s. John Graves Simcoe, the first lieutenant governor of Upper Canada, named it for the Great River Ouse of his childhood home in Lincolnshire, England.

The Eramosa meets the Speed in Guelph. The Speed in turn joins the Grand in Cambridge. The Nith flows into the Grand in Paris. Our own Conestogo slips into the Grand River in the village of Conestogo, twenty miles south of Paradise.

The Conestogo rises in a field near the village of Damascus, thirty-five miles northeast of us, at the edge of the Luther Marsh, a fifty-two square kilometer wetland prized as a waterfowl habitat and waystation for migrating birds. Situated in the Lake Erie Basin, the river runs through the most intensively cultivated land in the Grand River watershed. Very little of the area remains treed, and wetlands are scarce. This adds to Paradise's exceptionalism.

Named by Mennonite settlers for the Conestoga River in Lancaster County, Pennsylvania, the river went through various spellings in the 1800s. Conestogo came out on top. We, however, have always referred to our river as the Conestoga, as I have for the most part in this book.

The upper portion of the river drains a silty till plain that generates a significant amount of runoff, especially during the spring thaw. Collected behind the Conestoga Reservoir (a few miles downstream from the cottage) since the mid-1950s, this storage reduces flooding on the waterway below the dam. The lake covers nearly nine square miles or twenty-three square kilometers. This has resulted in a conservation area operated by the Grand River Conservation Authority (GRCA), which also administers the Grand River watershed.

Conestoga Lake consistently tests high for phosphorus, primarily from upstream field runoff. This promotes blooms of algae, and cyanobacteria produces an accumulation of murky buff-colored froth that sometimes floats on the surface of the river upstream. The reservoir also acts as a source of nutrients downstream. Water quality on the Conestoga often runs fair to marginal with elevated levels of nitrogen and phosphorus.

Still, thanks to the GRCA's continual conservation efforts, pond and snapping turtles, brown trout, pike, small and largemouth bass (both a species of sunfish), perch, walleye, and common carp all still manage to thrive in our waters.

❊ *16 June* ❊

AFTER A COOL, THIN DRIZZLE just before dawn, the day turns warm and sultry, the opening salvo of summer's impending heat. On this breathless and drowsy day, we watch the water-meadow for hours. No end to birdsong, with an added sudden sprinkling of Baltimore orioles. Wild purple irises sway among the riverside brush and sedges, like dabs of watercolor. Smooth, melted-butter marigolds fleck the short grass, wide white patches of Canada anemone spreading out from the feet of still burgeoning dame's rocket.

Over at Edna's Cottage the red squirrels up their game with ever more inventive schemes to reach the suspended bird feeders, and the chipmunks have begun eating peanuts from our hands. All in all, a gorgeous summer day of blue skies fading to cream on the horizon.

By late afternoon, the sky has gone pearly white. As we laze about at Castor's Landing, a robin, settled in a nest above us on a cedar limb that hung over the river, sends an alarm call that attracts a gang of crows. Already in harassment mode a couple of trees down, the crows scull to and fro against the gray skies. Tempers flare all around until finally, expelled by a very small, very brave song sparrow, the crow pack flaps off. In a short time, one of their number flashes out of the wilds across the river, on the heels of a great horned owl with a crow chick clasped in its talons.

What goes around, comes around.

Today's skies, blanched with heat and humidity, mesh well with June's birth gem, the pearl, and with both of June's birthstones— alexandrite and moonstone.

For centuries, we've valued the pearl, as glistening and iridescent as a summer heat haze. Composed of calcium carbonate crystals deposited in concentric layers, pearls, which can thus be dissolved in vinegar, arise within the mantle folds of shelled mollusks.

Natural pearls, extremely rare, occur spontaneously in nature. Hundreds of pearl oysters or mussels must therefore be gathered, opened, and killed to extract even one. Matching strands of natural pearls sell for hundreds of thousands of dollars. In 1917, jeweler Pierre Cartier exchanged a matched double strand of pearls he'd collected over many years—valued at one million U.S. dollars—for the Fifth Avenue mansion now housing New York's Cartier store.

Natural pearling, previously undertaken in many parts of the world, currently takes place predominantly in the seas off Bahrain. Australia also has one of the world's last remaining fleets of pearl-diving ships.

Cultured pearls from both farmed pearl oysters and farmed freshwater mussels make up the majority of pearls sold around the world. Most freshwater cultured pearls come from China.

Super-small, irregularly shaped keshi pearls result from errors in the culturing process. Tahitian pearls, often called black pearls, are valued for their rarity. True black pearls, which are rarely black, come in shades of blue, green, purple, and gray to aubergine, silver, and peacock (a mix of several different hues).

A pearl's luster depends on the movement of light within the translucent layers. Thinner more numerous bands produce a finer sheen. This iridescence results from the overlapping of strata, which breaks up any light falling on the surface. Though the ideal pearl has a perfectly round, smooth shape, a pearl's value in jewelry depends on a combination of luster, size, color, symmetry, and flawlessness. Of these, luster may take top prize, though in general, the larger the pearl the higher the value.

The Pearl of Puerto, the largest known natural pearl, developed in a giant clam found in the Philippines by a fisherman from Puerto Princesa on the island of Palawan. One foot (30 cm) by 2.2 feet (67 cm), the Pearl of Puerto weighs 75 pounds (34 kg). The second largest, the Pearl of Lao Tzu, also found in the Philippines, occurred in another giant clam, and weighs 14 pounds.

The English word "pearl" comes to us from the French *perle*, from

Latin *perna* meaning "leg," named for the mutton-leg-shaped bivalve. *Margaritiferidae*, the scientific name for the family of pearl-bearing oysters, developed from the Old Persian *mrgāhrīta*, meaning "derived from a shell," from which we get the name Margaret (Margarita) in Spanish.

It's said that a bartender named Santos Cruz invented the popular tequila drink—the margarita. While working in the Studio Lounge in Galveston, Texas, he was asked by American jazz singer Peggy Lee to mix her a simple tequila drink, which he did. Peggy's husband, Lee Barbour, named the drink after Peggy, which is derived from Maggie. Margarita is another nickname for Margaret.

The white, luminescent crystal moonstone, a sodium potassium aluminum silicate belonging to the feldspar-group mineral orthoclase, also echoes the hot humid skies of summer. The most common moonstone is the feldspar mineral adularia, named for an early mining site near Mt. Adular in the Swiss Alps, now the town of St. Gotthard Pass. Colorless, white, or pale green, brown, gray, or peach, pearly moonstones manifest an optical phenomenon called adularescence, also named after Mt. Adular. During moonstone formation, different alkali feldspars separate into thin alternating layers. As with the pearl, light falling between these strata scatters produces a billowy sheen that glows like moonlight on water.

The Romans and ancient Hindus both believed that moonstones captured light from the moon itself. The Greeks combined Selene, their moon goddess, with Aphrodite, a goddess of love, to give moonstone crystals the name Aphroselene.

Moonstone occurs all over the world from Australia, Austria, Armenia, Brazil, and Burma to India, Mexico, Madagascar, Norway, Poland, Sri Lanka, and the United States. Though absent from the state of Florida, the moonstone was designated the state gem in 1970 to honor the Kennedy Space Center's moon landings.

An oxide mineral, alexandrite, the second birthstone of June and one of the three main varieties of the mineral chrysoberyl, does not present the same lucent quality of the moonstone or the pearl. Yet this aluminite of beryllium offers another equally bewitching optical phenomenon. It magically changes color.

Like all chrysoberyls, alexandrite occurs in association with metamorphic deposits like dolomite marble and in mica schists. Weathered out of these rocks, alexandrite can be found in alluvial deposits like river sands and gravels.

Because of the presence of traces of chromium, alexandrite stones can appear emerald green, reddish, or orange yellow in color. They can also alter their hue in artificial light as compared to daylight. The color shift from red to green results from the intense absorption of light in a narrow yellow portion of the spectrum. This allows for the transmission of large bands of blue-green and red wavelengths. Most sensitive to green light and least sensitive to red, human vision interprets alexandrite as greenish in daylight, where the full spectrum of visible light is present, and reddish in incandescent light, which emits less green and blue light. High-quality alexandrite, extremely rare, ranges from green or bluish-green in daylight to raspberry red or purplish-red under incandescent light. The yellowish-green daylight shade of most stones will become brownish-red.

The history, discovery, and naming of alexandrite remains lengthy and controversial. The first discovered stone quite likely came from an emerald mine or the mica schists on the Tokovaya River, both in Russia's Ural Mountains. Forming the border between Europe and Asia, the Urals stand among the world's oldest existing mountain ranges. Known in medieval times as the Stone Belt, they arose millions of years ago in the late Carboniferous period, the result of the collision of a continent consisting largely of Siberia with the supercontinent that contained the majority of the world's landmass at the time. The name "alexandrite" derives from the Romanov Tsar Alexander I.

Beyond the Urals, alexandrite has also been found in Brazil, India, Madagascar, Tanzania, and Sri Lanka. Several labs have produced synthetic stones with the same chemical and physical properties. The largest known faceted gem, a 6.6-carat stone, resides with the Smithsonian Institute. The largest uncut gem-quality specimen, the Sauer Alexandrite, named after its discoverer, Amsterdam jeweler Jules Sauer, weighed nearly 54 pounds. Found in Bahia Brazil in 1967, its whereabouts and status are presently unknown.

<h1 style="text-align:center">❈ 20 June ❈</h1>

ON A SUBLIME SUMMER DAY, DEEP GREEN and sleepy, cloud puffs drift in from the far west across a vivid azure sky. All week long, blue jay babes have clamored in The West Woods by day, fireflies flashing over the water-meadow by night.

Two chipmunks now snatch peanuts from our fingers, sometimes sitting on our shoes, sometimes whipping up a pantleg, tiny feet faint as a feather. Unimaginatively, we've called the shyer of the two, a bushy-tailed beastie with a bald patch on the top of the head, Peanuts. Scarface, by contrast, the least fearful, sports a thin, smushy tail and a blemish on the right cheek. Quite the cache they must have assembled by now.

Such a perfect summer solstice day. Just a few short years ago, the Full Strawberry Moon fell on the summer solstice bringing a matchless fusion of fireflies and moonlight.

"Solstice" comes from the Latin, *sol*, meaning "sun," and *sistere*, "to stand still." For a few days either side of the summer solstice, the longest day of the year, the sun appears to stand motionless in the sky.

In many temperate regions of the world, the summer solstice, when one of the earth's poles sees its maximum tilt toward the sun, marks midsummer or the middle of summer. Other parts of the planet consider the summer solstice to be the end of spring and the beginning of summer. Either way, civilizations have celebrated this day for thousands of years.

❋ 23 June ❋

ALL CHANGELESS CHANGE, summer moves all things forward for the earth, growing out and up and in, living and dying in a cogent, green timelessness.

We pass today under blue skies, languid clouds, and a soft summer breeze.

Yet just two days ago, on Father's Day, a formidable amount of rain had fallen through the night, with occasional distant rumbles of thunder. When I woke, I caught such a rush of water that I thought the storm had doubled in strength.

I stepped outside to find that the river had jumped its banks, flooding to the base of the hill below Edna's Cottage, not twenty-five feet below where I was standing—higher even than the spring thaw. Water swamped the floor of The Willow Deck, lapping at the short steps up to our Greek-key shower. A state of emergency has been declared in Drayton.

Today, as we overlook the water-meadow in the early afternoon, the river slips by still glutted and muddy, barely contained. Dame's rocket has rebounded from the flood, bordered by oxeye daisies and lemony-yellow bird's-foot trefoil, backed by the mellow coos of mourning doves. Summertime birds flit everywhere, while a Baltimore oriole pair busily feed their single demanding chick, a mousy fluff-ball perched in a lilac bush.

After supper, we head for Black Bass Bend and sit from the gloaming through to a dusky ten o'clock. A kingfisher executes a string of impressive back-to-back dives off a riverside cedar limb. A hefty snapping turtle—one of three paddling about with a half dozen pond turtles—emerges and submerges in silence before making his way across the narrow far-side clay bank to rummage among the blue flags. In near darkness, we return to Edna's Cottage, disturbing roosting blackbirds who chirp and buzz and flutter above us in waves as we pass.

❊ *25 June* ❊

WE'VE NOW ENABLED THREE furry opportunists: Scarface, Peanuts, and Bob, who brandishes a patchy stunted tail and will squat on a knee for a treat. They wrestle each other for a handout at the drop of a hat.

They all want peanuts. And they want them now.

Of course, the time has quickly come for reining in the patter of tiny rodent feet across Edna's deck. So, we've trained them. Peanuts can only be had from someone seated on the park bench by the eastside bird feeder.

Scarface, however, did drop by Russell's Cottage one afternoon and waited while I fetched the container from Edna's shed.

In other faunal news, we've relaxed by the river several times now with no overt beaver sightings. Once or twice some smooth, silent swimmer, nose poking up above the waterline, has glided past Black Bass Bend and along the far shore to dive opposite the den.

The falling darkness prevented any definitive ID. But it was quite likely Beau.

In the last few days, we've spotted a large beaver on the river below Russell's, puddling about under the water-meadow's giant white willow—a thrilling and welcome surprise. The river down from the eastern rapids now often runs only knee deep, so with work on the dam suspended, perhaps they've moved house. Or perhaps a relative has moved in. Time will tell.

At this time of year, as we've seen, gangs of crows will on occasion hassle a predator—an owl or a hawk. Otherwise, they're on their own. Making a meal of a hatchling or fledgling, as they will, any errant crow in flight attracts a gadfly or two. Small birds, like our song sparrow, will dive-bomb them or dart in for a move-along-nothing-to-see-here peck on the backside.

Through the afternoon, blackbirds of all sorts waggle by the dozens along the south riverbank, plucking crayfish from the shallows. Working the soft bodies out of their armor, they wing them back to their nests.

One starling spent long moments extricating a tasty tidbit only to have a crow swoop in and steal it away.

By early evening, having fed the youngsters in their cedar tree nests, they begin to cluster in our skeletal elms for pre-roosting.

On this hot and humid day, we've kept the porch door and all the cottage windows closed against the heat. Clouds scud across the milky-blue sky with the hazy smudginess of an impending thunderstorm, though no rain has yet fallen. Everything under the sun lies in stillness. Lush, green, and expectant.

Despite the rising temperatures, our red fox makes a sudden reappearance, trotting to within ten feet of Dan as he lounges in Russell's swing. With a princely air, he sits and scratches and gazes about. Spying Dan watching him through binoculars, he jauntily lopes off into the north woods.

We've also had bullfrogs. Green and blue heron. A trio of raccoons at the westside bird feeder. Our very first sighting of an opossum, North America's only marsupial. All of them backed by that ultimate expression of high summer—cicadas.

Cicadas are related to leafhoppers. None of the seventeen-year periodical cicadas of the genus *Magicicada*, so prevalent below the border, live in Ontario, except near Windsor in the extreme southwest. Paradise cicadas belong to the annual genus *Neotibicen*, species *Canicularis*, the dog-day cicada (also known as the jar fly, heat bug or dog-day harvest fly). With a life cycle of two to four years, dog-day cicadas emerge every year from midsummer to fall on a staggered cycle. Their interlaced wings have green veins, especially noticeable near their base.

The sound of a male dog-day cicada is the song of summer. The high-pitched, loud, long, and lazy buzzing drone lasts for several seconds before fading away.

❋ *28 June* ❋

THIS AMAZING DAY BREAKS WITH a stellar robin-lead dawn chorus, coming on the heels of heavy, late-night showers. Such celebratory voices could only set the tone for a day of unwavering wonder.

A muggy overcast has spread west to east by early afternoon. Yet outside Edna's Cottage, a half-dozen red squirrels scurry after each other, spiraling up and down the walnut trees and vaulting through the canopy of maples and spruces. One enterprising fellow passes the time augmenting a stash of pinecones he's collected in the old outhouse. Carpe diem!

Over at Russell's, catbirds, wild canaries, orioles, kingbirds, flycatchers, red-breasted grosbeaks, and house wrens all flit over the water-meadow, a pageant of color and cheer. And at Wood's End, where the neighboring farmer has just slung up his cattle fence across the river, cordoning off the point of land where the river turns south, we admire a pair of eastern kingbirds feeding four scrappy, bald chicks. Their bulky nest of weed stalks, grasses, and twigs hangs suspended over the river on a long bare limb of the giant, white willow. Often perching on the barbed-wire fence, these sturdy dark-gray beauties, with creamy underbellies, neat, white-tipped tails, and pointed wings, will soar sky-high, and with shallow fluttering wing beats, snatch insects, midair.

Late afternoon, just before supper, two lively red fox kits, the likely offspring of the adult Dan had seen earlier, scuffle around the well with the innocent joy of babies everywhere. Mere moments later, as we sit once again above the water-meadow, a white-tail doe swims the river above Wood's End and heads for the cottages before sounding the alarm and melting back into the high grass.

As we set off for Black Bass Bend, the whirring purr of raccoons in conversation drops from overhead. We hold our breath, wide-eyed, as with soft trills and a deep curiosity, a mom and five kits, each barely a foot long, scoot backward down a sugar maple tree just west of Edna's and bolt off down the embankment.

Last year, after we discovered the body of an adult under Russell's porch (the likely consequence of some altercation with a coyote or a fox), three orphaned racoon kits scudded one by one out of an aspen tree on the north side, crying brokenheartedly for their mother. Over the next few days, we reveled in their company, as they feasted at one bird feeder or another. Ultimately, they vanished.

At least this little band still has a parent to guide and protect them.

Moments after we arrive at Black Bass Bend, one of the beaver kits pops up under the downed cedar tree below where we sit. Crossing the river, the youngster returns, padding out and up the bank to within ten feet of us. On hind legs, he sniffs and sniffs with great curiosity. Slipping back into the water then, he glides along the far shoreline toward the lodge and disappears. A breathtaking experience.

By nine o'clock, sunlight still tops the cedars on the east river bend. A mallard duck with six ducklings maneuvers as one to the far shore and toddles out in silence to nest for the night in the tall grass.

In the cool, damp air of dusk, we make our way back to Russell's. In tandem with the aria of a single cardinal exalting across the meadow and the hooting of a great horned owl, robins sing the sun down with unwavering, infectious joy. Through high hazy clouds in a mantle of rose and gold, the sun slips away, leaving fireflies below, bats above, and a wisp of ground mist swirling up from the river.

"Nature teaches us simplicity and contentment," Mark Coleman writes in his book, *Awake in the Wild*. "Because in its presence we realize we need very little to be happy."

"Hot July brings cooling showers,
Apricots and gillyflowers."
— SARA COLERIDGE

❈ *1 July* ❈

O CANADA! TODAY WE celebrate Canada Day, known until 1982 as Dominion Day. On July 1, 1867, the English parliament passed the British North America Act, recognized today as the Constitution Act. The four then-existing British colonies of Upper Canada, Lower Canada, Nova Scotia, and New Brunswick became united, as one dominion within the British Empire—a confederation to be called Canada. That seed blossomed into the nation-state we know today.

Pyrotechnics from sea to shining sea will be the order of the day. Here in Paradise, we've settled for a fistful of sparklers and the view of a few popping cherry bombs set off at the nearest farm.

This second month of astronomical summer in the Northern Hemisphere takes its name from the Roman general and dictator, Gaius Julius Caesar. July is his birth month. Before about 713 BCE, this month was called *mens quintilis,* "the fifth month" in the ancient Roman ten-month calendar. At that time, March kicked off the year, January chosen around 450 BCE.

After the assassination of Caesar on the Ides of March in 44 BCE, Rome teetered on the brink of civil war. While many Roman citizens revered him, most aristocrats looked forward to his condemnation as a tyrant. Looking for some stability, the Roman senate under Caesar

Augustus changed the name of Caesar's birth month to *mens iulius*, the "month of Julius." July is now the seventh month in both the Julian and Gregorian calendars.

In much of the Northern Hemisphere, we find that the hottest and most sultry portion of summer falls in July. This period of sweltering humidity is known as "the dog days." In ancient times, Sirius, the Dog Star, rose in the night sky just as this steamy summer weather arrived. As Sirius formed part of the constellation Canis Major—the Greater Dog—this summer stretch became known as the dog days. Today, though the precession of equinoxes has pushed the rising of Sirius into early August, we still keep to the ancient designation of dog days.

This morning, we wake to a mellow rainstorm, thunder muffled like garbage bins being rolled curbside. No monstrous cracks or commanding booms. And after that, only blue skies, the occasional shred of cloud, a soft breeze from the southwest, and a thick blanket of mugginess.

In the late afternoon, we walk through to Castor's Landing. A fisherman, car parked on the roadside by The Big Bridge, has just cast in below the far rapids above the beaver lodge when a striking merganser glides through from Black Bass Bend, with long graceful neck, rusty-cinnamon tufted head, reddish beak, and long streamlined grayish-white body. Leery of intruders, she bobs in the water, diving a time or two before sailing away back down below the rapids. In short order, she floats back, doddling offshore, and in time gathers the courage to slip along the far shore past the fisherman. Just then, he flings his line in with a resounding *plop*. The poor thing, desperate to be gone, sprints across the water flapping furiously. Collapsing into a breakneck paddle, she speeds out of sight.

Meanwhile, Beaudelaire materializes from below The Dam Rapids, making for the far embankment, out of sight of the fisherman. Hauling up a fallen willow branch from the shallows, he strips the bark and begins munching contentedly.

And then, when the fisherman finally leaves, we all go home.

❋ *2 July* ❋

HENRY JAMES ONCE WROTE in his novel, *Portrait of a Lady*, "Summer afternoon—summer afternoon; to me, those have always been the two most beautiful words in the English language."

And so, we have a Henry James "summer afternoon" kind of day. Just lazing about, we somehow still manage a bit of trimming along the path to Harold's Tea Deck, where we freshen the tea candles in the ceiling's beigy chandelier, fashioned as a sculpted ring of lotus blossoms.

Early this morning, nine white-tailed deer browsed for an hour or two in the meadow across the river where neighboring cattle will soon be released for summer grazing. By midafternoon, one lone doe ventures back to the riverbank for a drink. A red-winged blackbird couple, who must have had a nest in the tall grass, swoops in. Perched on grass stalks, they scream relentlessly, stab at her face, pecking and clawing, even touching down on her rump. The harassment finally gets the best of her, and she withdraws, leaping back to the safety of the cedar woods.

The great green day then bubbles over with birdsong and wildflowers. June's blooms have now been enhanced with black-eyed Susans, creeping bellflower, mallows, cranesbills, dogwood, great Angelika, pussy toes, and so many others.

Sadly, Paradise does not support either the larkspur or the waterlily, the two birth flowers of July. An annual species of the genus *Delphinium*, the larkspur belongs to the *Ranunculaceae* family. Members grow only in western North America, restricted in Canada to the foothills of the Rocky Mountains, the boreal forest, and the interior of British Columbia. The vibrant blue flowers, which provided a dye for Native American tribes, resemble the claw or spur of a lark. This gave the plant its name in Tudor times. All parts of the larkspur are poisonous. The seeds and new growth have the highest concentration of toxins.

The lotus or waterlily, which has existed upward of 145.5 million years, is also poisonous. An alkaloid called nupharin exists in every part of the plant but the seed and in some cases the tuber. Many cultures still boil or otherwise cook them for eating.

Native to tropical South America, waterlilies are a hardy perennial of the aquatic family *Nymphaeaceae*, genus *Nymphaea* that flourishes all over the world. Waterlilies have notched and disc-shaped leaves with a purple underside. These leaves grow from long stalks that attach the leaves to a stem rooted in the mud below. The rounded pad can reach twelve inches in diameter. Waterlilies blossom from May to September, the height of bloom falling in July. Fragrant eight-petaled starry cups in yellow, pink, blue, or white rise above the water or float on the surface, settling underwater to decay after about four days.

Both the family *Nymphaeaceae* and the genus *Nymphaea* derive from the Greek word *nymphaea* meaning "waterlily," a word inspired by the nymphs of Greek and Roman mythology. Nymphs in turn take their name from the Greek *nymphē*, meaning "young woman, bride, or young wife." The name "lotus" traces back to Latin *lotus*, Greek *lotos* (a term initially applied to a large variety of plants) and perhaps even further back to the Semitic word *lot* meaning "myrrh."

In ancient Egypt, the lotus, rising underwater out of the mud and opening into sunlight, suggested the sun's emergence from primeval slime. A metaphor for creation. The lotus thus became a symbol of divinity and the renewal of life, of the upper Nile itself, giver of life. Lotus blossoms accompanied many ancient Egyptian burials.

One July not long ago, we reached Paradise by way of the north shore of Lake Superior. We drove south and then east across the top of Georgian Bay and along Lake Huron's eastern shore. The placid beauty of the seeps, pools, and lakes along this route deepened with glorious gleaming blankets of *Nymphaea odorata* (*odorata* meaning "fragrant" or "perfumed"), the common North American white water or pond lily.

Sluggish as the Conestoga can be at times, we have no water placid enough and waterlilies have unfortunately never taken root.

❈ *3 July* ❈

THIS MORNING, FROM A DISTANCE, we watch a pair of chickadees bustling about feeding their young in a tiny, well-worn cavity nest in the apple tree just outside Russell's front door. So unlike the raucous demands of red-winged blackbird chicks, these young give out only a soft delicate cheeping, which both Mom and Dad reined in with a string of insects.

Much later, we barely arrive at Castor's Landing a couple of hours before sunset, when beaver Beaudelaire emerges from upstream. Executing a series of uncertain passes bank to bank, he sets off to forage in the far-side forest. Harvesting a giant fern leaf, he swims back to the den. On his second sortie, a muskrat passes him by, moving downstream to the shallows above The Dam Rapids, where with considerable enjoyment, he wriggles about on his back.

A swimming muskrat and a swimming beaver can be indistinguishable at dusk. But at close range, in the gloaming or in late afternoon, dust-brown muskrats move more quickly, head held high, body mostly visible. A skinny whip-like tail snakes back and forth or pointed backward near the surface of the water. Beaver, generally more of a dark chocolate brown, with a wide, flat, paddle-shaped tail, glide in utter silence, snout, eyes, and ears alone above the waterline.

Near ten o'clock, we head back to Edna's. A guttural growling stirs the darkness of the eastside bird feeder, moves up into the woods, and then off toward The Gully. I have only just reached the steps of Edna's deck when the deep grumble sounds again, this time from behind the cottage. A silvery, ethereal purring pours down from a white spruce, echoed in the cedar tree opposite. Our five raccoon kits scoot down, each in chirping conversation with their mother who had worked so hard to draw attention away from them. Mom at the helm, the five amigos slip off into the night.

❖ 4 July ❖

AMERICAN INDEPENDENCE DAY! On the fourth of July, 1776, the United States declared its liberty, with political separation from Great Britain.

Our own July 4, toasty and tranquil, proves a splendid summer day for celebration. With late evening, we witness a bewitching Full Buck/ Full Deer Moon, also known as the Full Elk Moon or the Full Rose Moon. Anglo-Saxons labeled this month's full moon the Full Hay Moon for midsummer's hay crop, the Full Mead Moon for the honey harvest, or the Full Wort Moon, for the gathering of *worts* or herbs to dry for seasonings or medicines.

Deer shed their antlers and grow them anew each year. In late July last summer, Dustin's partner, Marie Laure, uncovered a stunning pair discarded and half buried in the eastern cedar woods. We have them displayed high on Edna's porch wall. July is the month when the growth of these intricate, one-of-a-kind, branched bones with an initial coating of velvet reaches its peak.

Along with elk, moose, reindeer, caribou, and several other species, deer belong to the *Cervidae* family. Our smallest living deer, the South American pudu, weighs no more than twenty pounds and stands about fourteen inches high. The largest living deer, the moose and the elk, can reach six and a half feet, hoof to shoulder. At up to 1,800 pounds, moose and elk can weigh nearly a ton.

In honor of the Full Buck or Deer Moon, we catch one white-tailed doe browsing by the dead thorn apple tree left of the water-meadow. When we step out of Russell's in the early evening, she bolts across the river, clamors up the far bank, and races off into the woods, bellowing constant alarms. Down at Black Bass Bend later, a six-point buck crosses the river at The Dam Rapids and vanishes in the long summer grass.

Later still, the full moon crowns a magical, otherworldly night.

Not a breeze or a leaf stirs. A fine white mist glows and thickens over the river in moonlight, spreading over the water-meadow. Surreal and frosted tendrils move layer upon layer into the black forest, into the far hills, and to the foot of Russell's slope. Gentle rapids and the soft croak of frogs purl in its depths.

❈ 7 July ❈

JIM DOUGAN, A BOTANIST from Guelph, conducts another floral appraisal of Paradise today. He's already identified over 150 plant species. Some of them—beaked sedge, finely-nerved sedge, Michigan lily, and Canada clearweed—are rare in Wellington County. At least on the record.

The old growth forest across from Castor's Landing, rife with giant ostrich ferns, would make prime nesting for bald eagles, Jim says. They've already moved north with global warming, and we've seen several adult males pass through in recent years. Hopefully, one day we'll sight an eagle's nest across the river.

Birds flutter everywhere through the day: courting or feeding chicks; singing or frequenting the bird feeders. Robins hunt worms; Brewer's blackbirds hunt butterflies or grasshoppers. A stocky green heron, with a rufus chest and a glossy, greenish-black cap, fishes along the river on the sandy strip opposite the water-meadow willow. A sparrow-sized indigo bunting pipes in the trees all morning, raising a tiny head to the sky and emitting a bright lively song, sharp and clear, three or four quick, high-pitched notes on a loop. A wild canary in bright golden yellow then perches in one of the old American elm skeletons next to the silvery billed, cobalt-blue bunting—two brilliant warbling gems.

About eight o'clock, at Black Bass Bend, Beau harvests fern fronds from the wilds again. Two racoon youngsters scramble out of the sedges and pad along the far shoreline looking for crayfish. Crossing to the north side below The Dam Rapids, they join a fishing blue heron.

Most exhilarating of all, a white-tailed doe ambles out of the high riverside grasses escorting a tiny fawn, two or three feet tall and still spotted. We watch breathlessly as they negotiate the far side of the river, Mom pausing on occasion so the wobbling little one can catch up. Beyond where the north riverbank juts south, they cross over and head for the water-meadow.

❋ *9 July* ❋

THREE THUNDERHEADS EMBEDDED in a gray sky roll in midmorning over sunny blue skies. Two or three quick showers and they boil off, leaving behind a rising, red-hot mugginess.

In general, July brings the year's highest heat and humidity. This somewhat validates the ruby, a pinkish-red to blood-red variety of the mineral corundum (an aluminum oxide), as our July birthstone.

The word "ruby" comes to us from the Latin *ruber*, meaning "red." The ruby's color is produced by the presence of chromium. All natural rubies have imperfections, including needle-like inclusions called "silk" by which gemologists distinguish unprocessed stones from synthetic.

One of the traditional cardinal gems, alongside amethyst, emerald, diamond, and sapphire, rubies have been mined all over the world, though Macedonia is the only country in mainland Europe to have naturally occurring stones. For centuries, Myanmar served as the world's primary source, overtaken by Mozambique with the discovery of gem quality rubies in 2009. Kashmir has extensive reserves but only one working mine due to the lack of development. The rubies of Greenland, at about twenty-three billion years of age, comprise some of the oldest in the world.

A ruby of choice color, cut, clarity, and carat weight is of enormous value. Auctioned by Christie's in 2011, Elizabeth Taylor's jewelry included an 8.24 carat ring, which sold for US$4.2 million. A necklace for US$3.7 million. The largest mined ruby in the world, the Liberty Bell Ruby, vanished in a heist in 2011. The Sunrise Ruby, the world's most expensive, sold in Switzerland in 2015 for US$30 million.

As early as 200 BCE, rubies were being traded west along the North Silk Road from China. Other Asian countries placed rubies in the foundations of their buildings for good luck and Hindu astrology considered the ruby as a representative of the sun—totally appropriate for July's often weltering, midsummer days.

After a light midmorning shower fails to cool the air (as they've done so often in the past), we watch a punky belted kingfisher (*Megaceryle alcyon*) family hunting from the west line fence at Wood's End, cardinals and robins singing through the heat haze.

Megaceryl derives from the ancient Greek *megas* meaning "great," together with ancient Greek *kērúlas* meaning "fabulous seabird." *Alcyon* comes from the ancient Greek word *alkuŏn*, the ancient name for the kingfisher.

Striking, large-headed birds with shaggy Mohawk crests top and back and a thick daggerlike black bill, Mom, Dad, and a single young one perch in a tight line on the top rung of the barbed-wire fence. Sometimes in unison, sometimes solo, they plunge into the river head-first, like darts. With luck they reemerge with a fingerling, a minnow, or a crayfish. At other times, they hover on beating wings over the surface of the water, bill pointed downward, before executing a similarly impressive dive. Any sizable catch of four inches or more is taken to the white willow. With considerable pummeling against a tree branch, the prey is stunned and swallowed whole. Any indigestible parts, such as bones or scales, will be coughed up later as pellets.

Such a joy to watch these stocky solid beauties at work, with their slate-blue heads, white collars and underparts; broad, blue breast band; back and wings of the same blue-gray; black feather tips; and tiny white spots on wings and tail. Slightly larger than Dad, Mom also sported a chestnut belly band that extends down her sides, an example of reverse sexual dimorphism, a female more brightly colored than a male. The babe echoes Mom's tones with irregular rusty spots on a blue breast band.

Kingfishers find or fashion nesting holes in dirt banks slanted upward to avoid flooding. They also eat frogs, tadpoles, and other amphibians, as well as small crustaceans, insects, and reptiles, even mammals. The increase in spring heat waves from global warming now often threatens their nestlings.

The wild rattling chatter of a kingfisher whisking up and down the river is one of the sunniest constants of Paradise. Migrating south when the river begins to freeze—or even earlier—we always miss them.

After lunch, we slip on our wellies to install a handful of No Trespassing signs along the outer fence on the south side. We venture across the river at The Dam Rapids, entering a vast and overgrown wonderworld, sumptuous and wild. Thousands of shoulder-high ostrich ferns on the sheltered banks have coalesced into a sea of emerald-green. Ancient cedars and willows, some with six to eight sturdy trunks, soar overhead in a whisper of wind. We find a few wild strawberries and peachy-colored limpets along the water's edge. Well-worn deer paths meander beyond the boundary line into grassy farmland thick with thorn apple trees.

As we make our way back to Edna's, an owl shoots out from the top of a white spruce beside the cabin like a great, gray ghost on smooth and soundless wings. Then, across the river from Russell's, starlings by the hundreds begin to gather in the dead elms to hash over their day. Red-winged blackbirds and robins twitter across the water-meadow as the day closes.

❀ *12 July* ❀

ON THIS HOT, SULTRY DAY, we haul in a few slender cedar logs from the east woods to augment the timber roofing at The Willow Deck. On the river's edge, just up from Black Bass Bend, freshly gnawed cedar stubs, wood chips sprinkled at their base, mean the beaver are at work again. When ragged clouds gather overhead in a white watery haze, we retreat to escape the rising heat.

Outside Edna's west window, a lanky little cottontail has just hopped over to feast below the bird feeder when a red squirrel zips down the backside of the maple tree from which the feeder hung. The squirrel pops its head out from behind the tree and the rabbit leaps six or eight inches straight up into the air. The red squirrel then races back up the tree to do it all over again. The rabbit finally gives in and skitters off.

With early evening, a rush of wind careens through the thick summer canopy with a sound like falling water. A line of thunderheads brings a velvet rain that leaves the air charged with the deep earthiness of wet loam and pungent cedar. The breeze evaporates, leaving behind a surreal stillness into which birdsong erupts, and through errant drops of rain and a crystal-clear otherworldly amber glow, the sun slips away.

❈ *14 July* ❈

BY NECESSITY, INCIDENTS IN THE NATURAL world of Paradise, especially during the short summers, will repeat themselves. The cacophonous roosting of blackbirds in the east woods. The padding of raccoon families hunting crayfish along the river's south shore. Male red-winged blackbirds singing the sun down across the water-meadow.

But today, we witness a somewhat unique event.

After dropping off supper's food scraps at The Gully Bridge, we troop down to Black Bass Bend for a bit of an evening sit. Within moments of our arrival, Beau slips out to the opposite shore and begins to groom himself—a common yet fascinating procedure we've never witnessed before.

Sitting upright, flat tail in front between his back feet, he opens with a thorough scrubbing of face and tail. With dexterous front paws he rakes his fur—front, sides, and back—using hind feet to reach the more difficult spots.

A life-or-death necessity, beaver must groom themselves regularly to eliminate debris from their pelts and to waterproof them using an oil produced from their anal glands. A specialized toe on each hind foot known as a "grooming claw," with an additional horny growth between the true nail and the toe, functions as a finely serrated toothed comb.

Face and tail completed, Beaudelaire gives himself a belly rub with a hind foot, drawing up more oil. When he's finished the entire intensive process, he lumbers back to the water's edge and pulls up a cedar branch he'd stored just below the surface. Stripping the bark, he munches contentedly for some time before heading home. What a privilege to share such an intimate moment.

On this gorgeous summer day, blue and breezy, the water-meadow already hints of coming fall. Dame's rocket has gone to seed, replaced by the dusty purple buds of Joe-Pye weed, which will last into early autumn. Tall spikes of medicinal elecampane have now spread across the bottom of Russell's slope.

To the ancient Greeks, these two-inch flower heads, with bright yellow rays and central floral disc, sprang from the tears of Helen of Troy.

Queen Anne's lace or wild carrot, the ancestor of the garden carrot, has also thrown a scatter of filigree across any open ground. Tiny white flowers form flat-topped umbrellas, one miniscule dark-purple bloom at the center.

In addition, we have low-growing edible self-heal, a medicinal herb with tubular, lipped flowers in deep mauve, and common vetch, with trailing stems and clusters of magenta, blue, or white flowers. As with all legumes in the *Pea* family, vetches will add nitrogen to the soil. The blossoms of both seven-foot cow parsnip and six-foot water parsnip resemble Queen Anne's lace but for an umbrella of creamy flower clusters that are more widely spaced.

A medicinal herb brought to the new world by European settlers, St. John's wort has been known since ancient days as a remedy for ailments from insomnia to depression. The plant's name combines John the Baptist with *wort*, an old English word for "plant." St. John's wort appears around June 24—St. John's Day. Five golden petals, each with tiny black dots on the outer margins, have a knot of showy stamens shooting up from the center.

In the past, sprigs were hung over images of the saint or placed on altars dedicated to him to bring good health.

On the water-meadow and on the top of the north hill, we've seen that common milkweed has also come into bloom, two to four feet high with fragrant clusters of pink-purple flowers. Both leaves and the milk-like substance inside are poisonous except to monarch butterflies, who will only lay their eggs in milkweed stands. Day by day, these orange-black treasures flit over the meadow in the company of swallowtails, coppers, blues, crescents, admirals, sulphurs, skippers, painted ladies, and—most especially—cabbage whites, who favor Joe-Pye weed.

Cardinals pipe in from every direction. Last year, rose-breasted grosbeaks dominated. Today, starlings and red-winged blackbirds amass in the bare elms, parents perched beside buzzing babes who demand food with gaping maws and flailing wings. Trying to ignore the fuss, parents who flutter off are pursued relentlessly.

Sundown leaves us with a parade of high-piled clouds along the southern horizon, billows of bleached alabaster and ash topped with pale gold, coral, and pink cream.

❈ *17 July* ❈

THIS MORNING I WAKE UP IN A BIT of a blue funk. The last few days of intermittent overcast and sudden downpours have felt overly "fallish."

But out the west window as we eat a late lunch, a half dozen Brewer's blackbirds, a couple of Canada blue jays, three chipmunks, and two mottled brown cottontails feast together in harmony below the feeder. One of the chipmunks repeatedly charges the clump of blackbirds who lift off in unison again and again, wings flapping. Rabbit and chipmunk bolt after rabbit and chipmunk in what looks like great good fun.

An early afternoon check of the night vision camera brings us two fox kits and two baby raccoons, scampering in turn across The Gully Bridge. A skunk has cleaned up the wasp nest in an old bird feeder at Willow Deck, where last month's Virginia creeper clippings from the Rumble Tum Café in the village of Conestoga had begun to climb the railings. And the fresh birdhouse Dan nailed up two days ago has attracted a pair of house wrens.

When the glowing pastels of a double rainbow arch over the river through another gentle shower at day's end, my spirits get back on their feet.

❋ *18 July* ❋

ON THIS LAZY AFTERNOON, we take a late lunch to Castor's Landing. Salmon salad, chips and salsa with guacamole, pecan tarts, and wild blueberries. In direct sunlight, the air sizzles. But sheltered at the edge of the woods with a light breeze, we feel refreshed. High summer clouds scud above. A prop plane thrums. Songbirds trill, as two red-tailed hawks, calling to each other, spiral overhead on updrafts.

As dusk comes on, we return to watch the blackbirds gather around Russell's in preparation for roosting: grackles, cowbirds, Brewer's black-birds, starlings, and red-wings.

By eight o'clock, they single out four lofty elm skeletons. One behind us to the west at the top of the north hill. Two across the river, east and west. A fourth rising over the crest of the hill above Wood's End.

In time, dozens on the west tree to the right dart up and away, joined by others in swirls and flutters, merges, separations, and shape-shifting. And then all together, they stream off in a mass of motion to roost in the eastern cedar woods. A door has opened. A glimpse of the astounding thousands-strong performances yet to come.

The aerial ballet among blackbirds known as a murmuration often takes place during the winter months in more southerly locations. Here in Paradise, they go full tilt in late July or early August, after the breeding season and subsequent "child-rearing" affords more time and energy. Our participants include cowbirds, European starlings, and even the occasional robin (none of which belong to the *Blackbird* family) as well as grackles and both red-winged blackbirds and Brewer's blackbirds. During the day, smaller groups will fly off to forage, gathering again as the sun goes down.

A record roosting event occurred in Arkansas during a Christmas bird count in December 1964. The wide band of an estimated forty million roosting red-winged blackbirds streamed overhead for twenty minutes.

Such massed flocking might reflect the presence of a prime food source. Or the clamorous swooping and swirling along with the sheer numbers may confuse predators like hawks and owls.

But how do they do it?

Large-scale group behavior can either come from the top down (as from the unique authority of a leader) or from self-organization, individual actions scaling upwards. In 2013, a Princeton mechanical and aerospace engineer and her team, studying the phenomenon with Italian physicists, found that murmuration participants tracked about seven flock mates—their closest neighbors—and ignored the rest. Each magnificent seven affected nearby individuals, the synchronized gyrations and spins spreading by groups of seven through the entire assembly.

But how do they do it?

One theory that exploits the fact that birds see much better than humans, proposes three basic movement parameters: an attraction zone in which they move toward their neighbor; a repulsion zone in which they avoid their neighbor; and angular alignment, where they follow in their neighbor's wing flaps, so to speak.

But again, how do they do it?

❖ *21 July* ❖

FROM EARLY MORNING, we revel in full-on summer, lush and green. A robin-led chorus opens the day featuring a soloist with a uniquely creative delivery. Not your average robin trill.

Azure skies and lazy clouds define the day after that, lively breezes rustling through the trees. Just below the surface though, we sense a surge of activity—all the preparations necessary to survive or escape another cold season. Always and forever, "winter is coming." Even the spider in our shower, already twice removed, has once again slung up a replacement web, declining to move on.

Bob, who, along with chip-mates Peanuts and Scarface, had vanished over the past week, returns to size up the westside bird feeder from the lip of the tree limb six feet above from which it hangs. Free falling, he plummets to the plastic cover, inches over the rim, and pops down into the pan. A red squirrel—they're all Rocky or Pavarotti—scarfs up whatever seed remains, flinging himself in from the tree's trunk and then scolding from an upper bough. We've moved the feeder farther along the limb and extended the drop.

And then there's Winston, our latest faunal challenge. For days now the hefty raccoon has dismembered the suet holder strung up between two maples to the west. No matter how far out, he reaches in from the bole of a cedar tree and reels it in. A new feeder down the line with an exposed underside manageable to chickadees, nuthatches, woodpeckers, and such, has met the same fate. Avoiding hawthorn prickles, he fishes up the container, pries it open, and devours the contents. His sixth suet block this week.

Through a sprinkle of rain, the beaver continue their ostrich-fern harvest at Castor's Landing. Heron and kingfishers work both sides of the river and a troupe of swallows flit over the water in unison, dipping in for a drink, beaks brushing the surface like tiny plows.

Over the past several days, too, we've been following a lovelorn house wren outside Russell's. He's presented his mate with several splendid homes. Males will construct up to seven "dummy" nests from which a female will choose a favorite, adding finishing touches. Yet his lady has declined all offers, and he's been singing the blues from sunup to sundown.

But now, at eight thirty in the evening, as the river mist rises and the fireflies begin to glimmer, she's sprucing up a little something he threw together in one of the gourds of the swallow apartments on a pole above the water-meadow. So, he's singing for joy.

The Chippawa call the house wren *o-du-na-mis-sug-ud-da-we-shi*, meaning "big noise for its size." The perfect epithet.

❀ *24 July* ❀

THIS MORNING, THE WHOLE WORLD glimmers green on another blissful summer day. Rich and ripe, meadow grasses, some over six feet high, shimmer in wildflower green and gold, lilac and plum. Wind shadows dance in their midst. Breezes warm as bath water shift and whisper through canopies of walnut and maple, aspen and poplar, rippling the surface of the river into a cut-crystal glaze of silver. Behind the umbrellas of the white willow and above the southside cedar woods, midafternoon towers of creamy cloud drowse on the horizon, silent as sunshine. Honeybees bumble. Birds whistle and chirp. Cicadas buzz.

Into all of this splendor, two dozen Canada geese paddle soundlessly from around the west bend. Baffled by the line-fence, they skir as a flock back and forth bank to bank six or seven times, unable to fathom a crossing. With time, three of their more astute members make landfall one by one, each toddling under the lowest wire rung on the far side. The rest give up and climb out to bed down for the night in the tall grass. Half a dozen choose our north side. Tomorrow, it will be as if they never were.

An amazing gift befell us after that. We discovered a black vulture nest inside the cabin ruins east of Edna's shed. Mom and Dad with two nearly full-grown juveniles. As the babes were fledging, eggs laid in mid-April must have hatched in May.

They will stay with their parents for at least another four to five months.

The black vulture (*Coragyps atratus*), the only living member of the genus *Coragyps* in the *Cathartidae* family, is also known as the Mexican vulture, urubu, or gallinazo. Belonging to New World vultures, black vultures ranged from the northeastern United States into South America in the past. Global warming has brought them farther north and they are now regularly sighted in Southern Ontario, often migrating short distances to overwinter.

The word "vulture" derives from the Latin *vulturus*, meaning "tearer," a reference to the bird's feeding habits. The genus name *Coragyps* means "raven-vulture," a contraction of the word *corax* and *gyps*, which are the Greek names for those respective birds. *Atratus* meaning "clothed in black," comes from *ater*, Latin for "dull black."

Black vultures, with featherless, dark-gray, wrinkled heads and necks and short hooked beaks, live in scattered forests, nesting in caves or hollow trees, on bare ground, or in abandoned buildings. They generally raise two chicks a year, scavenging on carrion or eating birds' eggs or the newborn of livestock. They feed their young by regurgitation. Gliding and soaring on short stout wings, they locate their food with their sharp eyesight but may also follow turkey vultures who hunt with a keen sense of smell. Like other New World vultures, black vultures lack a syrinx and are only able to hiss or grunt, which probably explains why we were unaware of their presence for so long.

Such a gift to watch these two scruffy youngsters find their wings, perching on the cabin rooftop under the watchful eyes of their parents. Within a day or two they should be joining their parents' hunt.

In the gloaming, I take a stroll through the east woods on a flower hunt. I've just arrived at Black Bass Bend to feed the fish when a Canada goose family—Mom, Dad, and three goslings—coast in from around the east bend. As Dad assesses the situation, a red-tailed hawk sweeps down. Under a chaos of flapping wings and frantic honking, the attacker retreats. Together again, the family cruises to the opposite shore, where Dad keeps vigil at the water's edge as the rest trundle out to munch fresh grasses on the bank.

❊ 27 July ❊

A PRODIGIOUS THUNDERSTORM roars over just after midnight. With sluicing rain, thunder grumbles under the cracks of a war-zone bombardment. Tentacles mutter on, long after the apex has passed. Four thunderheads follow in quick succession. And so, with electrifying power and awe, July makes way for August, the downside of summer, with its Full Thunder Moon.

When morning clears to smudgy clouds, we slip down to collect more tea leaves from the mint patch on the shoreline below the beaver lodge. We find there a monarch butterfly chrysalis suspended beneath a milkweed leaf, in the very same area where Danielle had discovered a half dozen others just a few years ago. Having reached its translucent stage, the delicate casing reveals a magnificent full-grown adult, easily recognizable from its black, orange, and white pattern. She will dangle upside down several hours yet, forcing air and fluid into her wings. allowing them to dry, expand, and stiffen. She will then sit in sunlight to warm up, opening and closing her wings, before taking off.

And what a beauty she is!

Belonging to the *Nymphalidae* family, the monarch (*Danaus plexippus*) is the first butterfly to have had its genome sequenced. This will allow researchers to gain invaluable insight into its behavior. The name, believed to have been given by North American settlers in honor of King William III of England, reflects the king's secondary title, Prince William of Orange.

Oddly enough, *Danaus plexippus* refers to the mythological Greek king Danaus, who ordered his fifty daughters to murder their husbands, the fifty sons of Aegyptus, Danaus's twin brother, on their wedding nights. One of these sons was called Plexippus. All of this amounts to a convoluted explanation I don't quite follow, either. But there it is.

In late summer/early autumn, eastern North American monarchs migrate over twenty-four hundred miles to Florida and Mexico, returning in the spring by a corresponding multigenerational flight path northward.

Monarchs undergo a complete metamorphosis in four phases, from egg to larva to pupa to adult. On warm summer days, they can pass from the first to the last in as little as a month. The larvae or caterpillars molt through five stages of about three to five days apiece. This culminates in a final complex pattern of white, yellow, and black bands. They will then choose a safe place to spin a silk pad, and, hanging upside down for a day or two, they shed their skin to reveal a long, soft green chrysalis, which quickly compacts to become translucent. Over the two-week period of this pupal stage, the adult butterfly forms inside, the exact miracle we discovered in the mint patch this morning.

Adult monarchs only live from two to five weeks. Recent studies have shown that billions have vanished from overwintering sites in the last decades due primarily to loss of habitat. The milkweed plants essential for their reproduction have suffered from the extensive use of herbicides. Increasingly arid conditions brought about by climate change have also caused a decrease in hatch rates. Expanded breeding locations have increased the distance adults must travel to reach overwintering quarters. In addition, milkweed growing at soaring temperatures contains higher levels of toxins.

All of this makes today's chrysalis discovery, along with accompanying monarch caterpillars, especially joyful.

By midafternoon then, Dan strategizes anew against our Pavarotti nemesis. He attaches a sheet of weighted plastic to the outer side of the westside bird feeder, successfully preventing future red squirrel in-flights from the tree trunk.

No such luck with Winston, who went out on a limb, literally, opened both wire compartments and gobbled up his eighth suet block.

In the early evening, I walk through a gentle rain shower to The Gully Bridge. Three flocks of chattering blackbirds stream overhead into the east woods from their postings in the dead elms across the river.

One more sign telling us that summertime is falling down.

❊ *29 July* ❊

THROUGH A STILL AND OVERCAST white dawn, after-drops of rainwater patter on the grasses and leaves outside our bedroom window. Doves coo behind the occasional purl of a blackbird, robin, cardinal, or goldfinch. Clouds fragment to blue sky after that, and a light midmorning shower leaves behind another spate of bright sunshine. At eight o'clock, Pavarotti begins harvesting seed cones from the overhanging white spruce at Edna's. Fifty to sixty missiles drop with clapping thuds on the roof.

In this, high summer, crows have begun gathering in gangs to forage or to harass some interloping predator. By noon, a dozen churn around the water-meadow's white willow in a bid to dislodge a great horned owl. Surprisingly, all the squawks and scoffs fail to rouse a juvenile great blue heron on the shoreline opposite. For half an hour—often on one foot— he dozes or preens or studies his prey before slipping off downriver.

High above the path to the cabin, at the apex of a white spruce, we've just discovered a green heron nest. Likely the same adult seen fishing at the southside sandbar a day or two ago. One exquisite pale-bluish egg lies in pieces on the footpath below.

After sunset—a vibrant pink globe through rain-drenched clouds—a great horned owl materializes in the cedars by Edna's deck. Dan speaks to him, and he glides closer, not seen so much as sensed. A second shadow coasts into the maple tree right of the hillside steps. And so, we talk, the four of us. For forty-five magical minutes. Owl voices shift in the shadows with unseen movement. In the end, both melt into the night. A thrilling and utterly surreal experience.

❈ *31 July* ❈

EVERY BREEZE, EVERY SCAMPER of a red squirrel brings showery sprays from a spit of rain in the night. We'd placed a handful of peanuts on the walkway outside the bedroom window just before midnight, relieved to see the mother raccoon with her five kits stop by, everyone looking fit and healthy.

For the third time in as many days, we awake to Pavarotti's raucous spruce-cone harvest. Eight o'clock sharp. Dan's rodent wars then resume in earnest. A nylon cord strung up between two maples on the west side now holds two suet containers and one bird feeder. The flutter of kites at either end has dissuaded both Pavarotti and Winston.

Success! At last!

The chipmunks, too, have been contained. Bob, aka Shorty, is now satisfied to eat from the ground or from a hand, in the company of four fresh cohorts, mild-mannered Timmy, full-tailed Chiquita, Chippie Le Bond, and little Pepe.

After lunch, I settle under pearly flat-bottomed summer clouds to watch the water-meadow. A black vulture dozes for hours on a low limb of the dead elm beside The Willow Deck. Awakening, he gazes off toward the river a moment or two before stretching broad wings and flapping away.

At Castor's Landing late afternoon, Beaudelaire and family slip out to graze on the southside grasses for nearly an hour, while, on a boulder downstream, a stocky little kingfisher peers about with sharp beak, night-blue crest and body, and white collar. Wings beating above the water, he dives in after prey, with a 90-percent success rate. An osprey drifts overhead on long thin wings, and eight mallards, males and females, primp on the far shore between afternoon naps.

Sundown ushers in a mesmerizing blackbird murmuration in front of Russell's. The performance opens with incoming thousand-strong squadrons in a rolling rush along the south horizon. They sail overhead from all directions, spinning and shape-shifting in eerie unison. Flock by flock, they take up their posts, dropping like magnets onto dead elm crowns across the river left and right, on the hilltop behind us, in the willow trees below. New arrivals flow in on the soft whispers of a thousand wings.

In an aerial ballet of controlled chaos, bands fly in from opposite sides, combining and spiraling upward, a cascading black fountain with one mind, twisting and swirling. Living clouds of birds, flocks shift, merge, roil, divide, subdivide, alight, and lift off again. Rivers of birds in a complex, pulsating, harmonized whole, black bodies turn to the setting sun and vanish with a single synchronized hairpin turn.

At the edges of the river, east and west, smaller clusters of birds shoot down like arrows to snatch a drink of water, bathe, and rejoin the fray. Explosive chattering from one corner of the stage will suddenly cease before the whole tree sweeps itself clean, a thousand dark leaves fluttering off as one.

For twenty-five minutes, the ethereal dance roars on. The skies fill with birds. When darkness descends, wave on wave pours into the eastern woods to roost. The chattering fades to the sound of falling water, and then on into silence.

"It was August and the fields were high with corn."
— MELANIE GIDEON

❋ *1 August* ❋

A BEWITCHING STILLNESS USHERS in this, the last month of summer. Though on the cool side in the shade, radiant sunshine and a scatter of gray-bottomed clouds hold sway over much of the day. Lush green still stands in the high grasses of the water-meadow, now sprinkled with cornflower-blue chicory, white feathery-leafed yarrow, purple thistle, and orange-yellow hawkweed. The watery rush of early fall breezes rustles in the trees, all of which hints at the downside of summer.

August is the eighth month in both the Julian and Gregorian calendars. Named *Sextilis*—the sixth month in the original ten-month Roman Calendar—August became the eighth month about 700 BCE, when January and February were added before the month of March. Rome's second king, Numa Popilius, also gave the month twenty-nine days at that time. When he created the Julian Calendar in 45 BCE, Julius Caesar added two additional days. In 8 BCE, Caesar Augustus renamed the month to acknowledge several of the military successes he'd had during that month, including his conquest of Egypt.

The first of August denotes the third of the four cross-quarter Celtic seasonal celebrations, Lughnasadh, which falls halfway between the summer solstice and the autumn equinox and opens the harvest. Lughnasadh corresponds to other European fall festivals such as

England's Lammas and takes its name from the prominent Celtic god Lugh.

The Old Irish name for this festival, Lugnasad, combines *Lug* (the god Lugh) with *nàsad* (an assembly). Gatherings involved feasting, trading, matchmaking, athletic contests, and visits to holy wells, along with religious rites like first fruits offerings, bull sacrifices, and other rituals. Dances or similar dramatic performances probably symbolized Lugh's defeat of the powers of disease and decay (represented by the god Crom Dubh). These safeguarded the harvest.

Many Lughnasadh activities took place on hilltops or on mountains. Such customs endure in pilgrimages like the climb to the top of Croagh Patrick in the west of Ireland on Reek Sunday, the last Sunday in July. The early-August Puck Fair, in the town of Killorglin, county Kerry, Ireland traces back to at least the 16th century. Quite likely another survival of Lughnasadh.

In Irish mythology, Lugh established the festival as an athletic competition similar to the ancient Olympic Games and as a funeral feast to honor his mother or foster-mother, Tailtiu. A likely earth goddess who represented vegetation (much like Demeter in ancient Greece), Tailtiu had died of exhaustion after clearing Ireland's interior for agriculture. The Irish Celts held these funeral games each Lughnasadh at Tailtin (Tailteann), a townland now in County Meath. In Tailtin, at trial marriages called hand-fastings, couples joined hands through a hole in a wooden door. Such unions lasted a year and a day, at which time they could either be finalized or dissolved without any repercussions.

Lughnasadh activities often entailed burying a measure of the first corn crop on high ground as an offering to Lugh. Corn in those days meant the local cereal grain, barley corn, wheat corn, or oats, not the sweet corn or maize we know corn as today.

Few of us here in Southern Ontario would relish a harvest festival in early August. Summer is far too short as it is. Most of the region's seasonal celebrations fall in September or October, though the Drayton

Fall Fair is early this month. Lughnasadh's first fruits, however, can already be seen in blueberries, blackberries, peaches, and sweet corn. On the hilltop in Paradise, we have ripened chokecherries. Raspberries and blackberries flourish on the fringes of the water-meadow, and full-clustered elderberry bushes occasionally mark the verges of the hilltop road.

Above all, we have fields "high with corn." Both feed-corn for livestock and hybrid sweet-corn by the dozens, with names like Kandy Korn, Silver Queen, and—my favorite—Peaches and Cream. In fact, for lunch today, we had BLTs with fresh thin-skinned heirloom tomatoes, steamed Peaches-and-Cream sweet corn, and homemade elderberry pie. What could be better on a lazy, late-summer afternoon?

After feeding the chipmunk gang—Bob, Scarface, Peanuts, Timmy, Chiquita, Pepe, Haunches, Le Bond, and friends (while still satisfying the red squirrels), we drift down to Black Bass Bend. A third empty green heron egg has turned up on the pathway. We should have fledglings by the first week in September.

Many migratory birds have already set off for southern climes. Many others remain, among them robins, warblers, doves, grosbeaks, and blackbirds. Wrens, who are still busy with their second broods remain, and, of course, our year-round thriving regulars—cardinals, blue jays, chickadees, sparrows, and goldfinches. Above the constant murmur of the river, their calls still break the stillness. Slow-moving clouds float across the sky, while a pair of red squirrels argue in the cedars behind us, damsel flies and dragonflies spinning through the summer breeze.

When we return to Black Bass Bend in the early evening, after supper, the sky has turned a fall-ish pearl-gray, and light rain speckles the river, pattering rhythmically on the cedar trees. A family of kingfishers hauls up several fingerlings a piece on repeated dives from the bottom limbs of white willows.

At sunset, I slip over to the beaver lodge. Fresh repairs are evident. I stop off at Castor's Landing on my return. Beaudelaire emerges upriver, skimming the water's surface, probably curious about footsteps so near the den. Joined by his mate, they glide off downstream, toddling ashore just above The Dam Rapids, where they stretch up on their hind legs to gnaw sprigs off a half-downed fallen willow and swim them home through the deepening dusk.

For the Celts, a gentle rain on Lughnasadh meant blessings bestowed. Time to give thanks, as we do, to the spirits of the land, for another successful harvest.

❈ *2 August* ❈

MORNING BREAKS WITH SEVERAL hours of summer before chilly winds blow in a string of thunderstorms that leave early autumn behind. Gray overcast and a watery sun forge the backdrop for lots of critter activity throughout the day.

Cottontails munch by the well. Red-tailed hawks hunt over the grassland. A half-dozen turtles sunbathe on an exposed log at Black Bass Bend. There are voles in the water-meadow, a pair of ospreys overhead with fish in their talons, bull frogs and garter snakes. Wild turkeys strut through the east woods and a six-point buck browses on wild cucumber across the river.

With day's end comes another stunning blackbird show, dominated, as usual, by European starlings. Close to eight o'clock, murmuration bands have gathered in several elm trees. For the next hour, we watch as thousand-strong flocks soar and wheel across the sky, shape-shifting and crisscrossing, merging, fracturing, and then streaming into the cedars to roost.

Poetically referred to as "little star," the word "starling" actually comes to us from *sturnus*, the Latin name for the bird (genus *Sturnus*; family *Sturnidae*). The family likely originated in East Asia, where larger species are called myna birds.

Purposely introduced, the European starling has become a serious problem in many areas. They can cause hundreds of millions of dollars in agricultural damage each year, binge-feeding in our crop fields and at our livestock troughs. Highly social, their numbers have exploded for over a century. They now successfully compete for resources with native birds like chickadees, swallows, and bluebirds.

Starlings are, however, both extremely intelligent birds and superb impressionists. Pliny the Elder studied starlings, as did Julius Caesar. On April 12, 1784, Mozart wrapped up his Piano Concerto No. 17 in G. As the story goes, six weeks later, before the piece had been officially debuted, he heard a snippet with the last two G's modified—from a caged starling in a pet shop.

"That was wonderful," he wrote in his diary, transcribing the variation. He brought the bird home for a pet at the end of May. When it died three years later, he orchestrated a grand funeral in his garden, composing a bittersweet eulogy for the occasion.

Apparently, ornithologists can pick out distinctive patterns of starling song in music Mozart wrote in the years he kept this bird. Notes that rise and fall, twist and turn might be called a musical murmuration.

With blackbirds gone to roost, night closes with a visit from Winston and friends. They snuffle up whatever seed remained below the eastside bird feeder. A scuffle or two with grunts and growling, and they are gone.

Over the years, Winston has had several manifestations. One recent summer, when Dustin visited, a particularly hefty version dropped by Edna's over a series of late evenings. With our walkie-talkies, we kept Russell's up-to-date on any raccoon activity. Dustin was Brown Bear; Dan, Tubby Bear; Marie Laure, Moon Shadow; and I went by Grosbeak.

"Moon Shadow. Moon Shadow. Come in. This is Grosbeak. Winston is active. Repeat. Winston is active."

So, at eleven o'clock, Dustin and Marie Laure crept over and captured Winston's antics on their cell phones.

❊ 3 August ❊

SHOWING EVER MORE SIGNS OF SEASONAL change, another warm summer day of lazy clouds in a pale blue sky foreshadows early autumn by nightfall. Morning sunlight patterns the layers of crisp-leaved maple branches angled overhead as we sit like cats watching shadows shift on the water-meadow. The air feels as balmy as bathwater, charged with the scent of rain-dampened earth. Orange day lilies and jewelweed have added their singular beauty to the hillsides and meadow, and dozens of white cabbage butterflies flit among the hundred-shades-of-summer-green spread across the grasses, sedges, brush, and wildflowers below.

Originating in the Mediterranean sectors of Europe, the cabbage white (*Pieris rapae*) arrived by accident in Quebec about 1860. They now range across the entire continent. Their English name, "cabbage," is taken from the member of the *Mustard* family they typically frequent. *Pieris* refers to the whites and sulfurs of the butterfly kingdom, and probably arose from an ancient Greek muse of the same name. *Rapae* traces back to Greek *rapavi*, meaning "radish," another of the plants cabbage caterpillars feast upon.

In general, cabbage whites have two broods a year, the first in April/May, the second in July/August. Any Paradise spring hatchlings would meet with too severe weather, but summer butterflies abound. They prefer purple, blue, or yellow flowers, in which the water-meadow presently excels. There's Joe-Pye weed in dusty amethyst, golden elecampane, black-eyed Susans, and butter-yellow wild mustard on which they often lay their eggs. On cream-colored wings trimmed with tiny black dots, adults will convulse over the meadow for the three weeks plus that they live.

When a cabbage female rejects a cabbage male, they circle each other in flight, spinning higher and higher in fitful frenzies until the male loses interest and drops back to earth. We've seen them a dozen strong, climbing ever upward with frenetic swirls, breaking up, reforming, shattering by twos and threes, and then climbing again.

The blossoming of wild cucumber, native to North America, also alludes to the waning summer season. Their delicate tendrils can climb upward of twenty-five feet, especially across the river. Draped over the meadow and along the riverbank, their tiny white-to-cream flowers are a favorite of our white-tailed deer. Plants develop spiny green oval fruits encasing dark seeds. Wild cucumber also goes by the name of manroot, having a large tuberous root in vaguely human form.

A true harbinger of autumn, goldenrod, in the *Aster* family, has also begun to flower across the hillsides, streambanks, and flatland. Of the hundreds of known species—most of them native to North America— Paradise supports three: eastern late goldenrod, early goldenrod, and gray-stemmed goldenrod. Their bright yellow flower clusters will soon dominate our landscape, along with most of Southern Ontario.

Also new to the water-meadow, spikes of yellow sweet-clover—a grassland plant native to Europe—have added their soft subtle signature fragrance to late summer. Brought to the New World as a forage crop, sweet clover has spread worldwide. The whole plant can be dried for a tea that hints of vanilla.

As summer drifts toward fall, our seven-foot-tall angelica plants sprinkled across the lowland have begun to shrivel and fade. Related to carrots and parsley and used in cooking, candy making, and liqueurs, angelica can cause a blistering rash if its sap touches bare skin in sunlight.

By evening, thunderheads slide eastward along the southern horizon, their gleaming scoops of cream and ivory tinged with the ambers, corals, roses, and golds of sunset. Strips of thin black cloud inch like floating islands across their faces. Night advances, and after a brief thunderstorm, the air resolves to autumn coolness, rain tapping on the roof in fits and starts.

I have always identified the full moon of August as the Full Thunder Moon, in deference to the month's rampant thunderstorm activity. The Cree call this moon the Flying Up Moon, for all the fledglings finding their wings. Its more common name, from Ojibwe, is the Full Sturgeon Moon.

Lake or rock sturgeon (*Acepenser fulvescens*), a member of the *Acipenseridae* family (which has existed for over 135 million years), could be most easily caught by Indigenous people during the month of August. Once prolific from Hudson Bay through the Great Lakes to the lower Mississippi, these living fossils, the largest fish in North America, have now become one of the rarest. Intense harvesting in the 19th century, along with pollution of their habitat and breeding grounds, have decimated the population.

The origin of the word "sturgeon" is obscure, though we can probably trace it back to the Proto-Germanic word *sturjan* or *sturjo*, the name then given to this particular fish. Another possibility is the root word "stir," through Old English *styrian* meaning "to stir or agitate" and Old High German *storan*, "to scatter or destroy."

This likely alluded to the wild thrashing of a hooked sturgeon. Native mythology envisioned that a giant sturgeon in Lake Superior was responsible for that lake's notorious late fall storms, commemorated so beautifully in Canadian Gordon Lightfoot's musical tribute, *The Wreck of the Edmund Fitzgerald*. *Acipenser* comes from the ancient Greek word for the sturgeon, *akkipesios*, *Fulvescens*, from the Latin *fulvus* meaning "tawny or yellowish-red."

Actually more of a gray-green in color, with a spade-like snout and four whiskery sensory organs called barbels dangling near the mouth, lake sturgeon can grow up to seven feet in length and weigh up to three hundred pounds. Males can reach fifty-five years of age. Females, reproducing every four years after the age of twenty, may live up to one hundred and fifty years.

As if by magic, the Full Thunder/Full Sturgeon Moon emerges from behind the eastern trees close to ten o'clock, an orange giant slipping in and out of ragged purple/black clouds. Moonlight softens to pale lemon-yellow, reflected on filaments of fog that edge up from the river and ripple across the water-meadow.

❈ *6 August* ❈

A DREARY MORNING BRIGHTENS to clear skies, summery sunshine, and a fresh breeze by early afternoon. We plan to scout out the wilds of the southside once again. As I wait at Black Bass Bend for Dan to arrive, Rocky keeps me company, chattering away on the arm of an empty Muskoka chair. Probably some rodent demand for peanuts.

The Dam Rapids are a mere trickle, and we ford the river with ease, the odd slipup on a mussel shell or a mossy stone lying purpled in the shallows. Gnawed limbs on a fallen willow at the water's edge point to the beavers' continuing harvest. We leave them a half dozen freshly cut twigs.

Dense vegetation moves back from the shoreline, riven with occasional animal paths and deer tracks. Several eastern garter snakes, greenish, black, or brown with white or yellow stripes, slither through the tall grass and shrubbery as we move farther inland.

Native to North America as well as parts of Central America, garter snakes often hang out together. Researchers suspect they have specific "friends" with whom they spend the bulk of their time hunting down frogs, tadpoles, toads, and earthworms. Their scientific name, *Thamnophis sirtalis sirtalis*, meaning "bush (snake) that looks like a garter strap," combines the Greek word *thamnos* (bush) with *sirtalis* from the Latin *siratalis* (like a garter strap).

Though they emit a foul-smelling musk when stressed, when we were kids we would let their smooth soft bodies wriggle up our shirt sleeves.

Like most snakes, their beauty is in the eye of their beholder. Our eyes have always appreciated the garter snake's singular charm.

In a bank of emerald-green coolness, the sterile tapering fronds of ostrich ferns (*Matteuccia struthiopteris*) spring like ostrich plumes from the fringes of the forest, between glade shadows and thick riverside growth. *Matteuccia*, the genus of fern to which they belong, has this one single species, also known as fiddlehead fern or shuttlecock fern. Shorter fertile fronds, long and brown, have just begun to ripen. They will last through the winter, releasing spores in early spring.

The ostrich, one of the largest species of fern in North America, is resistant to spring floodwaters and can form vast colonies along riverbanks, as they have here in Paradise. The immature, tightly wound fronds of early spring, called fiddleheads, can be fried in butter and garlic if rinsed and steamed or boiled properly to reduce their bitter toxins. They have been eaten for centuries by Native Americans. A sweet and healthy vegetable, the taste resembles asparagus. Last year, Jim Dougan brought by several dozen taken on his spring sweep through the property.

Tall stalks of buttery yellow Jerusalem artichoke (*Helianthus tuberosus*), also called sunroot, sunchoke, wild sunflower, earth apple, or Canadian truffle, dot the south shoreline overgrowth, as they do the north. A species of sunflower native to North America, Jerusalem artichoke has been widely cultivated for its tuber, a root vegetable with a taste similar to artichoke. Gleaming yellow-rayed florets give off a light vanilla scent and the thick root, pale-brown to white, red, and even purple, has a crunchy texture when raw and can be eaten pickled, raw, or cooked.

So far as we know, Jerusalem artichoke has no confirmed relationship to either Jerusalem or the artichoke. Italian settlers to North America called the plant *girasole*, Italian for "sunflower." With time, girasole appears to have been corrupted to Jerusalem, though it's possible that the Puritans named the plant with reference to their belief that they were creating a new Jerusalem in what they considered a wilderness.

Orange jewelweed (*Impatiens capensistall*), also known as spotted jewelweed, orange balsam, or touch-me-not, another North American native, has also blossomed over the land. Common in bottomlands and along streambanks, they're scattered here along the water's edge, with coarsely toothed leaves and a cluster of splashy yellow-orange flowers like tiny slippers. A hooked conical spur juts from the back of each bloom.

The name touch-me-not may have come from the plant's seed pods. Five valves whorl back to expel the seeds with a mechanism called explosive dehiscence or ballistochory. This can be sparked by the slightest touch. The name jewelweed is likely derived from the leaves, which appear silvery underwater. Or because, being water repellant, they sparkle in sunlight when covered with dew drops or rain. Bright-blue jewel-like seeds that taste like butternuts may also be the source of the name.

A distinct charm of the wilds of Paradise this time of year comes from strings of climbing plants draped about like strands of beads. There's tufted or cow vetch, a long, trailing legume with one-sided blue-violet wild-pea-shaped flowers especially attractive to bumble-bees. Native to Europe and Asia, ours will be seeding soon, bright-green pods ripening to black.

Riverbank or frost grape, in the *Grape* family, is also indigenous to North America. The woody vine with typical toothy grape leaves has reached the canopy of the tallest trees in a quest for sunlight. Spring's small fragrant white or greenish flowers have already produced tiny, sour, blue-black berries down by Willow Deck.

Virginia creeper, an aggressive flowering vine also in the *Grape* family, has forked tendrils with small strong adhesive pads well adapted for expansion. Native to eastern and central North America, the modest greenish flowers of late summer have now become hard, round, purplish-black berries.

One of about twenty-five species in the *Bindweed* family—most of them indigenous to California—false bindweed or morning glory has wrapped riverside vegetation in its delicate beauty. A twining vine of spiral leaves, bindweed's eye-catching white or pink trumpet flowers emerge in late summer here in Paradise. Their seeds are toxic.

Lastly, ground ivy, also known as creeping Charlie or catsfoot, is an evergreen vine in the *Mint* family. This ivy has fan-shaped leaves and bluish-violet funnel flowers. Introduced around the world by settlers from Europe, ivy loves the moist shaded areas of our wildwood.

Going to seed now, ivy stems have drooped to deposit seeds or leaned to the earth where roots can attach themselves. The Saxons and later the English, who both brewed ale with ivy as a flavoring or as a preservative, called the plant alehoof.

All of these effusive beauties have added to the lush, free-flowing bounty of the southside wilds and other parts of Paradise as autumn approaches. However, once again, the land does not support either of the birth flowers of August—the chrysanthemum nor the poppy.

A short-lived perennial in the *Papaveraceae* family, the poppy, from *papavum*, the Latin name for the bloom, stands for beauty, strength of character, and peace. Vibrant but fragile flowers have a conspicuous whorl of stamens at the center. Ancient Egyptian physicians gave their patients poppy seeds for pain relief. Seeds contain small amounts of opium alkaloids, including morphine and codeine, derived from a milky sap found in unripe capsules. When harvested at least twenty days after blooming, these are generally no longer present. For obvious reasons, poppies symbolized sleep and death to the Greeks and Romans and served as offerings to the dead.

With about three hundred species, the gladiolus, from Latin *gladius* meaning "sword," belongs to the *Iridaceae* or *Iris* family. The giant one-sided blossom spikes seen in gardens today are the hybrid product of centuries of crossbreeding in four or five species. Wild glads have much smaller flower heads. We've already seen spectacular cut blooms in pink, red, mauve, cream, orange, yellow, and all the colors in between, in farm-stall vases, baskets, and buckets along country roads. Another sure sign that summer is on the wane.

We return to Russell's in the early afternoon. A brief thunderstorm that dropped little rain leaves the air keen and clear. The chickadees, still in the hollow of their tree nest, flit in and out feeding their second brood. Across the river in the cattle field, a reclusive mink charges a cottontail along the riverbank before slipping to safety in a clatch of driftwood on the shoreline. Drying maple leaves crinkle overhead. Cicadas buzz. And two dazzling monarch butterflies, silhouetted behind a maple leaf high above us, drop down to the high grass. Their abdominal tips coupled in mating, they flutter off into the gloaming.

As the sun goes down, blackbirds collect once again on their favorite staging trees. A passing flock of Canada geese punctuate the opening salvo of yet another stunning murmuration. Across the river, cowbirds join in for the first time. Sweeping and swirling in little brown pods a hundred strong, they shoot like arrows into the river for a quick sip or splash between stunts. Some of them briefly settle on the backs of grazing animals. One cow with a nursing calf has a half dozen lined up along her spine.

With the final encore, we light up the first fire of the season at Edna's. Not too long afterward, we drift off to the haunting watery whinny of an eastern screech owl.

❋ 8 August ❋

LAST NIGHT WE FILMED THE blackbird pageant from Russell's. In the opening moments, a great blue heron flew in, circled overhead and then settled for ten minutes on a giant elm stump near The Gully to preen and take in the action. After flock on flock had flowed off to roost in the cedars, we startled a red fox on the path to Edna's. A flash of russet red, he scrambled under the eastside log fence, a super-hero in a red cape.

Roaring winds in the night brought slashing-down rain just before dawn.

And then another hot, humid day opens up, filled with blue sky, sunshine, and toads, toads, toads.

All three species of the American toad (*Anaxyrus americanus*) descend from a South American incursion that took place before the creation of the Isthmus of Panama land bridge. *Anaxyrus* means "king or chief" in Greek, *Anaxyrus americanus* being the chief toad of North America.

Eastern American toads have become wide-ranging throughout Canada and the eastern United States. They hibernate through the winter in rodent burrows or dig themselves underground below the frost line, beneath large stones, logs, or root balls, surviving by absorbing moisture and oxygen from the soil. Breeding from May to July, they require a semipermanent water supply and tracts of thick vegetation, both of which Paradise has in relative abundance.

The metamorphosis from eastern American tadpole to eastern American toad culminates here in August. Large numbers of toadlets complete the change in sync, remaining near their ponds for several days before migrating en masse to higher ground, usually to sheltered areas flanking their birth marshes. Adults being predominantly nocturnal, juveniles make up the bulk of the many toads we've seen throughout the day.

Eastern American toads vary from yellow to brown or black and from solid to stippled. Their color may change with stress, temperature, humidity, or the dominant tones in their environment. These youngsters skittering about all day only differ by their shade of brown, usually a dusty umber. Wee, sweet things they are.

After an early supper of sweet corn and fresh tomato BLTs, we drop down to Black Bass Bend. We've all but despaired of any animal sightings when a majestic eight-point buck saunters out of the southside forest. Ever alert, with ruddy red-brown body and antlers still in velvet, he browses the wild cucumber cloaking bushes that rise higher than he stands. Then ambling back to the cedars, he vanishes.

❈ *10 August* ❈

THIS MORNING, WE WITNESS A breathtaking life or death struggle at the edge of the water-meadow. A cabbage butterfly, snared in a garden spider web slung low in the tall grass, puts up a fierce resistance.

Moving along the web's perimeter, the spider assesses and tests each of her lines in turn. She pulls them in with two or three forelegs and then lets each rebound. Eventually, line by line, for whatever arachnid reason, she cuts her captive loose.

At the end of a single strand, the butterfly flails in desperation. She finally frees herself and drops to the grass. The tip of one wing has been lightly damaged, but within the hour she's flown off.

Such a dramatic, primordial event tucked away behind the calmness of a brilliantly blue day. Had we witnessed a flicker of arachnid compassion? Had the struggle inflicted too much damage to the spider's web? Whatever the reason, we've never witnessed or even heard of such a miraculous event before and probably never will again.

Something equally gripping and seemingly primal befalls the dairy cattle across the river in the early afternoon. Nursing calves have been rollicking in the pasture for days. I'm hardly savvy to the ins and outs of bovine behavior, but today one young cow beyond the fence lumbers alone, the length of the woods and back, with constant mournful bellows. Perhaps she's lost her own babe.

By nightfall, the world has righted itself with the season's first surge of intense field cricket chirping. Another reminder that autumn is on its way.

Crickets belong to the superfamily *Grylloidea*, related to grasshoppers. They occur all over the world, but for latitudes north and south where temperatures are consistently lower than about 55 degrees Fahrenheit. The greatest cricket diversity has been found in the tropics. One spot in Kuala Lampur recorded eighty-eight different species, each with its own song. The largest member of the family is the two-inch long bull cricket.

Ontario has at least a half-dozen varieties. The most common, the fall field cricket (*Gryllus pennsylvanicus*) can be found from Canada to Mexico. The Latin word *gryllus* may have been borrowed from ancient Greek *grúllos*, meaning "a performer in an Egyptian dance, a caricature or comic figure." Such an accurate description that brings to mind Walt Disney's Jiminy Cricket with his spiffy top hat, spats, and umbrella.

Field crickets (an important food source for many forms of wildlife) hatch in the spring and mature in late summer, during which time they shed their skin at least eight times. Large black round-headed insects with long slender antennae and enlarged back legs for jumping, field crickets nest in tall grass or in piles of vegetative debris. They spend the day hidden in cracks or under bark, pebbles, fallen logs, or leaves.

Only male field crickets sing, most noticeably at night. They produce their brief, pleasant trills by briskly rubbing the edges of their forewings together. This serves to attract a mate so that eggs can be deposited before winter sets in. Their music intensifies by volume and speed in the fall, the cricket's last chance to reproduce. The rate of chirping, sometimes up to thirty calls a minute, depends on both the species and the temperature. The higher the temperature, the faster the chirp, a relationship known as Dolbear's Law. Adding forty to the number of trills produced in fourteen seconds approximates the current Fahrenheit temperature. For Celsius, count the number of chirps in eight seconds and add five.

Crickets conjure up warm summer evenings, soft summer breezes, wistful summer memories. We have great affection for our field crickets. (Unless, of course, one is singing right behind the bedpost at night.) They remind us, too, that their magical voices will soon be gone.

❈ *12 August* ❈

A NIGHT OF HEAVY RAIN LEAVES the day dull, gray, and dribbly. A short evening stay at Black Bass Bend turns up a great horned owl and a kingfisher. A great blue heron, still as a stalk of grass, inches into the river to hunt and preen.

Sprinkles of red and blue berries now dot the edges of the forest and the water-meadow. Dad's journals made note of Mom's chokecherry jelly this time of year. In the late '70s, he whipped up a batch of what he called screech—chokecherry whiskey. No word on the outcome or the quality, and I don't recall either.

Many of our migrating birds have already escaped the coming cold, though some wrens are still tending to their broods. The water-meadow, wrapped in beigy grasses and ruby-stemmed reed thickets, lies rich in goldenrod, Joe-Pye weed, wild cucumber, Queen Anne's lace, and day lilies. Hawthorns have just begun to turn yellow-green. The sugar maples, rasping like crumpled paper in today's fallish breeze, show patchy flashes of scarlet and cream. Poplars and aspens of olive and lemon yellow.

The birthstones of August—reddish-brown sardonyx, transparent ruby-shaded spinel, and olive-green peridot—seem to mirror these hues of late summer.

Sardonyx is a variant of onyx, the parallel-banded variety of the silicate mineral chalcedony. Agate is the curve-banded form. Sardonyx takes its name from Sardis, the capital of the ancient kingdom of Lydia in present-day western Turkey, where red onyx was first discovered. "Onyx" derives from a Greek word of the same spelling meaning "nail or claw." Pinkish, white-banded onyx sometimes resembles a talon or fingernail.

Found all over the world, onyx has a history as a prime medium in jewelry and carving (especially beadwork) that dates back to Egypt's Second Dynasty. Archaeology shows that the artwork of Knossos in Minoan Crete favored sardonyx or red onyx.

To instill courage, Roman soldiers carried amulets of sardonyx engraved with Mars, the god of war, into battle. English midwives in the past laid stones between the breasts of new mothers, believing that red onyx would ease the pain of childbirth.

Spinel, a glassy-to-opaque magnesium/aluminum mineral, comes in many colors, most commonly ruby red. Prior to 1783, when science differentiated spinel from ruby by chemical analysis, both went by the name of ruby. Transparent spinels were known as spinel-rubies. From the 18th century on, ruby referred only to the familiar red corundum gem. Spinel comes from the Latin word *spinella*, meaning "spine," alluding to the stone's pointed crystals.

Spinel and ruby are sometimes found together. A metamorphic mineral forged most often in metamorphosed limestones and silica-poor mudstones, spinel may also develop in rare igneous rocks, the magmas of which have a deficiency of alkalis relative to aluminum. Where aluminum oxide may produce a ruby, aluminum in combination with magnesia creates spinel. Synthetic spinel, glass-like but with far greater strength, has been used in military and commercial applications.

For centuries, mines in present-day Tajikistan have been the primary source of red and pink spinel. Stones are also found in Sri Lanka, Afghanistan, Myanmar, Vietnam, Tanzania, Kenya, and Madagascar. Since the turn of the 20th century, Myanmar, Tanzania, and Vietnam have also supplied vivid pink and blue spinels. Intense blue stones from the presence of cobalt have come from south Baffin Island since 2018.

Several spinels rank among the world's most notable gemstones. The Black Prince's Ruby, thought to have come from Kajikistan and to be one of the oldest baubles among the British Crown Jewels, was given to the Black Prince, Edward of Woodstock, in 1367. Also in that royal collection is the Timur Ruby, an unfaceted gem associated with the Emperor of Persia, who swiped it from India in the early 18th century. Returned to the Punjab in 1810, the gem fell to another invasion, this time from the East India Company, which then gifted the stone to Queen Victoria in 1851. Two years later, the Timur Ruby was set in a necklace.

Among the crown jewels of France, there is the Côte de Bretagne, a red spinel cut in the shape of a dragon under Louis XV. The bulk of France's royal bling, amassed between 752 CE and 1825, vanished, broken up and sold off by the third French Republic. The Côte de Bretagne, now on display in the Louvre, managed to survive, along with several other pieces.

The largest known uncut spinel, the Samarian Spinel, weighing in at five hundred carats or one hundred grams, also came from India. Stolen in the 18th century, the gem now forms part of the Iranian Crown Jewels.

The more familiar birthstone of August, the peridot, sometimes called chrysolite, is a magnesium-rich variety of the silicate mineral olivine. Peridot is one of the few gemstones that occur in a single color. Olive-green in the case of peridot. The depth and shade depend on the level of iron present and can range from golden-green to olive to brownish-green and—very rarely—a medium-dark pure green with no secondary tones.

Peridot and diamond are the only gems not formed in the earth's crust. They come from the molten rock of the upper mantle, peridot often in silica-deficient rocks like basalt. And because olivine exhibits a chemical instability at the earth's surface and movement upward from deep inside the mantle causes extreme weathering, most peridot olivine is found as small grains.

The mining of peridot began about 300 BCE on Egypt's Zabargad or St. John's Island, part of an archipelago in the Red Sea comprised of uplifted mantle rocks. It was called topazios at that time and was usually hand-hammered out of basalt. Peridot olivine is now found in other parts of the world, the San Carlos Apache Indian Reservation in Arizona being the primary source.

The origin of the name peridot remains unclear. The Oxford English Dictionary has "peridot" as an alteration of the Anglo-Norman word *pedoretés*, a kind of opal. Another possibility is the Arabic word *faridat*, meaning "gem." Ancient Egyptians claimed peridot could banish fears and ward off evil spirits and nightmares. In the Middle Ages, it was believed that such stones could cure depression.

Peridots can also be found in distinct entities called pallasite meteorites. Only sixty or so have ever been found. Peridots resulting from volcanic activity contain much higher levels of lithium, nickel, and zinc than those found in pallasite meteorites.

A rare class of stony-iron meteorites (at only 1 percent), pallasites date back 4.5 billion years to the formation of our solar system. In the molten state of their parents, heavy metals like iron and nickel sank to the center or the core. Lighter rocks rose to the upper layers of the mantle. Trapped for billions of years in the asteroid belt between Mars and Jupiter, these parent bodies further splintered as a result of endless collisions, producing the pallasite meteorites found on earth today.

Because of their formative history, pallasite meteorites carry the material from the boundary between their parent asteroid's metallic core and the olivine silicate in the lower mantle. Centimeter-sized crystals of olivine peridot are embedded in a nickel-iron matrix like cherries in a pie. The border between the earth's core and the earth's mantle would be much the same. Golden-green olivine crystals glitter like jewels when light shines through thin slices of these pallasites.

The largest peridot olivine discovered thus far is a sixty-two gram/ ten carat specimen from Egypt's St. John's Island. This gem is now in the National Museum of Natural History in Washington, DC.

As most pallasite meteorites, with their attendant peridot olivine, deteriorate in the earth's atmosphere, stable samples are scarce.

Indonesia's Jepara meteorite came to light during excavations for a factory in 2008. Thousands of years ago, the Brenham meteorite scattered three tons of debris across a wide swath of Kansas in the vicinity of Brenham and Greensburg. Over fifteen hundred years ago, beads fashioned from Brenham bits had been transported a thousand miles east by the people of the prehistoric Hopewell culture and were subsequently unearthed in southern Ohio's Hopewell mounds. The first modern-day discovery of Brenham meteorites occurred in 1882.

Dubbed the Space Wanderer, a thousand-pound fragment from 1949 is housed in the Big Well Museum and Visitor's Center in Greensburg. A 1,400-pound piece from 2005, believed to be in a private collection in Texas, remains the largest single aggregate of extraterrestrial semiprecious gems in the world.

Prepping for a water tank near the town of Esquel in northwest Patagonia, a local farmer dug up the Esquel pallasite meteorite in 1951. The 2000 Fukang meteorite, from the Gobi Desert in China, weighs

2,200 pounds. Split into five sections, it has a combined value of from US$30–50 per gram. Chile's 1822 Imilac stone likely came from a pallasite meteorite of up to a thousand kilograms that exploded over the Atacama Desert in northern Chile in the 14th century. Lastly, a farmer in northwest Missouri came across the Conception Junction meteorite, valued at US$850,000, in a hillside in 2006.

Back here on earth, I head up the hill just before midnight in hopes of a glimpse of the Perseids meteor shower, in progress since mid-July. The display will last through August 23 but peaks tonight through tomorrow night. Fifty to ninety meteors might cross the sky between moonset and dawn; "Raining fire in the sky" à la "Rocky Mountain High," John Denver.

Of course, the best viewing of meteor showers in Southern Ontario would be the dark skies around Lake Superior, the deep forests of the Bruce Peninsula, or the sandy beaches of Point Pelee. But those are not an option.

Coming at a time of often favorable weather, the Perseids, one of the most impressive and accessible showers of the year, easily brings several meteors an hour, long bright tails coursing across the sky, even in cities with extensive light pollution.

The Perseids take their name from their perceived point of origin to the northeast in the constellation Perseus. They are the result of the passage of the earth through the Perseid Cloud, a stream of debris ejected from the comet Swift-Tuttle on its 133-year orbit around the sun. Many particles have been part of the cloud for at least a thousand years, and most Perseids burn up in the earth's atmosphere while at heights above fifty miles. The peak of Perseid activity comes as the earth moves through the densest and dustiest area of the Perseid Cloud.

Several years after the passage of Swift-Tuttle in 1862, Italian astronomer Giovani Schiaparelli discovered and articulated this relationship between meteor showers and comet trails.

Poetically, some Catholics look on the Perseids as the tears of Saint Lawrence suspended in the sky. They return to earth once a year on

August 10, the date of his 258 CE martyrdom, when he was burned alive on a gridiron. Meteor experts expect that the Perseid shower of 2028 may reach from 250 to 1,000 meteors an hour. Gravitational forces from Jupiter will push the debris plume closer to the earth by at least a million miles.

Here on the north hilltop, a vague fringe of dusty cloud lies along the southern horizon where the lights of Kitchener glow. The odd shimmer of lightning flashes to the west. Within seconds of my arrival, despite the moon being only a week past full, I am blessed with two gorgeous shooting stars that sweep across half the sky above and disappear. Nearly thirty more fiery darts make for a glorious cosmic light show after that. Star-spangled in every way.

Walter J. Hoffman in *The Menomini Indians* states that the Menominee of the Great Lakes speak of meteors in this way: "When a star falls from the sky, it leaves a fiery trail. It does not die. Its shade goes back to its own place to shine again. The Indians sometimes find the small stars in the prairie where they have fallen in the grass."

❈ *14 August* ❈

TODAY PASSES COOL, GLOOMY, and overcast, with intermittent sunshine. A morning fog lies long and low in the bottomlands. Looking ever more like fall, much summer vegetation appears tired and limp. Goldenrod remains in force, but black-eyed Susans and daisies have both begun to fade. With each passing day, we see more leaf patches change color. Amber and ruby-red already tint the low bushes along the pathway to the east woods.

Timmy and friends still vie with the red squirrels and the blue jays to augment their winter peanut stashes, and migratory wrens flit about their nests. This morning, we watch a cottontail and a red squirrel munching together under the bird feeder by the west window. When the squirrel pops up on an old stump Dan has placed nearby, the rabbit shoots a foot straight up into the air. Very soon, they snack together as peaceably as before, just inches apart, until the red squirrel once again hops up on the stump, and the cottontail hurtles himself into space once again.

Down at Black Bass Bend, a mallard drake lowers his landing gear as he approaches. Catching a glimpse of aliens on the riverbank, he retracts his wheels and continues downstream. Beau slips into the water near the lodge just as an eight-point buck with a bum leg arrives to feast on the wild cucumber draped over the south bank foliage. We do our best to leave in silence, but a beaver tail slaps four times on the water as though four boulders had been tossed into the river. The buck, already obscured in dense jungle vegetation, vanishes.

One more outstanding blackbird performance opens at seven o'clock back at Russell's. In a grand finale, with tendrils of mist swirling up from the river, they soar and whirl. Great ribbons of birds, rivers of birds, wave on wave of birds flow east and west, north and south. Vague specks along the southern horizon grow and grow, coalescing to an undulating serpentine tide that spills across the sky. In the end, they all stream off into the east woods, as usual, to roost.

❈ *16 August* ❈

LAST NIGHT, THE WIND CAME UP JUST before dawn, rushing in the trees and dropping a light gentle rain that cleared to yet one more quintessentially bright and blue late summer day.

Botanist Jim Dougan stops by with recommendations for the scrap of muddy ground in front of Edna's shed. We'll try wild strawberries and a few more periwinkle and lily of the valley.

Lots of bird activity all day long—two ruffed grouse in the eastern woods; an osprey, black and white with thin M-shaped wings hovers over the river a half dozen times; a phalanx of geese in ragged V-formation, several dozen strong, follow the river east heading for Rainbow Cliff, one of their prime fall gathering spots.

Not much of a murmuration to speak of. No blackbirds gather in their usual staging trees. Distant black pods flow far south of the west bend. Skimpier flocks pass overhead. Along the main road south, birds have lined the utility lines. They must have heard about all the wings we ate at the Chophouse tonight.

❖ *18 August* ❖

ANOTHER BREATHTAKING DAY of high summer came to Paradise, toasty and humid, with a hefty breeze and sailing fluffs of creamy summer clouds.

Last night, about eight o'clock, bevies of blackbirds passed through. No settling on their usual perches, but flocks rippled along the tops of distant trees across the river. One throng of several hundred arrived from the south for an exquisite spiral dance beside the giant white willow. I watched from Russell's as scores of geese in V-formation honked overhead, circled once, and continued upstream.

The meadow lies flush with goldenrod and Joe-Pye weed, but for a wide oval powder-green plot where white wild asters will soon bloom. Flecks of deep-purple New England asters have already flowered across the fields and hillsides. Cicadas buzz. Crows and blue jays shout. A few elecampane and leftover orange day lilies persist along with Queen Anne's lace. Cabbage butterflies abound and wrens putter about their nests, though their young have all fledged.

A high point of the day comes in the early afternoon. I head off to The Gully to offer up the trout skin from our lunch to the raccoons living there, when red-squirrel chatter breaks out beside the cabin. I turn and hunkered up against the well-rotted bole of a dying willow, sits a female pileated woodpecker, stiff tail braced against the trunk—the first such sighting in Paradise.

Crow-sized at about fifteen inches, with a black-and-white striped head and brilliant-red pointed crest—or mohawk as it's sometimes called—she eyes me with deep curiosity. With her chunky, chisel-like beak, she's excavated a large rectangular cavity in the rotten wood and has been probing and prying, with her long, retractable, barbed and sticky tongue, snaring ants in their nests or wood-boring beetle larvae in crevices.

With two subspecies—northern and southern—*Dryocopus pileatus* belongs to the *Woodpecker* family *Picidae. Dryocopus pileatus* is the largest North American woodpecker, now that the ivory billed has been declared extinct. Pileated, from the Latin *pileatus* meaning "capped," refers to the bird's prominent scarlet crest. *Dryocopus*, the ancient Greek word for "woodpecker," combines *druos* (tree) with *kopos* (beating).

A prehistoric, raptor-like bird, she's hopefully taken a shine to our patch of old growth forest with its accumulation of large decaying but live trees. They're ideal for insect foraging as well as nest building. Pileated woodpeckers do not return to any previous home. Their abandoned quarters provide nests or overnight shelters for small owls, ducks, bats, or even raccoons. In their excavations, they also remove vast quantities of wood, speeding up both decomposition and nutrient recycling.

For half a minute or more we study each other before I continued to The Gully. When I return, she's moved on, of course. Global warming has allowed pileated woodpeckers to shift their territories farther north, so we're hopeful we'll see her or one of her dashing relatives in the near future. At the very least, we might yet hear the deep rolls of her resonant drumming.

By early evening, the skies have darkened with low distant rumbles of thunder. A great wind blows in the scent of rain. The temperature drops by twenty degrees and a mighty downpour leaves behind a line of tall thunderheads stretching along the southern horizon topped with amber, orange, coral, and red.

At Black Bass Bend, a doe and two raccoons make a dainty crossing at The Dam Rapids and disappear into the woods. A great gob of blackbirds gathers in the tops of the trees across the river, twittering and whistling. We've already seen their reflections on the water. Flock after flock flies in, and as the sun goes down and we leave for Edna's, we might have been herding blackbirds. Wide disturbed flittering flocks move before us like dominoes falling one after another as we make our way home.

❈ *20 August* ❈

WE'RE SITTING, MIDAFTERNOON, in front of Russell's on a perfect late-summer Garden-of-Eden kind of day. Shreds of cloud drift along the horizon, the air saturated with the subtle perfume of wildflowers. The meadow below and the maples above stand full of fall in a rustle of changing leaves. Slender seed-cones top the cedar trees. Joe-Pye weed has spread, goldenrod thickened. Spikes of white wild cucumber drape everywhere and shrinking day lilies lean out from the top of the hill. Doves coo. Cardinals whistle. Wild canaries chirp in rhythmic flight. A mallard mom floats downstream, her babes on her back, and a pair of male ruby-throated hummingbirds duel at the birdfeeder.

Just moments ago, six great blue herons, in family units, sailed in to fish in the shallows. Two juveniles have settled high in the white willows beyond The Dam Rapids, one at the apex of the largest tree, one lower down, though still thirty or forty feet up. They perch like roosting egrets.

Great blue herons are common near open water or in wetlands throughout much of North America, Central America, the Caribbean, and the Galapagos Islands. The largest heron in North America, *Ardea herodias*, a member of the *Heron* family *Ardeidae*, takes its scientific name from the Latin *ardea* combined with ancient Greek *erōdios*, both meaning "heron." The genus dates back fourteen million years. The oldest great blue heron fossil goes back to the Pleistocene age at 1.8 million years. The great blue heron in its present form is at least one and half million years old.

We've so often admired these splendid creatures from a distance. They might be standing motionless knee-deep along the shoreline waiting for fish; spearing prey with a lightning stab of their long sharp bills and swallowing them whole; wading on lanky gray legs; flying high overhead with measured wingbeats, neck curved, head hunched; scanning the river's depths from a flat boulder midstream; foraging in the riverside pastures.

Hunting by night or by day, the great blue heron prefers fish but will also eat frogs, turtles, insects, snakes, salamanders, field rodents like voles and gophers, as well as small waterbirds.

Our great blue herons arrive in Paradise from late March through early April, Southern Ontario being a prime breeding ground. They nest in colonies called heronries, grouped in tall trees near lakes or other wetlands, sometimes with other wading birds. The male selects a nest site for a single brood, frequently in a tree twenty to sixty feet high. The female constructs a platform from sticks brought in by the male. Chicks will leave the nest at about three months of age.

As with all great blue heron populations east of the Rockies, most of ours migrate to the Caribbean, Central America, or northern South America beginning in late September through early October, by day or by night, alone or in flocks. Because of their flexible diet, they can pass the winter farther north than most herons.

And what beauties they are! The adults fishing in the shallows by The Dam Rapids have slate-gray flight feathers tinged with azure blue. Their rusty-gray necks are streaked black and white in front. A pair of slate-colored plumes sweep from just above the eye to the back of the head, with more of the same on the lower neck. Back in the spring at the start of the breeding season, their now dull yellowish bills and gray legs both turned bright orange. The two youngsters, an overall dullish gray, are perhaps relishing their first far-flung outing from the heronry. They sit in quiet satisfaction on their lofty white-willow perches.

The prehistoric squawk of a great blue heron on the move, especially after dark, is one of the primordial splendors of Paradise.

In the coolness of early evening, we head to the river. Molted feathers litter the cedar forest at Harold's Tea Deck and beyond. These warm August days are prime molting season.

Most birds lose their plumage in spring, prior to the breeding season and again in the fall, in order to be in fine feather for winter. For indigo buntings, rose-breasted grosbeaks, American goldfinches, and others, the spring molt may be partial, involving just the head and body feathers that dress them up for courtship.

Feathers provide insulation and regulate body temperature for protection against heat, cold, or water. They camouflage or they express sexual dimorphism—the differences between male and female. Feathers play a significant role in courtship, territorial displays, and of course flying. Molted feathers also make good nesting material. Adult birds drop old, damaged, or worn-out feathers from the breeding season and grow new strong and warm ones for winter.

Feathers grow from follicles in the skin. A new feather, fed by blood vessels, will gradually push the old one out. A full molt takes on average three months. Over a one-year period every feather will be replaced with a new one. Small birds might molt in five weeks. Ducks, geese, and swans will lose all their flight feathers at one time, leaving them flightless and vulnerable to predators for a few weeks.

Molting requires a great deal of energy, so intense periods like nesting and migration are avoided. Some birds become less active with the stress and irritation that comes with molting. Wild canaries will even stop singing. We've often noticed the decrease in bird activity in Paradise at this time of year, though some of that no doubt involves early migration.

Some birds, like the house sparrow, the red-winged blackbird, snow bunting, and European starling, put on their breeding plumage without replacing a single feather. Instead, they are subject to feather wear. Molting just once a year, European starlings, dark with white speckles in the fall and winter, turn sleek and glossy-black in the spring and summer.

The fall molt blanketing the forest floor today comes from new feathers with bold white tips replacing old dark feathers. By next spring, the creamy tips that give them their spotty appearance will have worn away, leaving behind the iridescent purple-black of spring and summer. Containing melanin, which is resistant to abrasion, these dark feathers will not continue to wear away.

Blackbirds by the hundreds gather in the second and third banks of trees across the river. By ones and twos and threes, they drop to the water's edge like black darts, sipping and dipping, rising in unison to make way for the next group. Washing up done, they soar by the thousands, flock after flock overhead and out of the distant trees, to roost again in the cedar woods. As we head home in the glow of sunset, blackbirds chatter behind with the sound of sizzling bacon, like a far-off cheering sports crowd.

❧ *22 August* ❧

ON THIS GENTLE SHOWERY MORNING, we sit on Edna's deck, rain tapping on the roof. Elderberries have ripened, and wild New England asters, yarrow, self-heal, and hawkweed have blossomed among the fall-tinged grasses.

In the early afternoon, a handsome gray cat stops by, with soft, sleek coat and vibrant green eyes. We've had scrappy dime-a-dozen farm cats before, lurking like phantoms, skittish in the shadows. We've come to treat them as just another wild animal. But this one seems domesticated. We're hopeful he has a home nearby. Unfortunately, he's found our chipmunks irresistible.

We've been this way before.

In 2009, scruffy Mama Joad appeared from under the shower, a rough, tough stoic *Grapes of Wrath* feline, black and white with a botched and beaten cancerous right ear. Intensely leery at first, she eventually brushed her tail against my leg, allowed me to pet her, and she purred and purred.

The next day, Blanche surfaced from under Edna's deck. A long-haired gray-and-white beauty who within days introduced her four tiny kittens—three replicas of her genteel self, the last chestnut and white. From her demeanor, Blanche had been someone's pet, mindlessly dumped when they found her pregnant. Just a babe herself—and a Southern belle at that—Blanche reclined most of the day on a deck chair.

Encouraged by Blanche's boldness, Mama Joad brought forth her own litter of four. One a carbon-copy of Mom. One creamy with a pale, gray face. Two tortoiseshells, one with his mom's squared face. We gave them all milk and cheese and dry cat food.

We managed to get a portion of the menagerie to the Humane Society in Kitchener. They would not be euthanized as long as they were found to be healthy. Blanche went willingly and with ease. So young herself, she hadn't yet grasped the intricacies of motherhood. Her babes had zero interest in being relocated. Like jack-in-the-boxes, "springs" in their feet popped them right back out of whatever container we put them in. Finally, with Mom and three young ones at the bottom of a large plastic garbage bin, we drove them to Kitchener.

We learned later that Blanche's fourth babe had attracted the attention of a relative of one of the hilltop neighbors out walking his dog in the woods. If the kitten followed him up the hill when he left, he said, he would take it home. It had. And he did.

Mama Joad and family did not fare so well. We captured Little Runt once, the tortoise-shelled baby with his mom's boxy face. But he escaped under the deck, deeply betrayed. We never saw him, his mom, or his siblings again.

In 2017, sweet one-year-old Ginny, a well-groomed female yellow tabby, materialized, again unjustly abandoned. Accustomed to being indoors, she would rush to each opening of the cottage door. She walked the paths with us. She slept on a Muskoka deck chair every night. She greeted us each morning. Gratefully, the Humane Society in nearby Guelph took her in.

We'll see what happens to Smoky, the Great Gray Hunter.

One more mesmerizing blackbird murmuration closes out the day. From Russell's, I watch as a crush of birds fly toward me, shooting up forty feet away, like a waterspout. Flocks roll overhead in wide black waves. Massive, layered groupings moving along the southern horizon, left to right, right to left, and left to right again. Spinning as one sentient being, pods vanish and then pivot to become thick and solid again. In the end, they pour over The West Woods by the thousands, diving into the treetops.

❋ *25 August* ❋

THIS QUINTESSENTIAL LATE-SUMMER DAY of serenity and sunshine fills up with the lazy sound of crickets and the scent of ripening apples. In the early evening, at Black Bass Bend, a pair of young beaver (two brown heads above the waterline) cross the river above The Dam Rapids. They glide to within five feet of the gravel shoreline before diving. Then one by one, four antlered white-tailed bucks saunter out of the woods to graze on wild cucumber. Two of them pick their way across the river to be swallowed up in the tall grasses of the near side. The other two, enchanted by the beaver, spend several long *National Geographic* moments in fascination before melting back into the forest.

The evening's blackbird show launches at quarter to eight—the short program. Twenty mesmerizing minutes of circle, swirl, and undulate before slipping away to the woods. We give them a standing ovation.

At eleven o'clock, after an eastern screech owl has come and gone with soft whinnies and hoots, we climb the north hill for a magical display of the Northern Lights, not often seen in Paradise.

The best Canadian sightings of the Aurora Borealis fall, naturally, in the winter months, in the far north—in the Yukon, Iqaluit, or the Northwest Territories. Even there, December and January may prove too overcast. But Ontario does boast some exceptional viewing spots— Northern Manitoulin Island on Lake Huron, the north shore of Lake Superior from Thunder Bay to Sault St. Marie, Torrance Barrens Dark Sky Preserve near Gravenhurst in Muskoka's cottage country. All of these are just a tad too distant to reach on an evening.

Also known as the Polar Lights or the Aurora Polaris, the Northern Lights result from electrically charged particles (mainly electrons and protons from increased solar activity such as solar flares) carried on the solar wind and interacting with the earth's upper atmosphere. This activity produces dynamic light displays of varying hue and intensity— yellow and green to blue and red, based on the type of element involved, typically oxygen or nitrogen. Generally occurring in high-latitude regions around the Arctic and the Antarctic, auroras manifest patterns of light that dance through the night sky, shape-shifting from curtains and spirals to rays, flickers, glows, and flares. Solar activity runs in cycles of between eleven and fifteen years, beginning slow, reaching a peak, and then declining to begin the next sequence. They last peaked in 2014.

The name "Aurora Borealis," coined by Galileo in 1619, derives from the Roman goddess of the dawn, Aurora—who traveled east to west proclaiming the imminent arrival of the sun. Borealis comes from the ancient Greek god of the north wind, *Boreas*. Aurora Australis, the Southern Lights, were named from the Latin word *auster* meaning "south."

An aurora over Rome's port city of Ostia during the reign of Tiberius flushed so brilliantly blood red that soldiers on fire duty nearby raced to stamp out a blaze. The ancient Chinese had no settled word for the phenomenon. They named each occurrence according to its likeness. Stars like Rain. Sky Dog. Sword Star. Indigenous Australians often thought of the lights as bushfires in the spirit world, and Scandinavian mythology claimed them as the stored-up energy in glaciers broken out into flame.

The peninsula of Southern Ontario, lying so far to the south and with an over-abundance of light pollution and weather interference, rarely witnesses much of the high drama associated with the Aurora, though I once heard of green curtains rippling behind the CN Tower in Toronto. Tonight, the solar winds have blown in a bewitching pale-green glow on the northern horizon, and a mystical silver light shimmers overhead.

Much more than we could hope for.

❋ *28 August* ❋

THIS MORNING'S CHILL CONFIRMS that fall lies just around the corner, winter close behind. With distant thunder, misted veils of rain thread the south woods. The overcast lingers until late afternoon, when the air fills up with cool slanted sunlight, the scent of turning vegetation tinged with the cidery bite of ripening apples.

A harbinger of seasonal change, bird activity continues to diminish. Of course, chickadees, blue jays, and other year-rounders abound. A northern cardinal family dines at the west feeder, four chicks from their last brood with crests laid low. Dad wears vivid crimson, with a black mask and yellow bill, Mom in reddish olive.

Often migratory elsewhere, the eastern American goldfinch over-winter in Southern Ontario. Breeding in late July—aligned to the peak of their grain food supply—they're fledging their single yearly brood in August or even September and so are rarely seen at the feeders this time of year. They're out in the fields or feeding chicks. We see them flitting about with their wave-shaped flight pattern, a trill in the dipping phase. Some have also begun their autumn molt, dull buff and olive-brown plumage with pale amber face and bib replacing the lemon-yellow and inky-black of summer.

One of the earliest birds to lay eggs in the spring, eastern American robins, with their rich, reddish-orange breasts and tawny beaks, will be gone by mid-to-late September. Two full-grown fledglings with speckled chests have been scratching in the leaves outside our bedroom window. Alert for any insect movement, they snatch up leaves here and there, tossing them aside in the search.

Earlier, a dozen eastern American crows with iridescent black feathers, mobbed a pair of red-tailed hawks at Wood's End. Outside of nesting season, they usually travel in large numbers, gathering in communal roosts at night. Along with ruby-throated hummingbirds, mourning doves, belted kingfishers, and great blue herons, crows will remain here in Paradise for several more weeks.

As we feed the fish at Black Bass Bend in the late afternoon, a young double-crested cormorant alights in the willows, raising its wings. Circling and circling, the large bird settles and sits, circles again and settles again, its weight breaking branches with each landing.

Like all members of the *Cormorant* family, the feathers of double-crested cormorants are not waterproof. They must be constantly dried after swimming low in the water with just neck and head visible. A stocky, dark-gray bird with long neck, webbed feet, and a hooked bill, this youngster seems a bit lost, as well he may have been.

Late summer's shorter days brings dusk to the flats by eight o'clock. The evening's blackbird show opens at quarter to eight. Another brief but frenzied short program, twenty minutes long, focuses on the dead trees across the river at the west end. Great bands dash down to the river, spiraling up a half-dozen times to pour into the trees. Shadowy brown bodies rush to the surrounding cedars, dropping out of the sky like rain. Trees sag a foot or more under their combined weight. Great whooshing floods of birds in a final flurry stream overhead and into the east woods.

❋ *30 August* ❋

AFTER A DAY OF SHOWERY WHITE skies alternating with periods of smudgy sunlight, we find ourselves knee-deep in one more blissful late-summer day. Lazy cloud puffs drift through an azure-blue sky. Dad's journals mention snow flurries in late August 1965. So, once again, we've come out on top.

Smoky stops by this morning unfortunately hunting chipmunks. He looks fit and fed and well groomed. Geese gather at the bend above the Big Bridge as full summer shares the water-meadow with early fall. Ever-growing numbers of white cabbage butterflies dance over the meadow. Joe-Pye weed, darkened with age, now contrasts with the gauzy foam of white wild asters newly opened up in their allotted spot. We watch a kingfisher on the top wire of the west-side fence splash into the river a half dozen times to bathe.

At noon, we set off for lunch in Drayton, finding a black mass of milkweed tussock moth caterpillars chowing down on the few remaining milkweed plants at the top of the hill. They've stripped most of them bare.

Euchaetes egle—the milkweed tiger moth or milkweed tussock moth—belongs to the *Arctiini* tribe (the tiger moths), in the family *Lymantriidae.* Their English name comes from the caterpillars' hair tufts or tussocks, like tiny clumps of grass. The origin of the Latin *euchaetes egle* is unclear. *Egle* may have derived from Old Greek *aigle,* meaning "brightness or splendor," or alternatively from the Lithuanian word *egle,* meaning "spruce or fir tree."

Gray with clusters of black, white, orange, and sometimes yellow filaments, these common late-summer larvae feed on milkweed and dogbane, one generation per year in the north. They can be found from southern Canada to Texas and Florida.

Laid as eggs on the undersides of leaves by the gray female moths, milkweed tussocks feed in the dozens from June on. They avoid the sticky latex produced by both dogbane and milkweed by eating around leaf veins. This leaves behind only a lacy skeleton. Older larvae reduce the flow of latex to areas where they're feeding by cutting through the veins. They will eventually wander off in smaller groups.

Though monarch butterflies prefer younger milkweed shoots, tussocks present an existential threat. We're hopeful they haven't yet discovered the stretches of milkweed on the water-meadow and along the riverbank.

After a brief downpour in the early evening, a double rainbow tops the trees to the south. The atmosphere flushes gold as the sun slides behind purpled clouds. When The West Woods darkens, an eastern screech owl floats into the low branches of a nearby maple, resting five or ten minutes before moving on in silence. Within moments we catch its soft ethereal whinny echoing through the gloaming.

From inside Edna's Cottage, we discover—at long last—the culprit who's been raiding the west-side feeder. As we expected, a flashlight focused on the limb from which the feeder hung reveals Winston. No surprise there. Hauling in the feeder hand over hand like reeling in a fishing line, he snatches the thing in both front paws and dumps out the contents. Then, letting the line drop back, he scrambles down to snuffle up whatever seeds remained.

❊ *31 August* ❊

THIS DREARY, OVERCAST LAST DAY of August morphs into humid sunshine with high clouds and a summery breeze. Wild cucumber has withered on the water-meadow. Chickadees and chipmunks chirp. Cat-birds mew. House wrens and crickets and cicadas trill and buzz against a backdrop of apoplectic red squirrels. The wind rummages in summer-worn trees, nosing about in the grasses and reed beds on the meadow. Frothy, white wild asters have crept farther across their dusty green patch and elms have turned yellow. Aspens and poplars show hints of amber, maples of tangerine and red flame.

By early afternoon, we've gone over to Harold's Tea Deck for a touch-up cleaning. A white-tailed doe ambles up the adjacent hillock, just above the sign to Black Bass Bend. As does do, she melts into the woods.

Work complete, I set off for Edna's. Looking back, I see Dan standing in the tea deck clearing. A spotted fawn—quite possibly the doe's offspring—stands some thirty feet beyond him. Perhaps never having seen a human before, the fawn inches closer, coming to within ten feet of where Dan stands. On opposite sides of the tea deck, they eye each other before the babe saunters down the slope. Curiosity satisfied, she bounds down the hill, trots off into the lowland grasses of the gully wash, and disappears. What an amazing gift.

After supper, we puddle in the river in our Wellingtons, poking about the near shoreline to below our white willow matriarch where the water deepened. At the base of the tree, we are overjoyed to see evidence of a new beaver lodge, confirmation of a second colonist in the neighborhood. We putter our way back along the far side, sit on a rock midstream west of The Dam Rapids and watch one more outstanding blackbird show.

Returning from hunting in fall fields or whichever ones have been already plowed up for winter, thousands on thousands of birds pour across the sky in great dark flocks, raining again into the trees and into the river. In and out and up and down, twisting and turning, dissolving in synchronized flight, and popping out again. Wings whir and rush and hum.

Is it the thrill of flying? The contentment of companionship? Migration preps? Or just end-of-summer fun?

Eastern Chipmunk (Bob), May; photo by Marie Laure Fontaine

Watermeadow, June

Winston, Common Raccoon, June; photo by Dan Beeaff

Ostrich Fern in Wilderness, June; photo by Danielle Beeaff

Murmuration Dragon, July

Monarch Chrysalis, July;
photo by Danielle Beeaff

Belted Kingfisher;
photo by Dan Beeaff

Orange Day Lily

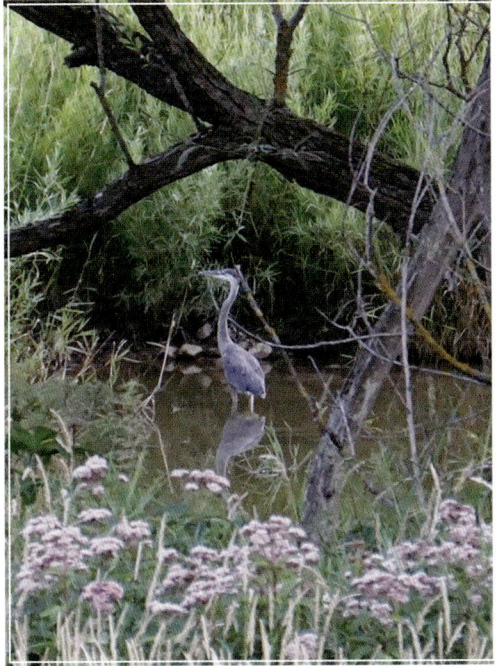

Great Blue Heron;
photo by Dustin Beeaff

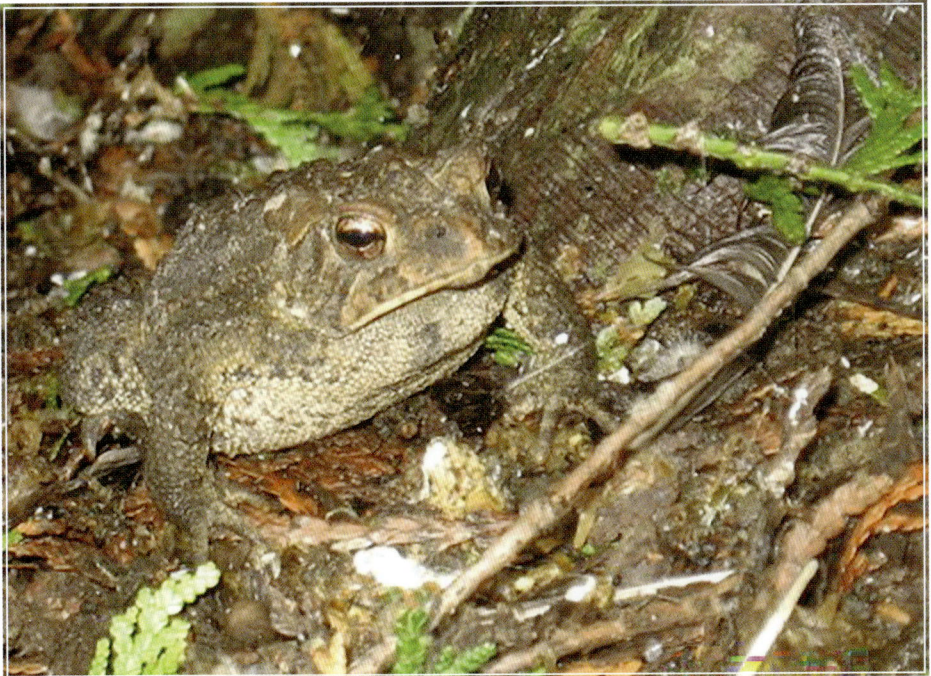

American Toad; photo by Dan Beeaff

Blue Damselfly; photo by Danielle Beeaff

Northeastern Wild Astor

Rufus the Ruffed Grouse

Eastern Chipmunk

The Dam Rapids, November

View East from The Dam Rapids, January

Part Three

AUTUMN

"And the sun took a step back . . . and autumn was awakened."
— RAQUEL FRANCOE

"This morning of the first September was crisp
and golden as an apple."
— J. K. ROWLING

❖ *1 September* ❖

SOMEWHAT CRISP AND SOMEWHAT GOLDEN, autumn has arrived; life in transition, summer to winter. Chilly evenings lie ahead with the promise of frost not far off.

Astronomical autumn descends on those of us in the Northern Hemisphere with the fall equinox when the sun idles above the equator, rising due east and setting due west. Day and night are nearly of equal duration all over the world. After that, daylight will decrease, nights lengthen, and temperatures will cool until mid-December's winter solstice. But the first of September marks the meteorological first day of fall. By this reckoning, fall will end for us on the first of December.

Prior to the 16th century, the word "harvest" described the autumnal season, derived from Old English *haerfest* and Old Saxon *hervist*, the period between August and November when major field crops ripened. As more and more people gave up working the land for urban environments, "harvest" came to refer to reaping activity itself, autumn and fall signifying the season.

"Autumn" comes to us from the Latin *autumnus*—archaic *auctumnus*—possibly from the Etruscan root *autu*, which has connotations for the passing of the year. *Autumnus* is derived from the Latin verb *augere*, "to increase" and *auctus* meaning "rich" as "in the rich season" and translated in Old French as *autompne*, in Old English as *autumpne*.

187

We can trace the alternative word "fall" back to old Germanic languages like Old English *fiaell* or *feallan*, and Old Norse *fall*, that suggested "a fall from a height." In 16th century England, "fall" came to denote the season, as a contraction of Middle English phrases like "fall of the leaf" and "fall of the year." This same concept produced "spring of the leaf" and "spring of the year." In the 17th century, English settlers to the New World took "fall" with them. While the word became passé in Britain, it prospered in North America in reference to harvest time and the shift to cooler weather.

September, the ninth month of the year in the Julian and Gregorian calendars, takes its name from the Latin *septem*, which means "seven," and *septimus* meaning "seventh." September was once the seventh month in the Roman calendar. After 153 BCE, the new year opened on the first of Kalendas Januarius (January), rather than the first of Kalendas Martius (March).

On this warm September day, after mild thunderstorms in the night, a subtle gloom descends, with leaden overcast and come-and-go showers. Midmorning, the sun breaks through, and gray-bottomed clouds scud across a deep autumn-blue sky. Against the stable greens of cedar and spruce, brilliant ever-expanding scraps of changing leaves in yellow, red, orange, and maroon rustle like tissue paper. The air fills with the earthy scent of forest and field.

At Wood's End, purple New England asters have spread across the water-meadow and the willow matriarch now leans farther south. The industrious resident beaver there swims about rearranging saplings and limbs to augment broken lower branches in the streambed. Chipmunks and red squirrels continue their own harvests, herons and kingfishers still haunting the shoreline.

In the countryside, soybeans plants lie yellow/brown in their fields, corn stands in crumpling lines, lower sheaves burnished beige, and colored leaves meld into forest fringes everywhere. Our apple trees on the hilltop sag with green and gold and striate-red fruit. Fallen bits have scented the air with a tangy ripeness, and opposite the cottage parking area, in a field where corn stalks have already been gathered in for silage, we watch a hundred Canada geese foraging in the stubble. Several other flocks, dozens strong, pass overhead in straggling V's, moving southwest, their long, black, white-ringed necks undulating as they flap over the treetops.

While we sit in stillness outside Russell's Cottage as the honey-hued full moon slips up behind the eastern trees, we call in two great horned owls for an evening chat. One sits high on a giant white cedar in The West Woods, the other in the white willow.

This year, the September full moon, usually called the Harvest Moon, will take the name Full Corn Moon, Full Fruit Moon, or Full Barley Moon, among others. A Harvest Moon—the full moon closest to the fall equinox—can be up to two weeks either side of that date. In 1987, the Harvest Moon occurred on October 7. Tonight's September full moon rises twenty-one days from the autumn equinox, which falls on September 22 this year. An October full moon appears only nine days from the fall equinox, so this year's Harvest Moon will move into October. A second full moon in that month, on Halloween—a Blue Moon—can also be called the Full Hunter's Moon, the customary designation for the full moon of October. The Harvest Moon can be either the last full moon of summer or the first full moon of fall. This year, it's the latter.

Another name for September's full moon, the Full Corn Moon, corresponds to the Indigenous time for harvesting corn. The Anglo-Saxons called the month *Gerstmonath*—Barley Month—for the same reason. A Maine *Farmers' Almanac* in the 1930s is credited with first publishing Indigenous full moon names, October's being the Falling Leaves Moon to the Algonquin.

When close to an autumn equinox, the full moon rises nearer sunset for several nights. In the days before tractor lights, the brightness of the Harvest Moon early in the evening helped farmers gather in their summer crops despite dwindling daylight. The angle of the moon's orbit relative to the earth's horizon causes the full moon to appear above the horizon faster than usual. The moon then rises at nearly the same time for several nights in a row. This provides longer harvesting hours. The farther north, the greater this Harvest Moon effect will be.

The golden-orange color of tonight's rising full moon results from the earth's atmosphere having a greater thickness toward the horizon. More blue waves scatter, leaving mostly red and yellow to reach our eyes.

We take the steps down to The Willow Deck and soak in the views out across the water-meadow and east and west to the cedar woods. Tatters of silvered moonlight break out below the trees, frosted on the meadow grass. Round and lustrous and now riding high in a clear sky, the moon shapes all manner of gray and black shadows across the landscape. The white ribbon of river, stalks and reeds, brambles and thickets, shrubs and trees, are silhouetted in sharp relief.

❈ *4 September* ❈

A HEFTY RAIN IN THE NIGHT, accompanied by great winds, leaves showers until midmorning, when a thin white gloom overlays the sky, vague patches of blue seeping through. While it's cool and dull for us through much of the day, autumn leaves flutter through the pearl-gray heaviness of a fall sky.

After lunch, we sit on Edna's deck. Five flocks of Canada geese fly over, each with a wild, rhythmic beating of wings, in small groupings of ten or twenty and once just a pair. They all honk madly but for the last contingent, which passes over in silent single file.

At the outdoor fireplace wood box, a red squirrel frantically works on a winter nest, hauling in twigs and leaves, mosses and grass, before a thunderstorm brings in low, black clouds. Roiling winds whip through the fading stalks on the flats and rattle tree branches overhead.

When the storm abates, we cross the river to examine what looks like pink orchids growing on the jungled shoreline just above The Dam

Rapids. The hooded pink flowers above a bank of stinging nettle turn out to be Himalayan balsam, also known as kiss-me-on-the-mountain or ornamental jewelweed when cultivated. An invasive annual species native to mountain areas near Kashmir, Himalayan balsam seeds, seed pods, shoots, and young leaves can all be eaten. The flowers have even been used to make jam.

With soft-green or red-tinted stems and foliage that when crushed gives out a strong musty smell, Himalayan balsam has glands below the leaflets that produce a viscous, sweet-smelling, edible nectar. Like common jewelweed, seed pods can burst with the slightest touch. These two attributes have given the plant its scientific name, *Impatiens glandulifera*. *Impatiens* is Latin for "impatient," *glandulifera*, a compound word derived from Latin *glandula* meaning "small gland," and *ferre*, "to bear."

As attractive as Himalayan balsam may be with its sunny-rose, snapdragon-like blossoms, we're not overly keen to find it's taken root in Paradise. Blooms will often successfully compete with native species and can, en masse, erode riverbanks.

We linger at Black Bass Bend an hour or so, startling a great blue heron who takes off with a loud croaky squawk, long legs dangling. The stream flows by languid and tea-colored, a quiet burble at the rapids where a bobbing snipe hunts the shoreline. Grasses have faded to buff brown and matte green now. Goldenrod is still strong and bright, but our Joe-Pye weed has darkened to dusty burgundy, with wild asters spreading in pale lacy white. The scent of wildflowers and ripening apples lies heavy in the air. In the woods behind us, dozens of terrestrial crayfish burrows have sprung up, consecutive rings in gray clay.

Another blackbird pageant opens about seven thirty—few of the twists and turns of previous performances, but large pods shoot into the water at Wood's End for drinks, soaring up into the trees. A shock of crows passes through the flocks flowing overhead, leaving frantic shrieks from one young murmuration participant who'd been seized mid-flight.

The sun dips behind a panorama of pink and coral clouds. Shortly after, a cool breeze rises with the pale, yellow-gold moon, and we return to Edna's Cottage.

❈ *5 September* ❈

THIS MORNING, SMOKY, WHO HASN'T been seen for several days, hunts down and makes off with a red squirrel. He's so fit and well-fed that we're hopeful it was a catch and release situation. So hard to watch, even if he's just doing what cats do.

We head for the river again at sundown. Autumn always sharpens spider time and we each take a walking stick to brush away all the gossamer strands slung across the pathway. Five orb spiders have already decorated the railings of Edna's deck. At Castor's Landing, two weavers, like jeweled broaches, climb webs that gleam silver in the setting sun. A spider's web has a tensile strength greater than steel with twice the stretch of nylon.

Sunlight still tops the eastern woods when a gentle rain begins to whisper on the river and in the forest behind us. Snapping turtles slip through the amber afterglow and a silver-gray drift of fog washes up against a great blue heron at The Dam Rapids. He stands in utter stillness on a flat rock midstream, head down, before stalking off along the far shoreline. Two others sweep overhead, primordial croaked greetings all around. As night closes in, we pick up a flurry of discordant squawks squeaking up from the dusky shadows on the river. Our green herons have fledged!

❋ 7 September ❋

ON THIS HUSHED AND CHILLY DAY, early fall excels. The river runs high, flat, and glassy. Trees stand old and tired but patchy with color, the elms golden. Papery crimson maple leaves twirl down from time to time. Pearl-gray clouds coast in from the west-northwest on a gentle breeze and crickets sing all around. Both cabbage whites and cicadas have declined.

Along with goldenrod and fleabane, wild asters and morning glories—the two flowers of September—now dominate the early fall landscape.

"Aster" comes to us from the Greek word *astēr* meaning "star," a reference to the shape of the flower head. Fall-blooming, leafy-stemmed herbs, asters belong to the *Aster* or *Composite* family *Asteraceae*.

Paradise supports five native wild-aster species. Magnificent New England asters—*Symphyotrichum novae-Angliae*, from *symphyotrichum* meaning "united hairs" and *novae-angliae*, "New England," light up autumn with their splashy, deep-violet, rose-purple, or lavender-rayed flowers, each with an orange-yellow center. Individual plants can grow up to six feet tall, with hundreds of showy flower heads. Bees and butterflies, especially monarchs, will all vie for its nectar before it succumbs to the first frost.

The water-meadow, hilltop, and forest fringes also support the western panicled aster, a lance-leaved herb with snowy rayed petals that can reach five feet. Panicle alludes to flowers that display in multibranched arrays. We also have calico or starved aster, a bushy plant whose cream-colored blossoms have centers that turn purple or brown with age. Calico asters make up that frothy wild-aster patch that always punches up the east end of the water-meadow this time of year. Swamp aster or red-stem aster resembles New England aster but with fainter-colored blooms, and arrow-leaved aster, also known as blue wood aster or heart leaf aster, has dense clusters of white flowers each with a pale-yellow center. Wild asters, along with the bright honeyed blooms of goldenrod and fall's painted leaves, are the heart and soul of early floral autumn in Paradise.

The name "morning glory" covers over a thousand flowering plant species in the family *Convolvulaceae*. Most of them open in the early morning and have closed by noon, though some may linger on cloudy days.

At least three thousand years before Charles Goodyear's discovery, ancient Mesoamericans used the sulfur in morning glory juice to vulcanize or harden rubber for bouncing balls. Aztec priests also exploited the plant's hallucinogenic properties.

The morning glory of Paradise—hedge false bindweed (*Calystegia sepium*)—native to both northern and southern hemispheres, proliferates by clonal offshoots that twine counterclockwise around other plants. *Calystegia* translates as "a covering cup," from the Greek *kalux* (cup) combined with *stegos* meaning "a covering." *Sepium* means "of hedges" or "of fences."

With clinging vines and broad leaves, false bindweed can smother or even pull down small trees or shrubs. Matte-green arrowhead-shaped leaves spiral around slightly hairy stems green to red. Funnel-shaped, vaguely lobed flowers, in white or pale pink with five darker stripes inside, have yellow corollas deep inside their throats. Also called white witch's hat and belle of the ball, morning glories have gilded the early fall landscape of Paradise for several weeks now.

By early afternoon, against a patchy blue sky, we watch a high-flying merlin zip over the browning water-meadow below Russell's. A small, robust falcon, merlin are swift and skilled hunters often called pigeon hawks in North America. They prey on small birds the size of a house sparrow, capturing most midair. In general, only one in twenty targets will be snared. This regal adult male, with blue-gray back, buffy, orange-tinged underparts streaked with black, and a blackish, white-tipped tail, is almost certainly making his way south on a fall migration that peaks in mid-September.

We don't often spot merlin. Paradise lies between their breeding grounds to the north and their wintering grounds in the southern and western United States, Central America, and northern South America. With impressive speed and agility, this gorgeous aerial acrobat tail-chased a startled song sparrow, who narrowly escaped.

Below Russell's Cottage, too, at the far west riverbend, Canada geese have continued to gather. A flock of ten or twelve sail over the north hill toward Wood's End just after lunch. Their leader announces their arrival. Someone on the river below answers, and they all dip a wing and drop to a lower level. This control tower maneuvering is repeated until they've all landed, at which time a cacophony of honking breaks out. Everyone is in meet-and-greet mode.

Just before bedtime, I speak with one of our hilltop neighbors. She confirms that Smoky, whose given name is Loki, belongs to a young couple at the nonworking farm at the east end of our hilltop road. They take in all sorts of rescue animals, an angora goat last year. Our loving, handsome fellow does indeed have a home.

❊ 9 September ❊

IN CRISP AUTUMN STILLNESS, we sit at The Willow Deck for lunch today. An early overcast, with mist in the trees, has resolved to sunshine, pearly gray clouds, and an errant spit of rain.

From a distance, geese honk on the river and crows caw. Apples on the water-meadow trees have filled the air with a ripened cidery sharpness. Teasles, burdocks, and thistles have all gone to seed, thorn apple trees dropping their leaves by the day. A cool breeze fingers the red-leaved bushes all around and squadrons of honeybees hum on the goldenrod and chicory. Even a bumblebee or two purrs through the autumn blooms. These winged Teddy bears have dense hair that allows them to survive in cold weather longer than most flying insects. We expect to see them flitting about for several more weeks.

From Edna's comes the occasional thump of a black walnut, coupled with complaints from a red squirrel we've called Aida. She's been burying peanuts all day only to have an astutely observant blue jay unearth them again.

By midafternoon, we spy one of the cows from across the river placidly munching meadow grasses under the giant willow on the flats. The owner and his daughter stop by when we ring them up. Having forded the river to give birth, the cow wanders upriver while the young woman fetches the newborn from the long grass and hands it off to her father. Together they redirect the inattentive mom back to the herd and then set about mending the fence.

In preagricultural days, early September opened up "driving down time," the return of domesticated animals to their winter quarters. Before long now, our cross-river band will be hustled back across the water to shelter in the farm's barn for the winter.

I meander down the path to The Gully in the early evening. The tang of apples charges the air above the musty fragrance of autumn foliage. A handful of chickadees twitter, crickets burr, and the wind rushes in the trees.

Everything in Paradise is in flux, all the time. And yet things have remained much the same through the decades. Through centuries; though millennia: the curve of the streambed, the sweep of the riverbank willows, the high grasses and the low.

"There's a spiritual quality to being out here," Bob Leverett wrote in *Smithsonian Magazine.* "You walk silently through these woods, and there's a spirit that comes out."

At Castor's Landing, surrounded by that spirit, we pick another bundle of mint at the river's edge. A muskrat paddles upriver, and several V's of geese squawk overhead, dark, ragged silhouettes across the paling sky. Hundreds of tiny insects bob over the water like flecks of dust. Kingfishers and great blue heron fish on the shoreline.

As the sun slips away, the river's surface turns buff brown. Leaves gleam against a failing light that pulls their colors after it as the western sky turns to pink and pearl. We return to Harold's Tea Deck, startling a ruffed grouse mom with four nearly full-grown chicks who scattered over the hillside.

The cool essence of night and still water creep ever closer along with the soft whinny of an eastern screech owl. Masses of blackbirds arrive with the synchronized flutter of wings, and as we make our way toward Edna's, the chirps and chatter of the roost fades to the distant sound of falling water.

❧ *12 September* ❧

LOKI SPRAWLS OUT ON EDNA'S welcome mat this morning. Fur brushed and burr-less, he's so utterly content that he even allows the chipmunks a peanut or two.

With neighboring alfalfa fields now in purple-blue bloom, autumn marches on. A beigy tint has washed the land, and here in Paradise knapweed and hawkweed have arrived. Hundreds of sunflower nubs atop the hill above the water-meadow stand ready to burst into blossom.

Summer songbirds and many butterflies have already gone. But— rather late in the season—the last few days of hot and humid weather have called up a Flying Ant Day. So many of the insects may appear in the same place at the same time that Flying Ant Day has become an informal designation. Flying Ant Season would be more appropriate. Depending on the weather, the phenomenon may occur more than once in the same area, or in different parts of the country, any time from June to September.

Ant queens can live up to ten years. On a Flying Ant Day, young queens and the males of the same species rise from their nests to begin their nuptial flights. Both have sprouted wings and are then called *alates*, a name given to the winged form of many social insects, especially ants and termites. On the wing, a queen, larger than the male, will mate with several partners before landing to start a new colony. At that time, she will also chew off her wings.

We spend the early afternoon in front of Russell's aiding and abetting two emergent colonies. Smaller insects have little difficulty getting aloft. But the larger ones struggle to climb the tall blades of grass needed for successful liftoffs.

A launch too often results in a crash landing.

As individuals step out, we scoop some of them up on twigs, transferring them to Dan's knee where they orient themselves toward the meadow, beat their tiny wings, and soar off like milkweed parasols. The air around us thickens with this dusting of new life.

With evening, a mass of blackbirds rolls in from the west to settle on the dead elms by The Gully. More flocks sail overhead with cascading swirls and dances. Within fifteen minutes, they've flooded back to the trees on the north hill for the roost, while a gaggle of Canada geese squawk past in the opposite direction.

❈ *13 September* ❈

A SOFT RAIN THROUGH THE NIGHT has faded away by early morning, when deep fog shrouds the landscape. Heavy in the trees, a blanket of silver-gray creeps across the water-meadow, beading the autumn webs slung up by yellow garden spiders. By noon, the day turns to a cold, ashen overcast. Not a leaf stirs. Neither does Loki, who spends much of his time curled up in one of Edna's cushioned Muskoka chairs.

Our non-migrating birds have begun to gather in wintering flocks. Wild canaries crowd the westside bird feeder and a half dozen adult cardinals swoop into the dead elms, accompanied by their chaffing offspring.

The river still runs high from recent rains. Over at Castor's Landing, after a ten-minute blackbird show wrapped up, a pair of female wood ducks bob about above The Dam Rapids, trailing a string of ducklings behind them. Then, just after sunset, when a biting wind has blown off the wintry cloud cover, we glimpse one or two shooting stars from the Epsilon Perseids meteor shower. (It had peaked on the ninth.)

And then the sky closes up again with cold autumn showers and we go back home.

❧ *14 September* ❧

LIKE FARMERS BRINGING IN THEIR SUMMER crops of hybrid corn and soybeans, the denizens of Paradise continue their own harvests. This morning, a red squirrel pounds spruce cones on Edna's roof again, gathering them at the base of the tree. Another does the same with fallen black walnuts. Near Harold's Tea Deck, a handful of cedars in the east woods now have bright yellow-green rings of cut seed-heavy cedar leaves circling their trunks, drying like new-mown hay.

Someone has overturned the pail of walnuts Dan and I had soaked for planting. The culprit has run off with every last one. Down at Black Bass Bend, the beaver clan are busy sailing willow withies back to the den for winter storage.

Still gleaming beside The Willow Deck, against the scarlet of Virginia creeper, goldenrod has begun to fade. The round stem-balls of the goldenrod gallfly (one of fifty species of gall makers) have formed on nearly every one.

Through much of the summer, stem after stem supported the sticky froth of bubbles we call "witch's spit," extruded from the anus of the spittlebug. Along with Joe-Pye weed, common teasel pods, long used to card or tease wool, have turned a dusty dark brown. By November, flowerheads will have withered to skeletons.

All the in-between spaces on the water-meadow are rife with daisies and jewelweed, with sky-blue chicory, fringes of orange-amber hawkweed, and the creamy foam and regal purples of the wild asters. The ribbon of sunflowers on the crest of the north slope at Russell's is now a sea of bright yellow, flower heads following the sun. A light wind, charged with the musty perfumes of autumn, shuffles through withering leaves, and while many of the thousand shades of summer green have faded, intense washes, tints, and tinges still lie on dusty beds of jade and chartreuse.

By evening, the blackbirds mesmerize once again, a flux of synchronized wings erupting from nanoseconds of silence. Flock on flock sally and retreat, ebb and flow, circle and disperse. At the top of the steps, where we meet our nearest neighbor out walking his dog, one participant, a young, speckled starling, lies limp and shattered in the grass.

The neighbor tells us that Loki's people have split up. Just last week. The young woman will stay on the farm until a new home in Elmira becomes available. The fellow has already moved up to Arthur, taking Loki with him.

A happy ending for Loki, without question. But still . . .

Loki's gone . . . one more time . . . Loki's gone!

❧ *16 September* ❧

ON THIS DULL AND DREARY DAY of heavy cloud cover, we head to the river about six o'clock in the evening. On the path east of Edna's shed, we startle our princely red fox. We eye each other for long moments before he trots up the hill and slips away. The flash of that bright and bushy red tail brings such comfort, as we've not seen him in some time.

At the river, six boisterous V-formations of geese flap overhead, reflected in the glassy surface of the water. Feathers glint in the struggling sunlight. The rhythmic rush of their wings surges through the tranquil evening air. The wheezing snort of a white-tailed deer alert from near The Gully bridge breaks the silence as we return to Edna's Cottage. Probably an allergic reaction to humans, Dan says.

With the red flicker of cardinals at the feeder and the blue flicker of kingfishers in the willows, we settle outside Russell's for sundown's blackbird pageant. Once again festivities have moved south. From a distant bend of the river, we hear the spirited cacophony as tiers of undulating birds drop onto the distant treetops.

As they migrate along river valleys, communal starling roosts can grow into the hundreds of thousands. Rest stops may last up to seven weeks. Southern Ontario is a major hub, with a quarter of a million overwintering birds. So, we'll likely see our flocks many more times.

With the blackbirds taking their show on the road, a few robins who often settle on the fringes of the roost have bedded down in the cedars around the tea deck. Their gentle trills will soon sing the sun down.

❉ *18 September* ❉

PALE SUNLIGHT TOPS THE EASTERN hill at eight thirty this morning. After a breakfast of scrambled eggs, toast, and peameal bacon, we hunker down on Edna's deck as a mist of rain in overtones and undertones splatters on the rooftop. Chipmunks loll about in the scrub pile on the slope below the cottage, munching spruce seeds. Red squirrels harvest peanuts, one stopping to gnaw a spruce cone as if cleaning up a cob of corn. When the drizzle diminishes, a thin breeze fractures the gray skies, allowing for cold sunlight to slip through.

The color in the maples and the aspens, in the walnuts and the poplars, deepens by the day. Queen Anne's lace has morphed to bird's nest, and hundreds of sunflowers sway across the crest of the water-meadow. The last hurrah of summer.

About eleven o'clock, we saunter through to Wood's End. Shredded clouds crawl across the sky, leaving the forest floor patchy with sunlight. Earlier, we'd marked a gathering of geese at the west bend, augmented by scraggly bands. But when we peer over the fence, only three adults are visible. They drift in utter silence, jostling together to eye the intruders, and then scud off again.

We inch closer. In an instant, with one off-key alarm call, out and up from beyond the curve of the river clatters upward of fifty geese in sudden, stunning coordination. They whirl overhead just once and set off for a safer berth.

By seven o'clock, blackbirds bluster over from the east, half of them coalescing into a tight ball. The other half make a sharp right turn, swirl to rejoin the flock, and then, with a rush of wings, everyone sweeps off to roost in the cedars. For several long seconds the sun sparkles silver on the river like shards of glass. Ashen clouds running across the sky turn to gold and the sun slips away.

❧ *20 September* ❧

AFTER NEARLY TWO DAYS OF unrelenting rainfall, the river jumps its banks this morning, hauling logs and limbs—and a basket-ball—on the current. The sluice of water runs nearly a hundred feet wide at the west bend. The water-meadow's white willow matriarch becomes an island, lower branches drowned in the deluge.

As we sit at the west end where the water has surged to the base of the Wood's End sign, Beau and his mate sweep down on the flood. They first struggle to shore on the far side. Beau dives twenty feet up from the fence crossing, emerges on an island that has lately been high ground. They've no doubt been here before and will make their way back to the den when the water drops. Fingers crossed that their babes have survived.

By midafternoon, well after the storm has passed, the floodwaters still roar, but at least they are back inside their channel. A mighty wind rises up then, with the sound of a passing freight train, and hundreds of downed walnuts pound the roof of Edna's deck. Everything near and far roils; a snapped branch rips on occasion from a maple or a willow. The wind still blusters in the darkness as the waning moon slips behind blackened clouds.

❁ *21 September* ❁

THIS BRIGHT AND BREEZY DAY begins with early morning fog and howling coyotes. We spend the late afternoon in an autumn walkabout, Castor's Landing to Wood's End, making our way down the hilltop road to duck into the forest near The Big Bridge.

At Castor's Landing, the river rolls by in pale brown silt, fifty to sixty feet wide. The volume of water stifles the gurgling of the eastern rapids, though not the caterwauling of the Canada geese amassing on the north side of the bridge. Next spring's ice-out will likely carry off some of the south bank cedars, whose gnarly toes have just now reemerged from the floodwaters. Sunlight glints on the deciduous trees to the west, some of them in crimson, some of them in amber-gold. Crickets trill and pond turtles pop their heads up left and right.

At Black Bass Bend, a white-tailed doe flashes through the grass across the river and disappears. From our vantage point, we see that one of the lower limbs on the lodge willow has sunk deeper into the stream and the fractured branches of a neighbor now skim the surface. At our back, bindweed threads through the terrestrial crayfish area and out front, scattered in the tall grass, red clover, St. John's wort, goldenrod, asters, chicory, and vetch, all careen in the wind.

From around the east bend of the river, a juvenile great blue heron stalks the shoreline. Reaching the drowned rapids, she attempts a crossing. Loose footing on the algae-covered bottom has her shooting her wings out a time or two to catch her balance. In the end, she gives up and flies off downstream.

Making our way to The Dam Rapids, we surprise a couple of white-tailed does savoring fallen apples just this side of The Gully Bridge. With whistles and snorts, they charge down the hill and splash across the river as we move into the stillness of Harold's Tea Deck.

But for the ground cover at the tea deck and glimpses of the river-bank and water-meadow, the cedar woods stay much the same from one season to the next. A few robins have begun their late afternoon chorus. Up from the river and down again, dragonflies and damselflies dart about like shimmering gems, as they have for some 250 million years.

Over at The Willow Deck, New England asters now reach over six feet high, Joe-Pye weed tall and straight, with dark shriveled leaves and fluffy beige seedheads like fuzzy umbrellas. Buzzing insects, mewing catbirds, and chattering kingfishers abound along with crickets, cicadas, and cabbage butterflies, monarchs, and painted ladies. Scarlet Virginia creeper has wound up against the small purple berries of frost grape. Hawthorns stand bare of their lemony yellow leaves and milkweeds have turned bisque. Clouds of white asters now stretch halfway to the river, surrounded by drifts of buff-colored grasses, and pods of geese sweep toward the intermittent prattling at The Big Bridge, where any sudden silence precedes a swoosh of wings. The air thickens with the scent of forest floor, musty leaves, overripe apples, nightfall, willows, and wet earth.

Back at Russell's Cottage, as the light changes and shadows deepen, a haphazard flock of blackbirds dances in from the west. Shooting into a dead elm across the river, they whip out again to swirl with undulating dark shapes, tendrils circling north and south, folding back on themselves and sailing into the eastern woods.

Each flock has its allotted time upon the stage:

"And now, direct form Apple Valley, give it up for the Dirty Dozens, performing 'Fly Me to the Moon.'"

And a flock of a hundred starlings punches in from the top of the trees on the hill above Harold's Tea Deck. Exploding in unison like fire-works, they reverse course. Ninety degrees down to the river, wingtip to wingtip, beak to tail. A hundred mini jets flying in formation. To the right. To the left. Left wing up. Left wing down.

What a night! What a show!

❈ *22 September* ❈

AN ALL-NIGHT RAIN USHERS IN A DARK and dreary overcast by morning. The river eats into the water-meadow once again. This day, the fall equinox, marks the end of astronomical summer, equinox dates varying from September 21 to September 24. Autumn will be with us now until December's winter solstice, the hours of natural light shrinking day by day.

Mist curls off the river like wraiths of campfire smoke, softening the woods near and far. Throughout the day, a watery sun is dulled by gray-velvet cloud cover. Only the amazement of saffron yellow in the bank of sunflowers at the top of the meadow's north hill could dispel the gloom.

❈ *25 September* ❈

THIS, THE OPENING DAY OF OCTOBERFEST, breaks out in chilled sunshine and azure-blue skies. An apt reflection of September's birthstone, the sapphire.

A variant of the mineral corundum—ruby is the red variety—sapphire consists of aluminum oxide with traces of iron, titanium, chromium, vanadium, or magnesium. We think of sapphires as being blue, but they actually come in many colors. "Fancy" sapphires can be yellow, purple, orange, or green. "Parti" sapphires have two or more different hues in one stone. The sixth hardest mineral known, sapphires have many non-decorative uses. In infrared optics, in watch crystals, and in electronics.

The word "sapphire" comes from the French *saphir*, from Latin *sapphirus*/Greek *sappheiros*—both of which mean "blue." Both also go back to the ancient Hebrew word *sappir*. Some etymologists go even further, believing *sappir* to be derived from the Sanskrit word *sanipriya*, *sani* referring to the god Saturn, *priyah* meaning "dear," hence, "sacred to Saturn."

Sapphires have long correlated with royalty, nobility, and the soul. To ancient Greek and Roman elites, blue sapphires provided protection from physical harm and envy. For clerics in the Middle Ages, they symbolized heaven. The Persians considered the earth to be nestled in a colossal sapphire that made the sky blue.

Gemstones have three chief attributes—hue or color, saturation or brightness, and tone or shade (light to dark). Blue sapphires, the most common and the most popular sapphire, can occur in primary blue or mixed with secondary colors, predominantly violet and green. And while they may exhibit tonal levels of lightness and darkness and vary by degree of vividness, all are valued based on the purity and saturation of their color blue, which results from a complicated transfer of electrons between titanium and iron ions.

Famous sapphires include the Rockefeller Sapphire, a 62.2 carat rectangular stone found in Myanmar and acquired by John D. Rockefeller from an East Indian maharaja in 1934. Recut and reset over many years, the Rockefeller Sapphire, first a brooch, was later fixed in a ring bracketed with diamonds.

One of the best-known sapphires, Princess Diana's engagement ring, a twelve-carat Ceylon sapphire surrounded by a diamond halo, became Kate Middleton's on her own engagement to Diana's son, Prince William.

Two of the largest gem-quality blue sapphires in the world are the Logan Sapphire (423 carats/84.6 grams) now in the National Museum of Natural History in Washington, DC, and the Siren of Serendip

(422.6 carats), a Sri Lankan sapphire in the Houston Museum of Natural History.

Unique star sapphires display a phenomenon we call asterism—also fitting for aster-rich September—in which intersecting needle-like inclusions following the underlying crystal structure of a stone produce a six-rayed star pattern when viewed under a single overhead light. The Sri Lankan Star of Adam is the largest known star sapphire, followed by the Black Star of Queensland and the Sri Lankan Star of India. At present, the sapphire world-record per-carat price rests with a Kashmir sapphire set in a ring which sold in 2015 for US$6.74 million, or US$242,000 per carat.

So, today, under a brilliant sapphire-blue sky, we plant a hundred tulip bulbs, parceled out among the wooden barrel planters at both cottages. We've been here before, losing most to hungry rodents. Still, it's best to stay positive.

At Black Bass Bend, in the early evening, several cedar trees flung over the water cling to the bank with a tenuous foothold. A willow to the left, around the bend, does the same. Beaver have burrowed there, accumulating a jumble of lodge poles, leaving their scrappy footprints in the mud. Two does emerge from the grasses and forest across the river and amble through the rapids.

In sundown's stillness, a deep rose-pink is mirrored on the surface of the water, trees rising through a dusky mist. An owl hoots and two raccoons make their way down a steep bank across the river. And then two more. The foursome paddle across. The first, a parent, doubles back to check on the kits and then idles midstream until they are all safely onshore. A fifth, perhaps the second parent, then pops out of the south shore grasses, swims across to join the others, and the family vanishes, as a racket of geese cross a corner of the sky upriver.

When the sky fades to deep purple, reflecting blue-black on the river, we make our way back to Edna's Cottage, as a three-quarter waning gibbous moon slips out above the eastern tree line.

❈ 28 September ❈

THROUGH THIS PERFECT BLUE-SKY DAY, autumn forges ahead. Painted leaves rain down at Russell's, the cries of blue jays, cardinals, chickadees, crows, and blackbirds reverberating in the crisp cold air.

At dusk, we settle in again at Castor's Landing. Striders and sunlight glint on the water's surface, gossamer spider webs string up everywhere, their lines wafting like wisps of down. A great blue heron lifts off from the vicinity of the beaver lodge, which had been heavily reworked after the month's recent flooding. In tandem, Beau glides to the far bank, lumbers out and up, and begins to rummage in the foliage. Losing his footing, he slides back to the shoreline, returns to the water, and disappears. We make out his mate idling midstream, on the lookout for Beau, much as she'd done in the spring. Three kits cruise into the upper shallows (a huge relief to know they had survived the recent flood). They make their way downriver, paddling directly in front of us.

After a time, as stealthily as we can and against a raucous outpouring of sloshes, splashes, and splatters, we head for Black Bass Bend in near darkness. Have deer crossed over at The Dam Rapids? Have a family of raccoons opened their nightly fishing along the water's edge?

Instead, we find the beaver family harvesting branch after branch from a fallen willow tree. As they work, dropping limbs into the river for transport to the den, they "talk" to one another, a high-pitched *cheechee* sound we've never heard before. The Ojibwe call the beaver Amik, Little Talking Brother, for this very reason. What a treat!

❃ *30 September* ❃

THIS CLOSING DAY OF SEPTEMBER breaks with the smoky silver of an overcast and wintry sky. A cold, cold rain falls through even colder winds, and the ground turns white with hailstones around noon. Cardinal babes hunker down, fluffed out at the west bird feeder to keep warm. Things dead and dying lie on the water-meadow among splashes of color. Little is left of summer now but that bank of brilliant yellow sunflowers blazing on the hilltop.

*"... crisp, misty, golden October, when the light
is sweet and heavy."*
— Angela Carter

❀ *1 October* ❀

OCTOBER TAKES ITS NAME FROM LATIN *octo* meaning
"eight," as before the insertion of January and February into Rome's Julian
calendar, October was the eighth month. This particularly bright-blue
sunshiny October day opens for us with a light frost. Blackbirds head out
for the day around seven, just as two eight-point bucks in the company
of a single doe come out to browse the long grass across the river. Their
winter coats, more gray than russet red, are already taking hold.

The ever-shrinking day closes with an extraordinary twenty-minute
murmuration either side of seven o'clock. Across a bleached-denim
sky streaked with strips of pink-pearl cloud, the birds stream in from
all directions, silent but for the multitude of collective wing beats like
a string of explosive sighs. Sheets of birds, long and wide, pass over the
water-meadow. Thin black lines traveled east to west and west to east,
bouncing through the air and crisscrossing from opposite directions.
One enormous clutch dips in front of us in unison as if to empty a plat-
ter of spare birds and then rights itself against a Full Harvest Moon that
peers over the gully hill. Audible against the distant chatter of the roost,
a great horned owl calls. All is quiet by seven thirty.

In the deep cold of midnight, we catch the full moon a second time.
It beams from a clear sky, high above Russell's Cottage, a phalanx of

geese silhouetted in front. From the white curve of the river in the west to the knobby sunflowers at Russell's, sharp and inky in the moonlight, a thousand shades of gray layers the water-meadow in charcoal and muted silver, ash and dove, dusty heather, slate, smoke, and raven's wing.

❧ *5 October* ❧

SEVERAL DAYS AGO NOW, morning unfolded with another cold overcast of low, gray, winter-like clouds—a warning of things to come. But since then, blue skies and sunshine have prevailed, the echo of summer days gone by. We call these unseasonably warm, quiet, hazy, cloudless days, with cold nights after the first frost, Indian summer. Often falling more than once from mid-September to mid-October—and sometimes into November—Indian summer can last from a few days to a week. Some years we have no Indian summer at all.

When the Northern Hemisphere was inhabited primarily by Indigenous tribes, Indian summer may have referred to their prime hunting and harvesting season. With the term presently related to pejoratives like Indian giver, other designations like false summer or second summer are obviously more appropriate.

Similar phenomena exist in large parts of Europe, from Germany's *altweibersommer* (old women's summer), to poor man's summer, Gaelic Ireland's "little autumn of the geese," or Turkey's *pastirma*—pastrami summer. (November is the prime time for making the meat from which pastrami originated.) Temperate South America recognizes the period as *veranito* (little summer) or *veranico de Maio*, May's little summer.

Yesterday's second summer day, the fourth of October, was also Wild Animal Day.

Enter Rufus, the ruffed grouse.

We've flushed out grouse by accident east to west across Paradise for many years, from the margins of the water-meadow to The Gully seep and the cabin ruins. Two of them materialize this morning outside Edna's. Presumed to be a male reclaiming his spring territory of six to ten woodland acres, Rufus successfully expels his competitor and then "speaks" with Dan for several hours with soft guttural cooing. He even accompanies him to Harold's Tea Deck and back, kept in line with the occasional swipe of a broom. He flutters to within one or two feet of us, supervising the assembly of a couple of new Muskoka chairs for Edna's deck.

And what a beauty he is! Splendid, feathered patterns in black, white, gray, and russet on his back, wings, belly, and fan-shaped tail, short rounded powerful wings, a triangular crest on his head. With a chunky yet slimmer and smaller body than most other grouse, Rufus sports the rich russet-brown color of his species brown morph. The other morph is gray.

Brown morphs have tails of the same pattern as the grays, mottled for camouflage with fine barring and a broad black band near the tip. But with a background of uniformly auburn plumage, on which dark intricately detailed bars and spots are arranged, brown morphs present with a more conspicuous tail. Male ruffed grouse generally have unbroken tail bands with several white dots on rump feathers. Females have a single spot, though otherwise males and females are difficult to distinguish.

The name "ruffed grouse" comes from the long glossy black- or dark chocolate brown-colored ruff of feathers on the sides of the neck, most prominent in the male. When defending territory or displaying for a hen, these neck feathers expand to a spectacular ruffle. In concert with a fully fanned tail, this makes the bird appear twice its normal size, as Rufus has demonstrated to us several times.

Non-migratory, one of ten species of grouse native to North America, and one of the smaller birds in the group, ruffed grouse breed from Labrador to Alaska and south to northern Georgia and Alabama. They thrive best in areas where snow covers the ground from late November to late March, burrowing in drifts for warmth. Isolated pockets of birds survive in the Black Hills of South Dakota and on the western slopes of the Cascades.

In New England and in much of eastern North America, they are sometimes erroneously called pheasant, partridge, or prairie chicken, and are quite elusive. At least fifty-eight tail color variants are recognized in the Upper Midwest, broken down into four general groupings: red, brown, silver-gray, and intermediate-gray.

The ruffed grouse (*Bonasa umbellus*), nicknamed "thunder chicken"—I love that—is the sole species in the genus *Bonasa*, in the family *Phasianidae*. The name is believed to come from Latin *bonus*, meaning "good," in combination with Latin *assum* meaning "roasted," resulting in nothing less than a good roasted bird. *Umbellus* derives from the Latin word for "parasol"—*umbella*—in reference to the bird's neck ruff.

Like most grouse, ruffed grouse spend most of their time in thick brush, foraging for dormant flower buds, leaves, insects, seeds, berries, or the catkins of birches, cherry trees, or aspens. They may emerge at times to dust their feathers on open dirt roads to get rid of pesky parasites. When surprised, they explode into flight on whirring wings. Males, solitary animals, bond with neither hens nor chicks, and spend their adult lives defending a patch of ground shared with one or two females.

A male ruffed grouse marks his territory by drumming, usually standing on a log, a stone, or a mound of dirt. A staging area is called a drumming log. This is one of the great joys of Rufus's company. He's thumped again and again—from the shed roof-top, from Edna's deck, and from the north hill stairs.

The sound is made by rapidly beating wings against the air. This creates a vacuum, as lightning does in producing thunder. The low-frequency sound, which begins slowly and rises to higher and higher speeds can be heard up to a quarter of a mile away.

Ruffed grouse drum throughout the year, longer and more often in the spring when cocks announce their locations to hens. A courtship and mating of just a few moments, filled with struts and hisses, with fanned crests, ruffs, and tails, ends with the male's complete desertion of the hen and subsequent chicks.

Here in Southern Ontario, ruffed grouse numbers have declined by 52 percent in the past few years as regrowth forests mature, depleting their food supplies, and eliminating their brushy understory shelters. Global warming has also produced deadly heat waves in the spring. These have increasingly put grouse nestlings at risk, along with many other wild youngsters. Heavy summer rains also threaten nest sites in scooped out pockets in leaf litter at the foot of trees, stumps, or clumps of bushes.

Brown morphs have always prevailed in warmer, more humid conditions, gray birds in areas with more severe winters. This makes Rufus—a brown morph in a deep Canadian winter—something of an anomaly. A canary in the coal mine; one more harbinger of climate change.

But for now, we can still revel in both his exquisite beauty and the great gift of his wild drumbeat.

❈ *8 October* ❈

AFTER SEVERAL MORE SPARKLING blue days and freezing nights, we've had a soft gentle rain since early this morning. Once again, Dad's journals through the 1970s, '80s, and '90s often speak of early October "rain mixed with snow flurries," "sleet flying at times," and "sheets of swirling snow." And—once again—we're grateful.

Despite the falling gray skies, we pick apples, bake a pie in the woodstove, and make applesauce. We even manage a walk to Black Bass Bend in an early afternoon drizzle. Rufus follows us down and back. Dan goes inside Edna's first. I follow. And with Rufus ready to join us, I have to shut the door in his face.

❋ *10 October* ❋

AT THE BASE OF THE NORTH HILL this morning, Rufus once again successfully challenges another interloper. Quite the standoff. A blur of battering wings, long nails raking on feathery four-toed feet. After supper, we carve his heroic likeness into one of our Halloween pumpkins.

It's so fully fall across Paradise now. Maples are crimson, tangerine, or gold, drifted leaves dancing in the still air or splayed at the base of trees. The brushy edges of the cedar forests stand as fiery remnants in red and rust and smoky amber. Grasses across the water-meadow and up and down the riverbanks wave dried wisps of bronze and cream, of russet, umber, taupe, and tan. All the varied hues of October's birth flowers—the marigold and the cosmos.

We know several groups of plants as marigolds, in the family *Asteraceae*. These include the pot marigold (*Calendula officinalis*), native to the Americas. Some species are now spread around the world. Marigolds are indigenous from the southwestern United States into South America.

The genus *Calendula* derives from the Latin word *calendae*, meaning "little calendar." *Officinalis* comes from *officina*, the traditional storeroom in an apothecary shop where the herbal medicinal plant was kept in Roman times.

Marigolds have finely cut leaves and showy, strongly perfumed composite flower heads, in gold, yellow, orange, or red, growing singly on the stem or in clusters. Among the most common cultivated varieties of those in the genus *Tagētes* are the Aztec or Mexican marigold, the African marigold, and the French marigold. With the pungent, musky scent of its foliage, marigolds, as borders, discourage common garden pests when planted near tomatoes, eggplants, chili peppers, tobacco, potatoes, and other vegetables.

The Latin word *tagētes* derives from the Etruscan prophet Tages, who legendarily sprang from the plowing of the earth. This likely speaks to the ease with which plants of this genus grow year to year, either from seed or from shoots already in place.

"Marigold" refers to "Mary's gold." Early Christians had a tradition of placing flowers on altars to the Virgin Mary. Much like the lily in Europe, this "flower of the dead" in pre-Hispanic Mexico still features in Day of the Dead celebrations in the New World.

The cosmos, a hardy herbaceous perennial or annual plant also in the *Asteraceae* family, blooms with a conspicuous cup-shaped ring of eight broad petals, each with three wavy teeth. A mass of yellow tubular florets comprises the center of the flower. The most common variety, *Cosmos bipinnatus,* known as garden cosmos or Mexican aster, though native to Mexico and parts of Central America, has been naturalized in the eastern United States and Canada. Garden cosmos blooms in colors ranging from pink, orange, purple, and red to lemon yellow, white, and maroon.

Spanish priests, who grew marigolds in their gardens, were so smitten with the elegant, organized layout of cosmos petals that they named the flower from the Greek word *kosmos,* reflecting the harmony of the universe.

Bipinnatus, meaning "twice pinnate," refers to the leaves being arranged on either side of a stem, usually in pairs opposite each other.

Neither the marigold nor the cosmos grow in Paradise. But their aura and their hue have infused the land with the spirit of autumn.

❉ *12 October* ❉

ON THIS BRIGHT AND CRISP AUTUMN DAY, we celebrate Canadian Thanksgiving. Officially recognized as the culmination of the harvest season since 1879, the day was codified as the second Monday in October in 1957.

Some historians credit Sir Martin Frobisher, English seaman and privateer, with the first North American Thanksgiving celebration, dating back to his 1579 voyage in search of the Northwest Passage. Others look to Samuel de Champlain's 1606 Order of Good Cheer, at Port Royal (now in Nova Scotia) in which French settlers shared a harvest feast with First Nations tribes. The Spanish dispute both claims, pointing to similar services in Spanish North America in the mid-16th century. Loyalist refugees to Canada from the 18th-century American Revolution quite likely brought with them Thanksgiving foods like turkey, pumpkin pie, and squash.

Our twenty-pound bird goes in the oven this morning at seven o'clock, quickly browns, and is covered with aluminum foil. Yukon gold potatoes, green beans, and Mom's dressing are heated on the stovetop at ten thirty. Butternut squash—cooked yesterday—goes in the oven an hour later. We sit down to eat at two o'clock. Apple pie with vanilla ice cream for dessert. Mom's spirit is definitely in the house!

By early evening, we trek off to Black Bass Bend. Two flocks of geese fly upriver in V-formation, a third in a long and loose line of disparate honking. After they've gone, a young doe picks her way across the rapids above the beaver lodge. She shakes herself off under a willow tree and wanders off downriver, where she browses the grasses before melting into the forest. A few minutes later, she peers out from behind a clump of cedars not fifteen feet from where we sit, before bounding back to the river and escaping to the other side.

Before bed, we prep the seeds from our three carved pumpkins and roast them in the oven. Tossed in salt, garlic, and a pinch of paprika, they're delicious.

❈ *13 October* ❈

ON THIS GLOOMY DAY, THE SUN wrestles its way out of over-cast skies for a brief moment that leaves wind rustling in the treetops.

Mist had covered the fields earlier, ushering in a sprinkle of rain. Mid-morning, we troop down to harvest another load of ripened fruit from the largest of the apple trees on the water-meadow. With so much of the crop out of reach, we beat them down with a dead hawthorn branch, leaving many on the ground for the deer.

We spend several pleasant hours afterward at Russell's, bundled up against the cold. Down on the river, a female mallard and ducklings paddle about by the old white willow while a pack of crows once again harasses a great horned owl. Several chickadees keep us entertained, hanging upside down eating thistle seeds.

These days, leaves brighten and color almost overnight. Red, maroon, gold, lemon yellow, apricot, crimson, ruby, and orange. Flaming and fluttering everywhere, they sometimes fall like rain. The Norway maples have developed their tar spots like broad black chicken pocks. Many trees have lost their foliage altogether and stand gray and twiggy on the fringes of the cedar forests. A hard frost early this morning froze some leaves to the deck and tabletops.

How absolutely autumn has fallen. Wild asters, sunflowers, and goldenrod have all gone to seed. No ants. No grazing cattle. No butterflies. No "harvest men," those gangling daddy long-legs so ubiquitous just days ago. Milkweed pods have burst. Their feathery parachutes drift through the muskiness of moldering leaves and overripe apples. There's occasional thumping from the east woods, and just a few days ago, he perched between us down at Black Bass Bend. But now Rufus, that singular flamboyance of autumn, has all but vanished.

❈ *14 October* ❈

ON THIS DAY IN 1972, according to Dad's journals, Paradise experienced "a heavy snow squall during the night." This morning, by contrast, a pale overcast brings us intermittent rain, and hefty winds strip more leaves from the trees. After the recent temporary reprieve of a second summer, we've been warned again that winter is imminent.

Meadow grasses have browned to russet and umber. Corn stumps in farm fields have gone crispy. And though many migratory birds have left, down at Black Bass Bend, as we peel apples, a long-legged great blue heron glides downriver and a chattering kingfisher executes several spectacular nose-dives.

Once again, the colors of the season mirror the gems of the month—opal and tourmaline. Opal, a form of silica deposited at relatively low temperatures, manifests in fissures of almost any kind of rock, most commonly sandstone, marl, basalt, rhyolite, and limonite. Being amorphous, that is without the crystal lattice of an ordered atomic structure, opals fall into the category of mineraloids. The crystalline forms of silica rank as minerals. Opal can be transparent, translucent, or opaque, depending on how stones developed. Black opals are the rarest. White, gray, or green are the most common.

Opals come in two broad groupings: precious and common. As a stone is turned in white light, precious opal displays flashes of color called iridescence. Silica spheres produce these internal hues by diffracting the light that passes through the microstructure of the stone. The regularity of the sizes of these spheres and their arrangement determines the quality of the stone. Gemologists call this phenomenon "play of color."

Natural opal refers to polished stones of precious opal. Precious opals too fragile to produce a natural opal can be combined with other minerals to form composite opals. Precious opal is restricted for use in jewelry by its sensitivity to heat, a subtlety caused primarily by its high water content. It also scratches easily.

We use the term opalescence to describe the milky, hazy sheen of common opal, which does not show any play of color. Common opals include milk opal, a milky bluish-to-greenish stone, which can occasionally be of gemstone quality; resin opal, with a honey-colored resinous sheen; wood opal, formed by the replacement of organic material in wood with opal; gray or brown menilite; hyalite, a colorless, transparent opal also called Muller's glass; and geyserite or siliceous sinter, a form of opal deposited around hot springs or geysers.

Fire opal, also in the common opal category, displays bright green flashes. Mexican fire opal comes from the state of Querétaro in Mexico, which is the most famous source. Opaque blue-green Peruvian opal, often called blue opal, also belongs in this classification. Blue opal can also be found in Oregon, Idaho, and Nevada.

In antiquity, when opal was prized as being extremely rare, the only known European source lay beyond the frontiers of the Roman Empire in Slovakia. One of the primary present-day suppliers of opal is Ethiopia. North Africa reportedly manufactured opal for tools as early as 4000 BCE. The first gem quality opal came from North Shewa Province in 1994.

Australia is today's other chief producer. Miners unearthed a vast deposit in the 19th century near the town of Coobere Pedy in South Australia. The world's largest and most valuable gem opal, the Olympic Australis, weighed in at 7.5 pounds. It came from the Eight Mile opal field in Coobere Pedy in 1956.

In the Middle Ages, Europeans believed that opal, holding all the qualities of the gemstones represented in its color spectrum, brought good fortune. In 1829, Sir Walter Scott published a novel—*Anne of Geierstein*—in which a baroness died shortly after a drop of holy water turned her powerful opal talisman colorless. Thereafter, people began to associate opals with bad luck, even with death. Within a year, the sale of opals in Europe dropped by 50 percent and remained low for over twenty years.

Adapted from the Latin *opalus*, which first appeared in Roman references around 250 BCE, the word "opal" probably originated with the Sanskrit work *úpala*, meaning "jewel." The Greek derivative *opállios* means "to see a change in color."

Famous opals, besides the Olympic Australis, include the Andamooka Opal or Queen's Opal, presented to Queen Elizabeth II; the first named opal, the Burning of Troy Opal, a now lost gem given to the Empress Josephine by Napoleon I; the Halley's Comet Opal, the world's largest uncut black opal; the Galaxy Opal, listed as the world's largest polished opal in the 1992 *Guinness Book of World Records*; the Sea of Opal, the largest known black opal; the Fire of Australia, the "finest uncut opal in existence"; and, my favorite, Beverly the Bug, the first known example of an opal with an insect inclusion.

Tourmaline, a usually clear crystalline silicate mineral in which boron binds with various elements from aluminum to sodium and potassium, can be found in most colors of the spectrum. Black is the most common. The presence of iron produces black to bluish-black to deep brown tourmaline. Magnesium results in brown to yellow stones. Lithium forms gems of almost any hue from rich reds to emerald greens, intense blues, and brilliant yellows. Tourmaline stones may also be bicolored, tri-colored, and—rarely—electric blue and neon green. Pink tourmaline results from prolonged exposure to natural irradiation.

The name "tourmaline" comes to us from *tōramalli*, which in the Sri Lankan language Sinhalese means "mixed gem." Not recognized as a distinct mineral until the 1800s, tourmaline stones previously had been identified as rubies, emeralds, sapphires, or other esteemed gems. In the mid-20th century, finds in Madagascar and Afghanistan supplanted the famed California tourmaline mines of the previous century.

As a mineral group, tourmaline stands as one of the most complicated silicate minerals. It has three basic varieties: schorl, dravite, and elbaite.

Schorl, the most common form, brownish-black to black, lies at the sodium/iron end of the stone's spectrum. This comprises 95 percent of all natural tourmaline. The name "schorl," in use prior to 1400 CE, takes its name from the village of Schorl in Saxony, Germany, now known as Zschorlau. Black schorl tourmaline had been uncovered in a nearby tin mine. Until the 19th century, both schorl and iron tourmaline referred to this mineral.

Dravite or brown tourmaline, the sodium/magnesium member of the group, is named after the Davra River in Austria and Slovenia, where this tourmaline was first found in 1884.

Elbaite—lithium tourmaline—is named for the island of Elba in Italy, one of the first places to analyze lithium tourmalines. Most gem-quality tourmalines are elbaites.

Highly regarded in jewelry making, tourmaline is often faceted to create sparkle. Some forms change color when viewed from varied directions. Others have magnetic properties. Red and pink have the lowest magnetic susceptibility, bright-yellow, green, and blue elbaites, the highest.

Today's opal sky passes overhead with no play of color. Remnant crimson and caramel still flutter in the treetops and all across the landscape—bottomland and beyond—schorl tourmaline's charcoals, ochres, and umbers tinge grasses that will all too soon give way to the shadowy blues and stark blacks and whites of winter.

❄ *16 October* ❄

EARLY MORNING'S SOLID, ASH-BOTTOMED overcast holds the heaviness of winter. Someone mentioned wet snow by the weekend. A cold, gentle rain springs up at dawn, clearing to sunny skies by early afternoon. The day then closes on us with layers of sunlit cloud in bright neon pink mirrored on the face of the river, still running high from recent rains. As farmers chop down their dried cornstalks, the drone of farm machinery rumbles in the distance. Some will spray the mulch back onto the fields. Some will collect the grindings into huge bins that lumber alongside the cutters.

Down from Castor's Landing, with mud trails to the river, the beaver have finalized extensive renovations to their lodge. Stacked twigs and small branches sprawl atop a base replastered to fend off coming snowfalls. Hundreds of geese stream south in haphazard V's. Fading purple patches of New England asters fleck the meadow. At the edges of the cedar woods, deciduous trees shed more foliage every day, while the surrounding fields have been ploughed to a deep rich umber fringed with the gold of elms and aspens, brilliant reds in sumac and maple.

An Iroquois legend tells of ancient hunters who killed the Great Bear (Ursa Major). The great beast's blood dropped crimson on maples, sumac, dogwoods, and sassafras. The cooked flesh and fat turned the leaves of aspen, elm, willow, birch, beech, and hickory to bisque, amber, and gold.

The reds of autumn actually arise from trapped sugars in leaves exposed to the near-freezing temperatures of fall. Yellow/orange pigments, present year-round in most trees, are concealed in summer by the green pigment chlorophyll. These carotenoids and xanthophylls emerge when the decreasing sunlight of autumn causes chlorophyll to break down.

But more simply said by Henry David Thoreau in an 1842 letter written to his friend Ralph Waldo Emerson, "Every blade in the field, every leaf in the forest lays down its life in its season as beautifully as it was taken up."

❋ *20 October* ❋

THIS BRIGHT AND BREEZY DAY holds off another threat of snow but feels too cold to spend much time outdoors. The river reaches almost to the top of the line fence and migratory robins still chirp across the meadow and back among the cedar trees. What can they be thinking?

In this month of transition, we pass an hour or so outside Russell's, watching the last bits of summer fade away. The most energetic participants of the day, our Aidas and our Pavarottis, engineer a confrontation at the westside bird feeder after lunch. One intrepid red takes on a black interloper twice his size. (All over the world, red squirrels are losing ground to blacks and grays, which carry a deadly virus.) Scrambling up a spruce tree in pursuit of his adversary, Pavarotti successfully evicts the rival, nipping at the rodent's back legs and tail. A conquering hero for another season.

After midnight, we wrap up in woolen blankets and fur-lined parkas and brave the icy air for the Orionid meteor shower.

Just above Sirius (the brightest star in the night sky), the Orionids' radiant lies in the constellation Orion, especially in the club area. They constitute one of two showers caused annually by Halley's Comet's return to the earth's inner atmosphere. The other is May's Eta Aquarids. The sun vaporizes parts of the comet's ice covering, causing fragments to break away. These particles continue on the comet's 148,000 mph trajectory and appear as the glowing trails of incandescence we call meteors or falling stars. The Orionids excel among meteor showers for their beauty, brightness, and speed, especially in the hour before dawn. Halley's Comet, named after astronomer Edmund Halley, only makes a showing every seventy-five years. This celestial marvel passed through the inner Solar System in 1986 and will reappear in 2061.

This year the entire Orionid display will stretch from October 2 to November 7. In mid-October, with optimal conditions, it could top out at ten to twenty meteors an hour. The Orionids are visible all around the world over a large portion of the sky from late evening onward. Some years have seen from fifty to seventy shooting stars an hour.

The night's waxing crescent moon sets before Orion rises in the east, which eliminates any light competition. Keeping away from street-lights (of which we have none) and finding a location with an open sky (more of a challenge) are key. With a viewing line to the southeast between two poplars, we position our Mazda in the hilltop parking area, lie on our backs on the hood, and wait a half hour for our eyes to adapt to the darkness.

A fringe of cloud dusts the horizon. Otherwise, the sky is clear and pinpricked with a sprinkling of stars. In two frigid hours, we clock twenty extraterrestrial beauties. The first, a large yellow fireball, burns across the sky with a streaking tail about a foot long. The last, shorter but directly overhead, dazzles with a tail that glitters like falling stardust. In between, scratches and flecks and scrawls flash in nearly every quarter of the sky.

A remarkable performance.

❈ *25 October* ❈

ALMOST EVERYTHING HAS TURNED brown and bleak as we slip from late fall into early winter. An all-day splatter of cold rain that fell from blank skies keeps the river rising and rising and rising.

❈ *31 October* ❈

ALL HALLOWS EVE, ACCOMPANIED by the full Hunter's Moon. A Blue Moon as well, this being the second full moon of the month. The next Blue Moon to fall on Halloween will be in the year 2039. Best to appreciate it tonight.

Seen from the top of the north hill, the moon, in burgundy and old gold, sits on the eastern horizon looking out on fields shaved bare of crops or ploughed up to dark chocolate-brown for winter. Within the hour, down below, the same light, now gleaming brassy white, slips out from behind The Gully trees, gilding the river and the water-meadow in dusty bronze.

Also called the Full Travel Moon, the Full Dying Grass Moon, and sometimes the Full Blood or Sanguine Moon—not to be confused with the Blood Moon of a total lunar eclipse—the Full Hunter's Moon takes its name from a combination of Anglo-Saxon, Germanic, and Native American sources. By autumn moonlight, Indigenous hunters could track and kill prey that would help sustain them through the winter: rabbit, red fox for pelts, or summer-fattened white-tailed deer.

The Full Harvest Moon and the Full Hunter's moon both rise thirty minutes later each successive night. Other full moons have a fifty-minute interval. This leaves sunset and moonrise in close proximity, a prolonged period of natural light that allowed farmers to complete the harvest and hunters to more easily spot the game animals that glean the fields. In pre-industrial times, the Full Hunter's Moon held a place of high honor as an important feast day throughout the Northern Hemisphere.

The post-harvest European celebration known as Samhain to the Celts—the supposed precursor of Halloween—also took place at this time of year. A Gaelic festival signaling the end of the harvest season and the beginning of winter or the dark half of the year, Samhain opened on the evening of October 31, the Celtic day beginning and ending at sundown. A cross-quarter day midway between the autumn equinox and the winter solstice, Samhain is first mentioned in Irish literature from the 9th century. It is likely much older. These holy days stand as one of the four Gaelic seasonal festivals, the others being Imbolc, Beltane, and Lughnasa.

Samhain, pronounced *SAWwin*—*Sauin* in Manx Gaelic, *Samhainn* or *Samhuinn* in Scottish Gaelic—derives from Old Irish *Samain* or *Samuin*, possibly from the Proto-Indo-European word *semo* meaning "summer," a reference to summer's end, from *sam*—"summer"—and *fuin*—"end." Other scholars trace the origin to the proto-Celtic word *samani* meaning "assembly."

At Samhain, crops had been gathered in, fields lay fallow, and the gates between life and death were flung open. Great gatherings, hilltop purification bonfires, contests, and feasting marked the day. After six months in high summer pastures, cattle were driven down to overwinter in the lowland. Some would be slaughtered. The boundaries and barriers between the physical world and the spirit world weakened or blurred at Samhain. Spirits, fairies, and other supernatural beings—now believed to be the remnants of pagan gods—could pass more easily into the present.

Ancient burial mounds served as similar portals for the souls of the dead. Some Neolithic passage tombs in Ireland—including the Mound of the Hostages on the Hill of Tara and Cairn L at Slieve na Calliagh—align with Samhain sunrise. This attests to the day's profound and archaic importance. Guising also probably played a large part in Samhain festivities, villagers going door-to-door costumed as animals or shape-shifting monsters like the Pukah, a supernatural being who received harvest offerings.

By the 1st century CE, Rome had conquered the greater part of Celtic lands and would rule them for over four hundred years. In that time, several Roman festivals appear to have merged with Samhain celebrations. One, Feralia, a late October commemoration of the dead, honored Pomona, the Roman goddess of fruit and trees. Pomona's symbol, the apple, may have been the inspiration for Halloween's apple bobbing tradition.

Evidence suggests that 1st century CE churches in Ireland and Northumbria held a feast on November 1 to commemorate all Christian saints. Over time, All Saints' Day, or All Hallows Day, melded with Samhain (the evening before) becoming All Hallows Eve. In the Middle Ages, turnips carved to ward off evil spirits began to appear on All Hallows Eve.

The actual word "Halloween," or Hallowe'en, dates only to about 1745. The New World did not widely celebrate Halloween until Scottish and Irish immigrants, many fleeing the Irish Potato Famine of the late 1840s, brought the traditions with them. The turnip gave way to the larger and softer native pumpkin, which we've found much easier to work with. By the end of the century, pumpkin carving, recorded as early as 1837 and associated with the harvest in general, had become specific to Halloween.

And so here we are. All Hallows Eve. A time when the darker side of humanity too often triumphed. When collective memories of animal cruelty and witchcraft trials carried the day, expressed so powerfully in the poem, "The Witch," written by Jim Hohenbary.

THE WITCH

The old crone stirs the kettle. Tangled limbs
Crowd the full moon, wild roof
Of shadow and silver; a trembling fever.

Wolves prowl on padded paws, heads low,
For silent prey. She whispers words
Over dry herbs, crushes them in water.

She draws small bones from her bag,
Once blue, and shakes them. More words.
She leaves the drink, thick with dregs,

Against the fever, the fire, for payment;
But none can name her parents. Crows,
Some say, land too much upon her sill.

Is this why, then, you will tie the stone
Around her ankles and drown her?
No. You indict the glassy eye of dying,

Branches that snap in busy shadow,
Howl and reply across the ravine, herbs
Without names, all the new moon hides;

And so, in deep water, eyes to the shore,
You bind her frail wrist and sink the crone
Because the night itself
is untouchable.

Comedian Bob Zany has given us a lighter side of Halloween that we'll stand with today.

"Halloween is a simple metaphor for life. Seize every opportunity to fill up your bag with free stuff."

"Wild November come at last beneath a veil of rain."
— RICHARD HENRY STODDARD

❈ *1 November* ❈

ALL SAINTS DAY (All Hallows Day or All Souls Day) ushers in November, autumn's last rapt breath before winter sets in. November marks the eleventh month in both the Julian and Gregorian calendars. Its name, from the Latin *novem*, meaning "nine," comes from earlier days before January and February were added to the Roman calendar.

This morning, we find ourselves knee-deep in late fall, on a foggy, wet, cold, and dreary day. Grasses everywhere stand brown and brittle, trees bare-limbed but for the stable moss-green of the cedar woods. Across the water-meadow, still dappled with bushes and reeds in red and gold, the river is swollen from rainfall to the north.

How fittingly that topaz, one of the two birthstones of November, reflects autumn's dying daubs of color. One of the hardest natural occurring minerals in the world, the silicate mineral topaz, colorless or with a grayish tint in its natural state, becomes golden-brown to orange-yellow with impurities. Commonly found with igneous rocks, topaz crystalizes in granite pegmatites or in the cavities of rhyolite lava flows like those at Topaz Mountain in western Utah.

In the Middle Ages, the name "topaz" referred to a large assortment of yellow gemstones. Most experts believe "topaz" came down to us from *Topázios*, the Old Greek name for the small island of St. John's in the Red Sea now called Zabargad, once a source of peridot and the yellow olivine called chrysolite. Before the advent of the modern science of mineralogy, these minerals were often confused. Alternatively, the name may be related to the Sanskrit word *tapas*, meaning "heat" or "fire."

In ancient Rome, topaz protected travelers. I like to think that our cottage denizens, some of whom are still in the throes of migration, would have been included.

The less valuable gemstone of November, citrine, a transparent silicon dioxide also known as the light maker, gives off the bright yellow hue of lemon. The French word for lemon—*citron*—gave citrine its name. A variety of quartz, citrine can range from pale yellow to brown. A superstition that citrine brought prosperity led to its alternative names—the merchant's or money stone. Cut citrine and yellow topaz are virtually indistinguishable to the eye, though topaz is considerably harder.

November's flower, the chrysanthemum—from Greek *chrysos* (gold) and *anthemom* (flower)—began to bloom back in mid-September.

We see them everywhere now. From farm stalls and nurseries to grocery store shelves and roadside kiosks.

Perennial, herbaceous plants, mums come in many colors, all flowerheads simple rows of rayed petals with a center of yellow disc florets. We've cultivated chrysanthemums since at least the 5th century BCE. The first Imperial Court Chrysanthemum Show took place in Japan in the year 910 CE. Cultivars came to America in 1798 when Colonel John Stevens imported a variety known as dark purple from England.

The heady aroma of mums ranks right up there with wood smoke, ripened apples, and musty leaves as one of our prime harbingers of late autumn.

And so, as the days in Paradise grow ever shorter, the atmosphere ever more turbulent, fields and forests are suffused with the muskiness of decaying vegetation. Our tenants hoard resources, prepare to endure hardship and privation, or continue to gather for primal migrations to warmer climates.

Yet even under this day's dull sky, the water-meadow and the fallen pastures beyond the river's edge still dazzle with autumnal hints of topaz, citrine, and chrysanthemum.

❈ *3 November* ❈

WIND AND WILD TURKEYS.

Despite heavy, wintery clouds and a smudgy sun, much of this day looks and feels like the onset of spring, though grasses hold only a faint hint of green. Tattered foliage in rust-red, scarlet, orange, and amber still clings to a handful of trees, which for the most part stand shivering bare and gray in an icy breeze.

Earlier, we watched as two great flocks of ring-billed seagulls circled overhead on the hilltop. A phalanx of Canada geese squawked over as we started down the steps.

Over at Black Bass Bend, just after four o'clock, six plump wild-turkey hens wander off into the woods just up from Castor's Landing. Dark beauties all, wary and magnificent, with long necks, long legs, bare heads and chestnut plumage, barred wing feathers and a coppery sheen on rump and tail, the latter tipped with cream.

We leave the warmth of the cottage later on for a frigid 41 degrees Fahrenheit at Black Bass Bend. The river in icy army-green is running high, rippled on the surface by the wind to move upstream against the current. Willows across the water, stripped bare, harbor thin, mixed flocks of black-capped chickadees, northern cardinals, and Canada blue jays.

It's hard not to feel melancholy and intensely mortal at this time of year.

"*Winter is coming.*"

❈ *4 November* ❈

SUNNY AND CALM THIS MORNING, temperatures rise to nearly seventy degrees on Edna's inside porch by early afternoon.

Yesterday, two of our Castor's Landing beaver sliced silent V's through the glassy surface of Black Bass Bend in the late afternoon. They dove soundlessly midstream to enter their lodge.

The full moon of November, which falls late in the month this year, is also known as the Full Beaver Moon. Beaver are especially active with winter lodge preparations and the building or repairing of dams, as we've noticed over the last several days.

Though beaver are predominantly nocturnal, our own clan have been out and about, at work or at play, as early as two o'clock in the afternoon. This very day in 1978, Dad's journals record that he and Mom walked down to the beaver dam around three o'clock. New digs were being raised on the riverbank just around the bend. That would be the current lodge at Castor's Landing. They'd watched the dam's day-to-day construction several years earlier, a structure that washed away in the spring floods of 1982 and was never fully rebuilt.

Beaver do not hibernate. Each autumn, they roof their dens with a layer of mud that ices over with the first heavy frost. Branches and boughs, sprays and sprigs are piled on or near the lodge—usually above water—where an accumulation of winter snow insulates and keeps the food supply from freezing. Beaver are partial to the inner bark of aspen and poplar. But birch, maple, black cherry, oak, beech, and ash will also do, as will cattails and waterlilies. Beaudelaire and family have a strong preference for willows and ostrich ferns.

After the spring thaw, animals may leave the lodge and roam freely until autumn. They return then to gather in a stock of winter food. The offspring of Paradise beaver have moved upstream or down over the years, throwing up new homesteads. We learned just recently that a new dam has been built around the west bend. The primary lodge, the one dating back to 1978, has remained occupied year-round. Paradise would be less by far without our resident beaver.

❊ *7 November* ❊

WONDERFULLY COZY IN HERE at Edna's Cottage, especially with the severe damp chill outside. Chickadees and cardinals have found our thistle and breadcrumbs at the west-side feeder, and a band of Canada blue jays dunk and dip in the bird bath below. One solitary brown cottontail munches on the withered grasses still left around the well, while a pair of red squirrels scold from the top of a bared sugar maple.

In a sprinkle of freezing rain from overcast late-fall skies, we stroll to Black Bass Bend in the gloaming. Beau is swimming branchlets of fallen willow to the lodge for winter storage. The river moves languidly through the gloom, banked by buff-colored grasses. Steeped in a deep spirit of wildness, we shelter in the woods in wintry stillness. Bare-limbed willows and dark cedars clack all around in a stiff, northeastern breeze.

Robert Bly, in his poetry anthology *News of the Universe, Poems of Twofold Consciousness*, speaks of "a consciousness out there so powerful it's dangerous." Author and journalist Richard Louv echoes this notion when he writes in his *The Nature Principle, Reconnecting with Nature in a Digital Age*, "Just beyond the veil of rain, we feel a presence for which we have no name."

The Japanese call this ancient primordial sensibility *yugen*, a profound awareness of the universe that triggers feelings too deep and mysterious for words.

If you've spent any time at all in nature, you may have already sensed *yugen* on an old-world moor at night. In a vast star-filled night sky. In a high-country meadow. On an empty Pacific beach. Or it may have manifested for you as a polar bear on the tundra, a condor in the Peruvian backcountry, a great horned owl in a spruce tree.

"A glimpse of that vivid, poignant, unreclaimed world which hovers on the horizon, broods above lake-water, lurks in the shade of isolated thorn, cries in the wind," writes Margaret Ithell Colquhoun in *The Crying of the Wind: Ireland*.

It doesn't take much for the power of *yugen* to manifest. Listen to the wild whenever you can. It's calling you.

❈ *11 November* ❈

WE WAKE UP THIS MORNING to snow flurries. Snow flurries! The first of the season!

A radiant shower, crisp and crystalline, dissolves much of the cold gray day and leaves behind a pristine freshness. With a light breeze, tiny flakes swirl in the air all day long. Only the water-meadow lies dusted by nightfall.

This day—Remembrance or Poppy Day in Commonwealth member countries, Veterans Day in the United States—evolved out of Armistice Day, first observed on the grounds of Buckingham Palace in the early evening hours of November 10, 1919. World War I had officially ended with the signing of the Treaty of Versailles on June 28, 1919. But "the eleventh hour of the eleventh day of the eleventh month" marks the time in the United Kingdom when the armistice went into effect.

On Remembrance Day, we celebrate the lives of all those in the armed services who made the ultimate sacrifice in the line of duty. Here in Paradise, we choose to remember and be thankful for *all* creatures great and small who have given their lives that we might live.

"The greatest peril of life lies in the fact that human food consists entirely of souls," arctic explorer and anthropologist Knut Rasmussen wrote in his personal journal, quoting Inuk hunter, Ivaluardjuk.

The earth is a dynamic living organism, alive with energy. The life force of the planet flows through and connects all things.

"I am a part of the sun as my eye is a part of me," D. H. Lawrence says in *Apocalypse*, his last written creative work. "That I am part of the earth, my feet know perfectly, and my blood is a part of the sea."

❋ *17 November* ❋

TODAY, EARLY MORNING fog gives way to a blank, white sky that brightens by degrees with an icy wintry sun. Barely a leaf can be seen in the distant fringe of trees. The frosted reeds and grasses on the water-meadow shiver, muted and dull under cold sunshine and a crawl of black-bottomed clouds.

As we finish our breakfast, three does, one with an injured front leg, amble up the bank from below to munch on a scatter of fallen apples by the well. Sleek beauties all, dressed in their gray-brown winter coats.

We keep to the cottage through the greater part of the day. In the early hours of the eighteenth, I straggle up the hill to view the Leonid meteor shower. Blessed with a rare, clear, late-autumn night sky, they prove well worth the climb.

The Leonids, known for spectacular meteor storms, radiate from the constellation Leo, for which they are named. They're associated with the comet Tempel-Tuttle. As the comet's frozen gases evaporate in the heat from the sun, solid particles are thrown off. Showers occur as the earth moves through streams left from previous passages of the comet. A fast-moving tide, the Leonids impact the earth's atmosphere at seventy-two kilometers a second. Annual Leonid showers can deposit twelve or thirteen tons of debris across the entire planet.

On average, the Leonids offer up five to nine meteors per hour. They will peak this year around November 18. Some showers spread out over the days to either side, the specific peak changing every year. Leonid meteor storms—larger outbursts of meteorites—occur about every thirty-three years. These can often exceed a thousand meteors an hour. What an extraordinary gift that would be. Beyond imagination.

We humans have noted this particular meteor shower as far back as 900 CE. The storm of 1833 came with mythic proportions. Data compiled as the storm abated showed more than 240,000 meteors streaked over the affected region of North America east of the Rockies over the nine-hour event. That storm resulted from the earth's direct impact with the dust trail left behind by the passage of Tempel-Tuttle in 1800. Several Native American tribes reacted. The Cheyenne signed a peace treaty and the Lakota Sioux reset their calendar.

The Leonid's passage in 1866 and 1868 saw thousands of meteorites per hour in Europe. The storm in 1998, comprised of larger particles, produced a rain of fireballs; 2001 and 2002 brought three thousand meteors an hour. Can you imagine?

Meteor rates are determined by the impact with previous dust trails. The shower of 2008, for example, one of the higher rates at over 100 per hour, resulted from an encounter with a debris trail deposited in 1466.

"The Leonids they were called," Cormac McCarthy writes in his novel *Blood Meridian*. "God how the stars did fall . . . from their origins in night to their destinies in dust and nothingness."

My own Leonids encounter—predicated on a paltry ten to fifteen flybys per hour—fizzles by comparison. Yet the experience is a haunting one. On a clear cold night, a billion icy lights hang in the firmament just out of reach. Nearer stars glitter like mica on a black-sand/chipped crystal beach. Fourteen brilliant microseconds of profound mystical beauty flash by in just under sixty minutes.

❄ *27 November* ❄

AFTER ADVANCING WITH A PRODIGIOUS northwest wind, a dull drizzle turns to snow flurries in blue predawn light. Tiny flakes swirl well into midmorning. Every leaf has fallen from every branch. A hazy bank of twiggy trees stands shivering in the distance, and the river glimmers with a glazy border of ice. Edna's windowpanes have blossomed with a wonderland of hoarfrost etchings. Feathers and ferns and flowers. Lichen and lace.

A first snowfall blankets the earth with hushed enchantment and peace. After that, at least for me, the novelty quickly fades. If winter must come, let it come. Keep the dampish buildup and the soggy intervals to a minimum.

Just short of two o'clock, we enjoy a second full Thanksgiving dinner, this one on an American schedule. From on (and in) Mom's woodstove, the aromas permeate every cottage nook and recess. A twenty-pound turkey browned and crisped. Fluffed mashed potatoes. Green beans. Baked butternut squash. Bread and onion dressing. Whole cranberries. And deep-dish apple pie.

The celebration of Thanksgiving in the United States has a long and convoluted history. But it all turns on gratitude. Gratitude for a bountiful harvest. Gratitude for the joys, the triumphs, and the gifts of the previous year. Up against the early onset of winter, Canadian Thanksgiving falls on the second Monday in October. But living much of the year in Tucson, Arizona, we also adhere to America's fourth Thursday in November.

Wherever and whenever, to be grateful is good for your health.

❈ *30 November* ❈

FOLLOWING AN ALL-NIGHT RAIN, another crisp morning breaks. And now the Full Frost Moon—the Moon of the Falling Leaves, the Moon of Storms, the Full Beaver Moon—has frosted our world with a silvery arctic chill.

Winter is here.

Part Four

WINTER

"Winter is putting footsteps in the meadow."
— ROMAN PAYNE

"The crisp path through the fields
in this December snow . . ."
— DYLAN THOMAS

❈ *1 December* ❈

WE WAKE UP TO THE BLACK and white of winter this morning, with a film of snow and brisk whiffles of wind.

The first of December marks the start of meteorological winter, the three calendar months with the lowest temperatures. In the Northern Hemisphere, this corresponds to December, January, and February. The coldest average temperatures typically fall in the latter two. Today's morning high of 31 degrees Fahrenheit is plenty cold for my liking.

Until the month-less winter period that followed was divided between January and February, the too-often grim month of December was the tenth month in the Roman calendar. Now the twelfth and last of the year in both the Julian and Gregorian calendars, December originated with the Latin word *decem*, meaning "ten."

I've never been a fan of the season. Arriving in Paradise just before noon, I sit in the car at the top of the hill cursing the weather until, cheered by another twinned swirl of seagulls spiraling overhead, I gather courage and inch my way down the staircase.

Stoked with homemade vegetable soup, we slog down to The Dam Rapids after lunch and sit for a freezing half-hour. The river runs wide and glassy through the frosted air, delicate ice etchings at the margins and scattered bits of snow on the rock-bound rapids. Up from the river's edge, where snow covers the shoreline on either side, runs a sprawl of high russet grasses and reeds. Thickets of twiggy black winter trees back up against a marbled winter sky.

Our frogs, bats, snakes, groundhogs, and more are all in hibernation.

Voles and mice and others have hunkered down under a layer of insulating snow. Rabbits, red squirrels, beaver, and deer all abound, though they're rarely seen. Their footprints often grace the muddy woodland paths.

Chipmunks, nestled in their dens, will sleep a few days to a week and then wake up for a snack. Raccoons do likewise, sheltering during cold snaps but otherwise out and about. On especially cold nights, skunks gather to sleep in communal burrows, plugging the entrance with leaves or grass.

At day's end, we deck out a small Christmas tree on Edna's oak bureau, using garlands, red ribbons, and a handful of old-time ornaments we'd found in the attic last spring while insulating the ceiling—hazelnuts wrapped in tin foil with matching hooks, strands of red and gold bells made from old metallic milk-bottle lids, strings of raw elbow macaroni, silver snowflakes, pipe cleaner Santas, and thin plastic icicles. Instead of our usual space heaters, we light both the fireplace and the woodstove, so that a deep cozy warmth counters the frigid outdoor gloom.

The word "winter" comes from Proto-Germanic *wintru*, possibly connected to the Indo-European root word *wed* meaning "water." (No doubt both a deluge and a blizzard lie in our future.) The winter sun climbs to a lower altitude in the sky than does the summer sun. Sunlight glances off the earth at an oblique angle, dissipating heat and limiting the amount of radiation striking the earth's surface. So now our winter days will grow ever shorter. Darkness will abound and much of life will lie dormant in a harsh and frozen landscape, while death stalks the land.

In the paralleled cycles of nature and life, morning and spring-time bring birth and renewal, evening and winter old age and death. But winter always harbors hope and the possibility of rebirth. Ancient myths have reflected this dichotomy through the ages.

In Greek mythology, for example, when Hades, the god of the Under-world, kidnaps Persephone, Zeus orders her immediate return to her mother Demeter, the goddess of the earth. But Hades dupes Persephone. Zeus then decrees that she will spend six months with her mother and six months with Hades, during which time Demeter, depressed, neglects the earth, leaving us mortals with the bleakness of winter.

And again, Gwyn ap Nudd, the ruler of the Otherworld, steals the Welsh maiden, Creiddylad. Her lover, Gwythr ap Greidawl, fights for her release each May Day, a contest representing the struggle for dom-inance between winter and summer.

In the winter of 2010–2011, La Nina gave us snow cover into May. I want no part of that. No ice on Lake Superior into June, as in the long-ago 1607–1608 season. For me, winter's snowmen, snow angels, ice skating, and tobogganing pale against hypothermia, snow blindness, noroviruses, seasonal depression, black ice, influenza, and wayward icicles.

❄ *8 December* ❄

TWO INCHES OF WET snow blanket the world this morning. Lacy flakes still swirl down when I go out for photographs at eight o'clock. Every treetop, every twig and bough, brightens the gray dawn, and hillocks gleam. *Animals must be about*, I think. And glancing toward Russell's, my eyes meet with a white-tailed doe's. She freezes mid-munch on an apple unearthed from a handful I'd brought down from the hilltop yesterday. The half-eaten fruit drops soundlessly from her mouth. I slip quietly back inside. She has, of course, vanished when I look out the west window.

Falling snow flickers through the bare maples as we fix break-fast. Two cottontails by the outside well nibble errant tufts of brown grass that poke out above the crunch of snow. A red squirrel bounces about in the tree limbs, and a lone coyote trots across the white water-meadow below.

Paradise denizens, as they do everywhere else, confront winter using a variety of strategies. We have no large migrating ruminants like caribou, reindeer, or bison. But some of our birds—orioles, mallards, hummingbirds—make seasonal journeys, as do our ladybugs. Four flocks of Canada geese had squawked over well before daybreak—stragglers awaiting this first firm snowfall. Many of our birds, however, do not migrate. Cardinals, woodpeckers, blue jays, chickadees, and juncos are all chowing down at half a dozen bird feeders.

Our groundhogs, wood frogs, bats, bumblebees, garter snakes, and snails prefer hibernation, a state of reduced metabolic activity during which both body temperature and heart rate are lowered. Snoozing away the season, these animals emerge only when warm weather returns.

Weasels, white-tailed deer, jackrabbits, and snowshoe hares take on winter by changing the color of their fur. Blending with the snow, they become less vulnerable to predators. Aquatic animals, like our beaver, mink, and muskrat, have double-layered coats. The heavy winter pelts of white-tailed deer, coyotes, and raccoons—shed in spring for better cooling—improve heat-retention during a deep Canadian winter.

Taking advantage of insulating properties, deer mice, moles, voles, shrews, and other rodents spend the winter months burrowed under a layer of snow.

With tiny drifting snowflakes still fluttering through early afternoon, we follow the tracks of rabbit, squirrel, red fox, and raccoon down the path and over The Gully Bridge to the river. Beau makes a brief appearance at Black Bass Bend before diving out of sight.

❧ *10 December* ❧

SNOW SQUALLS THROUGHOUT the night swell to an early full-blown blizzard by nine o'clock, when we get up and fix breakfast. Gusts of wind screech at the fireplace chimney. Swirls of stinging snow-pellets lash the treetops and pound on the window casements. Under the torrential onslaught of snow-laden winds, rising snowdrifts shift and ripple like sea-sand.

After raging for half the day, the wind finally subsides. Large congealed snowflakes rain down in a glut of whiteness. This curtain of coalesced haze obliterates all things near and far. Snow piles softly and soundlessly on forest and flats and wraps the air and the earth in a thick silence.

Such a day of bleakness, when winter's intense cold grips the outside world, underscores the warmth inside—a prism of Christmas lights draped along the mantel, coal-oil lamps burning on the buffet, the blaze of a hearth fire. All of this gives rise to that soothing concept of comfort the Danes call *hygge* (pronounced *hoo-ga*). The charm and simplicity of a cozy atmosphere.

Hygge derives from the Norwegian word *hugga*, which also gave us the English word "hug" and is loosely translated as "comfort." With its adjectival form *hyggelig*, *hygge* promotes gratitude, contentment, togetherness, safety, security—a focus on the present moment, whether through a mug of hot chocolate, soft blankets, firelight, a woodland walk, or stargazing. What *hygge* feels like is more important than what it looks like.

At its core, *hygge* is a pragmatic way of creating a sanctuary in the midst of real life. And couldn't we all use more of that? Especially in a deep and dark December.

❊ *11 December* ❊

THIS MORNING, UNDER RADIANT blue skies, brilliant sun-shine burnishes a snowscape two feet deep into an ocean of glitter. A thousand gray-black tree limbs, wrapped in a muffle of alabaster, pierce an atmosphere as bracing as ice water. The high white tops of the cedar forests cloak their bare understories in darkness.

By midafternoon, we venture to the river, which was partially frozen and overlain by a sheath of snow slivered by furrows of open water. No paw- or clawprint breaks the primal beauty of a dazzling blue and white winter day.

On our return, the sun sets in a frosted silver glow. The earth and the air take on the hushed powder-blue of winter's dark hour—that space between sufficient light to work and the lighting of lamps. The ethereal blue of night drapes over freshly fallen snow.

We're all accustomed to the sky colors of summer sunsets. The chrome-yellows, the golds, the ambers, saffrons, and lemons; the corals, magentas, and crimsons; the salmon-pinks, mulberries, pomegranates, and wines.

But the prevailing note of the sky is blue, a hue less often extolled.

"A splendid body of color," John C. Van Dyke writes of the color blue in his amazing memoir, *The Desert*.

Steel blue, teal blue, lilac blue, royal blue, cobalt blue, indigo blue, navy blue, turquoise, and ultramarine.

Day and night, the very air of winter is blue. So, December's blue birthstones—lapis lazuli, turquoise, and tanzanite—set the perfect tone for this, the first month of winter.

Tanzanite is a variety of the mineral zoisite (a calcium aluminum hydroxyl sorosilicate). It formed around 585 million years ago, created by the plate tectonic activity and intense heat in the area of what is now Mount Kilimanjaro. Discovered in July 1967 near the Mererani Hills of Tanzania, tanzanite was given its name by Tiffany & Co. in 1968. It was then chosen by the American Gem Association in 2002 as a December birthstone. In 2010, Tanzania banned the export of any raw tanzanite of more than one gram in weight.

In its natural state, tanzanite is most often russet-brown. Heat eliminates this brownish veil and brings out the blue-violet tones generated by the presence of small amounts of the mineral vanadium. Depending on the orientation of tanzanite crystals, its color may be a rich royal blue, violet, or burgundy. The blue is more evident under fluorescent light, the violet under incandescent light. In Tanzania, new mothers wear blue beads in hopes of promoting healthy, positive lives for their newborns.

Lapis lazuli—lapis for short—is a deep-blue metamorphic rock that has been valued through millennia for its vivid color. Though its primary component is blue lazurite or sodalite, most lapis lazuli is mottled with white calcite and/or the brassy metallic-yellow of pyrite.

The name lapis lazuli derives from *lapis*, the Latin word for "stone," and *lazuli*, the genitive form of medieval Latin's *lazulum*, which in turn traces back to the Persian name for the stone, *lajevard*. Etymologically, *lazulum* is the root word for "blue" in several languages, including the Spanish and Portuguese *azul*.

Cave deposits of lapis lazuli in the Hindu Kush Mountains of Afghanistan's Kochka River valley have been worked for over six thousand years. They were the lapis lazuli source for ancient Egyptians, Akkadians, Assyrians, Babylonians, Greeks, and Romans. Lapis was ground up for Cleopatra's eyeshadow, inlaid in Tutankhamun's funeral mask, fashioned into beads and amulets, and incorporated in daggers and bowls uncovered in the third millennium BCE royal tombs of the Sumerian city-state of Ur.

Exported to Europe at the end of the Middle Ages, powdered lapis lazuli—ultramarine—became the era's finest and most costly blue pigment. Renaissance and Baroque masters like Titian and Vermeer saved it especially for the robes of the Virgin Mary. Today, gem lore links lapis lazuli with good luck and healing.

The last of December's birthstones, turquoise is a hydrated phosphate of copper and aluminum. One of the first gems to be mined, turquoise has been highly regarded for thousands of years. Powder-blue, sky-blue, turquoise, or yellowish-green, this mineral may also be flecked with pyrite or dark, spidery limonite veins.

Found most often in arid regions, natural turquoise may line or encrust fractures in volcanic rocks associated with iron oxides. In the United States, turquoise often forms as a byproduct of copper mining.

The word "turquoise" dates to the 17th century. Originating in the French *turquois*, meaning "Turkish," the stone is believed to have been first brought to Europe from the mines in Persia (Iran) through Turkey, along with other Silk Road items. Pliny the Elder knew turquoise as *callais*, the Aztecs as *chalchihuitl*.

Mined for millennia, Iranian turquoise, found between layers of limonite and sandstone, is known in that country as *perozah*, meaning "victory." The brilliant blue turquoise domes of Iranian palaces symbolize heaven on earth.

Sinai turquoise, found in sandstone overlain by basalt, has been quarried on the coast since at least the days of Egypt's First Dynasty in 3000 BCE. It adorned jewelry and inlaid articles like Tutankhamun's death mask.

Though mining is not profitable today, nomadic Bedouins will on occasion dislodge turquoise deposits with handmade gunpowder. Sinai turquoise, mined by Egyptians for so long that it's referred to as Egyptian turquoise, is generally greener than Iranian, and when magnified, its surface is speckled with dark blue discs not found anywhere else.

Much American turquoise is low quality chalk turquoise subjected to treatments like waxing or dyeing. Greens and yellows abound in some areas due to high levels of iron. Pre-Columbian miners from as far away as Central Mexico worked outcrops of turquoise particularly in California and New Mexico. The Anasazi of Chaco Canyon, Arizona, the ancestors of today's Pueblo Indians, appear to have prospered from the trade and production of turquoise objects.

Nevada, with over 120 mines, produces varying shades of blues, greens, and blue-greens. Some of them are webbed with brown or black limonite. Turquoise found in the seams, veins, and nuggets of Cerrillos, New Mexico's mines—among the oldest workings in the New World—is among the best quality on earth. Two Arizona mines—the Sleeping Beauty Mine in Globe, which ceased production in August 2012 to focus on copper production, and the Kingman Mine, which operates outside that city next to a lucrative copper concern—are renowned in the industry.

Civilization has for centuries looked upon turquoise as a holy stone, fashioning this third blue harbinger of good fortune into amulets, pendants, and fetishes.

But we have no need tonight for a block of lapis lazuli or a trinket of turquoise.

We have only to glimpse the frosted world outside Edna's window. In a midnight snowfall draped in rich lapis lazuli, turquoise, and tanzanite blue, we capture and absorb their power and their beauty. We call upon good fortune to carry us through these our darkest days.

❋ *13 December* ❋

BLEAK, BLEAK DECEMBER. Dark and dreary. Sleet and slush. No clear skies to grace the Geminid meteor shower tonight. Two weeks from the full moon would have given us a midnight filled with stars.

Unlike other major meteor showers, which have been monitored for centuries, the Geminids were first observed relatively recently, in Manchester, England, in 1862. They appear every year, December 4 through 16, peaking from two o'clock tonight. Sunset occurs so early in December that they are in full swing by nine o'clock. This makes them one of the most active, reliable, and accessible of earth's meteor showers. Emanating from the constellation Gemini—now at its highest point in the night sky—they streak by every minute or two, all night long, and can be spotted anywhere in the sky.

The Geminids are thought to result from the earth passing through debris from a mysterious object known as the asteroid 3200 Phaethon. Asteroids disintegrate differently from comets, and so some experts now consider Phaethon to be an extinct comet, a dark, inert lump of rock from which most of the ice covering has evaporated. Being mostly rocky material that travels more slowly than other showers, Geminid meteors flare more brightly across the heavens, fired up by friction with the earth's atmosphere.

A sharp crystalline sky evades us tonight. And though I've layered up against this uncommonly early winter weather, ragged clouds and an arctic chill persist. There will be no reward for straggling up the hill in the dark and the cold.

Maybe next year.

❋ *21 December* ❋

ON A SOGGY, GRAY DAY a set of acrobatic red squirrels fly about in the bare trees off the eastern pathway. We crunch our way down to the river. Crisp russet grasses poke about here and there. Tufts of straw fringe rimy patches of dirty compacted snow. Flocks of chickadees flit through the blackened understory of the cedar forest. A phalanx of Canada geese slice through an icy mist overhead, belatedly heading south or perhaps just moving down the river, which flows deep brown below the rapids. Beau, hunkered on the shore above, slides silently into the water and disappears under a thin layer of ice as we approach.

Today marks the winter solstice, the first day of astronomical winter in the Northern Hemisphere. Winter will last now, officially, until the mid-March spring equinox. Also known as mid-winter, or the hiemal or hibernal solstice, the winter solstice occurs when the earth's axis tilts farthest away from the sun. This results in the shortest day and the longest night of the year. As the season progresses, our days will lengthen and our nights contract. With December's sun at a lower altitude, sunlight strikes the earth at an oblique angle, bringing less solar radiation to the earth per unit of surface area. Sunlight must also travel a longer distance through the atmosphere to do so, thus dissipating still more heat. In high latitude areas like Paradise, real winter often proceeds the solstice, as well we know.

The winter solstice has been hallowed from prehistoric times. A primary sightline at Stonehenge indicates the winter solstice sunset. The entrance to Newgrange, a Neolithic burial chamber in Ireland, aligns with the winter solstice sunrise. This and other ancient sites may have reflected the symbolic death and rebirth of the sun—a timeless celebration of light.

As dusk descends, the solstice sun, cloaked in silvered splendor behind a frost of winter clouds, slips behind The West Woods. And once again, we light our lamps against the encircling gloom.

❈ *25 December* ❈

CHRISTMAS DAY! Bright and blue.

Overnight, a glitter of fresh snow envelopes the world. Branches great and small are flushed with crystal. Sunlight shimmers on open stretches of the river. Spirited flocks of chickadees, cardinals, blue-jays, and juncos bustle at the bird feeders. Red squirrels chatter from the maple boughs above and cottontails nose about for scraps below.

As dawn breaks, three flocks of geese honk over, one following the river south, one sailing over The West Woods, one flying eastward high above the water-meadow, stragglers chasing after. The boundless peace of Christmas courses through our day, sunrise to sunset.

The flower of December, the ancient spiny-leafed European Holly, a staple of Christmas décor, does not grow in Paradise. However, other late-season berries provide similar food for our wild winter tenants. Nannyberry shrubs with shiny serrated green leaves produce a rainbow of colored fruits from light green to pale yellow and pink. All in the same cluster. These darken to blue/black through early winter. The bright cherry-red berries of the creeping evergreen common cranberry also grow on the fringes of the water-meadow. Most of these have already ripened.

❋ *29 December* ❋

A BROODING, MOURNFUL melancholy hangs in the air all day long, the sky gray and gloomy. Tendrils of ice fog reach up from the water-meadow's broad flats to creep across a fresh sprinkle of snow that has settled thickly in furrows and hedgy mounds. All day long, tiny flurries come and go from a broken sky. A light breeze slithers up and down the bare maples, walnuts, and aspens—at least until nightfall, when the full moon climbs up into the sky.

The Full Long Nights Moon, Full Cold Moon, or Big Winter Moon is the last full moon of the year. Midwinter nights are lengthy indeed. The moon, now sitting opposite a lower sun, lingers longer above the horizon.

The aroma of baked ham, sweet potatoes, and asparagus suffuses Edna's cozy quarters as we pack away bits and pieces of another Christmas gone. And then I gear up to hike over to Russell's to savor the full moon in all its splendor.

Just as I arrive at the crest of the slope above the water-meadow, the moon tops the eastern woods. And oh, what a marvel spreads out before me then! Silver-blue light slides up and down the mantled embankment, shimmering more deeply in snow-laden grottos, glistening on the boughs of the surrounding trees. A magical luminescence of lapis lazuli. Blush and glow expand in the still air.

I stand spellbound. Utterly bewitched.

Snug in the cottage again, I come to terms—at last—with this season of adaptation and change.

❊ *31 December* ❊

EIGHT INCHES of snow fall throughout the day, streaming into a cold and blustery New Year's Eve. Tomorrow another year arrives. But for me, any reflection and renewal will have to come from the inside looking out.

"Blasts of January would blow you
through and through . . ."
— WILLIAM SHAKESPEARE

❈ *1 January* ❈

HAPPY NEW YEAR!

A milky blue sky greets us this morning, before a wall of gray snow blows in to thicken the air through the rest of the day. And now, as the sun sets behind the wintery haze, a bitter wind is shuffling and reshuffling the crests of the snowdrifts, shaping and reshaping the last black patches of open water on the river.

January, the month of new beginnings, originated in Roman mythology. Janus (*Ianuarius*) is the Roman god of the doorway (*ianua*, in Latin). Looking both ways, Janus sees the years come and go. To reconcile time with the 365-day lunar year, the semi-mythical successor of Romulus, Numa Pompilius, added the months of January and February to the Roman calendar in 713 BCE.

Looking both ways is one thing, but I'm never really primed for January in Paradise. Gone are those olden, golden days of snow forts and snowball fights. Of toboggan runs down The Gully hill. Of ice skating on the river, frozen feet propped on the open oven door afterward for the tingle and itch of the thaw. Decades back, my brother Ebe remembers driving up from Kitchener in early January to shovel snow off Edna's roof. He always relished sliding off the back into an enormous snowbank. Dad would sometimes plant a live Christmas tree on the flats or burn the brush pile on New Year's Day—if the weather allowed. And in the late 1960s, when he was still hunting with bow and arrow, we even managed moose steaks in Paradise one frigid New Year's Eve.

All bold and adventurous occasions in their day. We're wiser than that now. Or maybe we're all just getting older.

❈ *10 January* ❈

SOMEWHERE BEHIND TONIGHT'S WINTER haze sails the Full Wolf Moon. The Saxons knew bleak January itself as the *Wulf-monath* (the Wolf Month), a time of starvation and want. All over the Northern Hemisphere, through the deep drifts of January, wolf packs once prowled, generating much fear and loathing among our ancestors.

Fittingly for this month of perpetual snow and cold, January's birthstone, the garnet, represents constancy. Garnet describes a group of closely related silicate minerals found in a variety of color from red, orange, yellow and pink to green, brown, and purple. The term most often refers to the dark red forms of almandine and pyrope which have been used since the Bronze Age for jewelry and abrasives. Red garnet necklaces adorned Egyptian pharaohs and the Romans used garnet signet rings to stamp wax for securing documents.

"Garnet" comes to us from the 14th century Middle English word *gernet* (dark red). *Gernet* in turn was borrowed from Old French *grenate*, from the Latin word *granatus* (from *granum* meaning "grain seed"), a possible reference to *pomum granatum* (pomegranate). The vivid red seed covers (arils) of pomegranate fruit are similar in shape, size, and color to red garnet crystals. In stone lore, garnet fosters good health and happiness. Not altogether a bad thing when January's persistent depression threatens.

January's flower, the snowdrop or galanthus (from the Greek word *gala* (milk), *ánthos* (flower) is a small genus of about twenty species of bulbous perennial herbaceous plants in the *Amaryllidaceae* family. Two long linear leaves bracket a single, small drooping bell-shaped white flower.

Native to Europe and the Middle East, snowdrops have been known under various other names, among them Candlemas Bell and White Lady. *Galanthus* took root in 1753. Brought to the British Isles by the Romans, snowdrops have been naturalized in Europe and North America. They often form large, creamy-white drifts in early springtime. In colder climates, they may even flower in winter, emerging through the snow. Synonymous with hope, snowdrops set themselves in delicate balance to garnet's persistence.

Today, the surface of the river is frozen solid, the water-meadow shrouded in nearly two feet of drift. In shallower spots, individual blades of grass protrude through the glaze, lightly dusted with snow. Somehow, I just can't rouse myself for another white winter walk.

❖ *20 January* ❖

THIS MORNING WE'VE BEEN GIVEN one more pure and glistening country snowfall. I'm grateful to at least be able to sidestep the slush and grime of the city in this the coldest month of the year.

Out the westside window, winter has draped the bared trees, Russell's rooftop, and the dips and hollows of the water-meadow, in a crystalline blanket. The sky is a wash of gray. I can almost hear the crunch of my boots on the footpath. Like broken glass. Like granulated sugar. And though tinged with wood smoke from Edna's fireplace, the smell of cedar permeates the air, leaving it clean and sharp. The magical simplicity of a black-and-white winter surrounds us.

Snow absorbs 60 percent of sound, so I know, without stepping outside, that a deep serenity has wrapped the winter trees as they stand mute and regal in silvery brown. The peace is palpable. All is right with the world.

But all is not as it seems. At this point in time, the planet's numbers don't look good.

Here's the latest from a recent episode of the CBS news program, *60 Minutes*. "Vanishing Wild" aired on January 2, 2023.

The human population was deemed too large for the earth to sustain—in 1970.

In 1991, one salmon species was under threat. In 2023, fourteen species were at risk.

In the past fifty years, 69 percent of the earth's wildlife has collapsed.

To maintain the earthly lifestyles we've grown accustomed to would require five more earth-like planets.

Since 1968, humanity has taken over 70 percent of the planet's land and 68 percent of its water.

In South America alone, the abundance of life has fallen 94 percent since 1970.

Over the four billion years of life on earth, there have been five mass extinctions in which 75 percent of the then known species disappeared.

Regrettably, most experts believe that we are in the midst of a sixth extinction event, the worst since the disappearance of the dinosaurs. Moreover, the rate of this extinction is a hundred times faster than any that has come before it.

We are on the brink of losing many common species we've long taken for granted. The polar bear. The snow leopard. The Bengal tiger. Kangaroos. Orangutans. Humpback whales and sea turtles. In the Pacific Northwest, salmon have declined at an alarming rate, taking with them the many predators that feed on them. Eagles. Minks. Otters.

In fact, as Stanford biologist Paul Ehrlich has said, we are killing our way of life. In the next few decades, without the necessary political will, we will destroy our lifestyle. Not through any volcanic eruption or an out-of-control asteroid—this mass extinction will be of our own making.

The challenge then is to save the third of the planet that remains wild. Little success stories, like the sixteen acres here in Paradise, must count for something. Each is a grain of sand on a beach. So, it's incumbent upon each of us to champion their preservation. ". . . to dance for the renewal of the world," as Robin Wall Kimmerer writes in her amazing book, *Braiding Sweetgrass*.

The winter world outside Edna's window seems hushed and lifeless today. But it's all happening just out of sight, as we would see if we dug a little deeper into those snowdrifts.

All winter long, voles and shrews and mice burrow through the soil just below the snow or through tunnels of arched and frozen vegetation, looking for stored plant seeds, berries, and nuts, or insects in leaf litter. Our fully hibernating toads, frogs, bats, garter snakes, bumblebees, and groundhogs remain insulated from the cold in lairs and dens where the temperature remains relatively stable due to snow cover. In a more hospitable "anchor climate."

Forty percent of the earth's land is snow-covered at one time or another. That blanket is vital to the survival of many plants and animals. Snow allows the temperature of underlying soils to remain warmer. Without it the ground would freeze.

Scientists are just beginning to explore this previously unknown winter ecology. In 2013, biologist Jonathan Pauli and ecology professor Ben Zuckerberg, both from the University of Wisconsin-Madison, coined the term Subnivium (Latin *sub* meaning "below," and *nives* meaning "snow") to describe this below-the-snow eco-zone. This subnivean layer has long been known by the Inuit as *pukak*, the airy space between the ground and a snowpack. Nature's igloo.

Pukak requires six to twelve inches of fluffy snow for creation. Snow full of air pockets provides insulation from heavy winds and plunging temperatures. Once again, however, the experts voice alarm about climate change producing a less stable subnivium; about heavier, wetter snows reducing air spaces and increasing carbon-dioxide, which could suffocate the animals living there.

So, despite my personal abhorrence of a harsh Canadian winter, I'm a newborn fan. Bring it on.

"When God was making the months,
I think February was a mistake."
— UNKNOWN

❈ *1 February* ❈

A CRUSH OF ICE TOPS THE RIVER this morning. Snow-covered wedges and slabs have rammed up and over the near bank where snow mobile tracks crisscross the water-meadow. All the world lies in gray and white. Frigid and bleak. *Helmikuu*, the month of the pearl, is what the Finnish poetically call February. With a mid-month thaw, melting snow on twigs and tree limbs might form droplets that would refreeze into tiny, ice pearls.

February takes its name from the Latin *februum*, meaning "purification," related to *Februa*, the purification ritual once held on the fifteenth of the month in the old Roman calendar. February days were lopped off at regular intervals in the distant past. This resulted in a twenty-three- or twenty-four-day month. With time, *intercalaris*, a twenty-seven-day month, was inserted after February, to realign the year with the seasons. February gained a twenty-eighth day, as it does under our present Gregorian calendar, when *intercalaris* was abolished with the Julian Calendar. A leap year then occurred every fourth year.

The first day of February also opens Imbolc, a Gaelic festival cele-brating the start of spring. The most common explanation for the name "Imbolc" is that it comes from the Old Irish *I mbolc* (Modern Irish *I mbolg*) meaning "in the belly," referring to the spring pregnancy of ewes.

Imbolc, as the cross-quarter day halfway between the winter solstice and the spring equinox, probably emerged from the Neolithic Period. Some passage tombs in Ireland, like the Mound of the Hostages on the Hill of Tara, align with sunrise around both Imbolc and Samhain, autumn's cross-quarter day.

Imbolc, associated with the pagan goddess Brigid in her role as a fertility goddess, celebrates hearth and home, the onset of spring, and the lengthening of days. Candles and hearth fires reflected the power of the sun as its warmth and light strengthened through the following months.

Christianity adapted to Imbolc by establishing St. Brigid's Day in its place. St. Brigid crosses, made of rushes woven into a four-armed equilateral cross, were hung over doorways, windows, and stable entrances. These crosses welcomed Brigid and guarded against fire, lightning, illness, and evil spirits. They remained in place for the entire year. Figures of Brigid were paraded house to house. Beds were laid out for the goddess, along with food and drink. And Brigid was invoked to protect homes and livestock.

Imbolc conjures up the promise of spring. Still in the depths of winter, we can take some small comfort in that.

❈ *2 February* ❈

A HAZE OF BLUE SKY ON THIS—GROUNDHOG DAY— has softened the edges of winter. Imbolc celebrations often included divination, especially as to the weather. The Celtic custom of watching for snakes and badgers to leave their winter dens may be a precursor of this day.

In a similar tradition, the divine hag of Gaelic lore, the Cailleach, collected firewood for the rest of the winter on Imbolc. If she intended that winter last a good while longer, she made the weather bright and sunny, the better to gather and cache. Villagers were relieved then to see Imbolc break with foul weather, for the Cailleach was still asleep and winter was almost over.

Today, shadows rule. A groundhog, if one could be roused, would undoubtedly glimpse his shadow—however faintly—and retreat. The Cailleach is on the hunt, winter firmly in tow. At least for another six weeks.

February's blossom is the violet, a name derived from the Middle English/Old French word, *violete*, from *viola*, the Latin name for this common purple flower. The *Violet* family contains nearly six hundred different species, most of them found in the Northern Hemisphere. With scalloped, heart-shaped leaves, violets have five petals, four upswept (two per side), and one broad, lobed lower petal that points downward.

The color purple represents not only royalty, power, and confidence—as in the imperial robes of Rome—but also a modest spirituality. The goddess Diana changed one of her nymph companions—all of whom had sworn themselves to chastity—into a violet to protect her from the relentless pursuit of Apollo, Diana's twin brother. Christianity associates the violet with the modesty of the Virgin Mary.

The elusive scent of the violet, a major component of which is a compound called ionone, temporarily desensitizes receptors in the nose. Unfortunately, this attribute does not extend to February as a whole.

In keeping with the violet as February's color scheme, amethyst, a purple variety of quartz, is the gemstone of the month. The name originates in the Greek *amethystos*—*a* meaning "not" and *methysko* or *methustos* meaning "intoxicate."

The ancient Greeks believed that amethyst protected against drunkenness and wore amethyst amulets to that end. Carved amethyst wine goblets served the same purpose. Used in jewelry making from at least the time of the early Egyptians, amethyst also adorned medieval European soldiers, affording them protection in battle.

Yet another silicate mineral, amethyst occurs in colors from pinkish violet to deep purple, with occasional secondary hues of red and blue. Irradiation, iron impurities, and other transition metals or trace elements produce violet tones. All amethysts may darken with irradiation or fade if overexposed to light.

Top quality amethyst has been discovered in many parts of the world. Brazilian stones formed as large geodes within volcanic rocks. The largest opencast amethyst in the world is found in Lower Austria. New World amethyst has been uncovered in the Mazatzal Mountains of Arizona, Amethyst Mountain in Texas, and Yellowstone National Park, among many other locales. The largest amethyst mine in North America is located in Thunder Bay, Ontario, on the north shore of Lake Superior.

Amethyst is counted among the five prized cardinal gemstones, along with diamond, sapphire, ruby, and emerald. Paler stones like the light lavender amethyst called Rose de France were considered less valuable. The highest-grade amethyst known is the exceptionally rare Deep Siberian, incomparably suited to be February's gemstone.

Amethyst symbolizes piety, humility, and spiritual wisdom. All of these might just see us through this the shortest month of the year as it stretches out oppressively before us.

❈ *15 February* ❈

"HE WHO LOOKS LONG ENOUGH, SEES MUCH," naturalist Louise de Kiriline Laurence has written in her book *The Lovely and the Wild*. It's that kind of day.

A pea-soup fog settles on the countryside this morning, after storms over the past several days combined to dump eight to ten inches of new snow. Gazing out the west window much of the day, we watch feathery flakes shower down for hours, silent and thick. Maples, aspens, and elms all rise majestically under cloaks of gleaming white. In the distance, the cedars brood, their understories shadowed and obscured.

Winter birds flock everywhere. Glints of cardinal red, canary yellow, and Canada jay blue spark through the trees.

Late in the afternoon, as the skies clear and dusk deepens, we feel compelled to drift about in the gloaming and saunter through to the east woods. "Saunter" seems the perfect word for this winter's day wander. The etymology of the word is obscure, but I like to think of it much as Samuel Johnson did in his 1755 *A Dictionary of the English Language.*

Johnson thought the word "saunter" derived from the French phrase *aller à la sainte terre* (to go to the holy land) and described idle people who roved about the countryside asking for alms under the pretense of going to the holy land.

A Paradise winter invites idleness. But while we're not much into begging, we do feel, as always, that stepping into Paradise is to tread on holy ground.

<h2 style="text-align:center">❈ 25 February ❈</h2>

FEBRUARY IS OFTEN THE MONTH of the heaviest snow. Having only twenty-eight days in most years, it is also the only month of the year that can pass without a full moon. Way back on February 9, the Full Snow Moon or Full Hunger Moon rode high in the night sky. Full and frosty, it slipped behind a black lace mantle of bared branches.

Tonight, ice crystals twinkle in the still air as lamplight spills from the cottage windows like muted sunlight.

Very soon now, this month will usher in another spring, that optimistic season of action when everything happens at once. The land will rejoice. Refreshed. Renewed. Once again, bridging the gulf between the human and the divine like a Navajo sandpainting, nature will recreate a cosmogenic mythology and return us to a world center where all things move in harmony, bound by a cosmic code through which the seasons turn.

"I believe in God beyond God," writer Joseph Campbell has said in his seminal book, *The Hero with a Thousand Faces*. Through all the seasons, February to February, that's the prayer we have for Paradise and for the world—a receptive meditation that engages grace, emotion, thought, and imagination.

Be still and know.

Sit and wait.

For very soon, we will revel once again in the peace of wild things.

"To know fully even one field or one land
is a lifetime's experience . . .
In the world of poetic experience,
it is depth that counts, not width."
— PATRICK KAVANAGH

Epilogue

I AM ENVIOUS OF AUTHORS AND NATURALISTS who are so fluently specific about the natural world. Those who "dwell among the particulars." Those who immerse themselves in the struggle, who emerge bloodied and war-torn to give us the up-to-date nitty-gritty of exactly how things fare with the sperm whale or the highland gorilla, the Amsterdam albatross, white rhino, or giant panda.

American writer/journalist Brenda Ueland once wrote in her book, *If You Want to Write: A Book about Art, Independence and Spirit*, "The creative impulse of Van Gogh was simply loving what he saw and then wanting to share it with others." That has been my own much simpler goal in producing this book.

The door between two eastern white cedars that opened for me so long ago has never closed. But in the spirit of changeless change, the neighboring farm family no longer slings up their fence at the west bend of the river. Their cattle no longer graze that former south pasture. Repairs to the culvert on the main road left the creek passage too low for

271

them to negotiate. So, our kingfishers no longer dive from high wires, though they do still perch on the lower limbs of the water-meadow's giant white willow. The white-tailed deer and other denizens of Paradise now have a larger wildness through which to roam.

Our fireflies, our toads and frogs, our cabbage whites and monarchs, and our red fox and muskrats have all declined. The apple tree beside Russell's has been removed for safety reasons, taking with it a chickadee nest that had been in use for countless seasons.

And in these days of global warming, December rarely sees much snow. The beaver no longer work to any great extent at The Dam Rapids. The stones and limbs they tinkered with through the years since their last dam was washed away have formed a barrier on the far side of the river large enough that the land filled in behind. Great expanses of green and russet grasses now wave and ripple there throughout the summer and early fall. And we have never again seen that primordial denizen, the piliated woodpecker.

After daughter-in-law Marie Laure's first visit, she was reluctant to return; the experience had been so profound, restful, and energizing. She had said, "How could it ever be repeated?"

"The cottage is always like that," my son Dustin assured her.

And this is true.

Each and every year, we rediscover the joy, excitement, and mystery of the natural world.

We even gained a fresh perspective when Dustin recently flew a drone over the property. East to west, north to south, we marveled at its depth, width, length, and wildness.

As people age, they may become despondent with the passage of time. The world they once lived in is dying or has already died to them in so many ways. But new worlds are constantly being born. It's the quality of the time we spend in the natural world, not the quantity that matters.

"An awakened soul knows that God is in a blade of grass, a morning glory by the window, a wren's egg," says an aphorism I once read, without attribution, on an inspirational calendar.

U2's "Red Flag Day" from their album *Songs of Experience* says that, "Paradise is a place you can't see when it's yours." We have been so blessed from the beginning to be aware of, witness, acknowledge, and appreciate our very own Paradise through time.

Look for yours.

However large or small. Look around you wherever you are. What might you have taken for granted? What might you see if you moved more slowly, if you breathed more deeply?

Carol Sletten, author of *Three Strong Western Women*, writes, "We are always and forever allowed to linger in loveliness." And Wilfred Pelletier and Ted Poole state unequivocally in their book, *No Foreign Land: The Biography of an American Indian*, "Wherever you are is home and the earth is Paradise. Wherever you set your feet is holy land."

Acknowledgments

I AM ETERNALLY GRATEFUL to my mother, Edna (Ott) Ebertt, and my father, Russell Ebertt, for their foresight in purchasing these sixteen acres of Paradise in 1957, sharing the cost with my uncle Wilken Lavery and his wife Esther (Ott) Lavery, my uncle Harold Ott, and my maternal grandfather Alvin Ott. Though they are no longer with us, without them Paradise as it stands today would not exist. Mom and Dad protected and maintained the property for many decades, and my dad's cottage journals were an indispensable part of an accurate portrayal of the property, past and present.

First and foremost, then, I would like to thank my husband Dan for his steadfast love and encouragement, especially during the writing of this book. His incomparable creative and practical contributions to the growth and blossoming of Paradise cannot be overstated.

My children Dustin and Danielle Beeaff—more recently with their partners Marie Laure Fontaine and Chris Stephenson—have enjoyed stays on the property from their childhood, always and ever contributing to our wildlife adventures, some of which are recounted in this book. I am forever grateful for their love, creative input, and genuine interest and care for the land.

Many thanks to Dave Eveleigh who has been our go-to man for many years for construction, renovation, and artistic embellishment in Paradise, as well as for many of the necessary preparations for a cottage stay. His brilliant designs have included—but are not limited to—The Willow Deck, Harold's Tea Deck, outdoor and indoor showers, and a variety of staircases. We would be lost without his creative input, skill, maintenance, and expertise.

I am so grateful that my brother, David Ebertt, has always seen to various necessities ahead of any stay in Paradise. Ebe makes sure that the rain barrels are full, the electricity is turned on, and the fridge and freezer are plugged in. Stays are hassle-free because of his vigilance. He also did a stellar job on the new crossing at The Gully.

Botanist Jim Dougan provided us with a thorough and intensive floral inventory of Paradise lands, from the cedar forests to the water-meadow.

Special thanks to Rufus, the Ruffed Grouse, who invited us into his world. Rufus showed us that we can all strive for a subtle and joyful appreciation of and interaction with the bounty and beauty of nature, no matter how fleeting.

In addition, I am honored and grateful to be able to include a variety of short quotes in the body of this book. Words of wisdom and beauty, these are acknowledged where they occur in the text, in support of the narrative or as epigrams.

Thanks to these inspirational figures for permission to quote more extensively from their work: Rabbi Abraham Joshua Heschel; Diana Beresford-Kroeger; Wendell Berry; Robinson Jeffers; Fenton Johnson; Terry Tempest Williams; and Jim Hohenbary.

Many thanks to my amazing publisher Brooke Warner of She Writes Press, to my project manager Lauren Wise, my editor Lorraine Fico-White, interior designer Tabitha Lahr, and SWP's Creative Director Julie Metz for producing a book of incomparable beauty and appeal.

And lastly, but surely not least, I would like to thank you, my readers. I hope that you not only enjoy this book but that you may find a small bit of Paradise in your own life. If you were moved in some small way by *Infinite Paradise*, please consider posting a review on one of your favorite websites.

About the Author

DIANNE EBERTT BEEAFF is the award-winning author of six previous books. She has been a freelance writer for many years, beginning her career in magazine journalism. She is a member of many writers' organizations including Arizona Professional Writers, the National Association of Press Women, the Authors Guild, and PEN America. As an artist, Dianne works primarily in graphite and watercolor, and her work has been shown in a variety of local, national, and international galleries. She lives primarily in Tucson, Arizona, with her husband Dan.

Dianne's work may be seen at
www.debeeaff.wordpress.com

Looking for your next great read?

We can help!

Visit www.shewritespress.com/next-read
or scan the QR code below for a list
of our recommended titles.

She Writes Press is an award-winning
independent publishing company founded to
serve women writers everywhere.

swp